THE JESUS ADVENTURE

Copyright © 2024 by Ian Millar

Published by Kudu Publishing

All rights reserved. No portion of this book may be reproduced, stored in a retrieval system, or transmitted in any form or by any means—electronic, mechanical, photocopy, recording, scanning, or other—except for brief quotations in critical reviews or articles, without prior written permission of the author.

Unless otherwise specified, all Scripture quotations are taken from the Contemporary English Version (CEV), copyright © 1995 by American Bible Society. | Scripture quotations marked CEB are taken from the Common English Bible, copyright © 2011 by Common English Bible | Scripture quotations marked CJB are taken from the Complete Jewish Bible, copyright © 1998 by David H. Stern. All rights reserved. | Scripture quotations marked ESV are from The ESV® Bible (The Holy Bible, English Standard Version®), copyright © 2001 by Crossway, a publishing ministry of Good News Publishers. Used by permission. All rights reserved. | Scripture quotations marked GNT are from the Good News Translation in Today's English Version- Second Edition Copyright © 1992 by American Bible Society. Used by Permission. | Scripture quotations marked GW are taken from the GOD'S WORD Translation Bible, copyright ©1995, 2003, 2013, 2014, 2019, 2020 by God's Word to the Nations Mission Society. Used by permission. All rights reserved. | Scripture quotations marked HCSB are taken from the Holman Christian Standard Bible®, Used by Permission HCSB ©1999, 2000, 2002, 2003, 2009 Holman Bible Publishers. Holman Christian Standard Bible®, Holman CSB®, and HCSB® are federally registered trademarks of Holman Bible Publishers. | Scripture quotations marked ISV are taken from the International Standard Version Bible, copyright © 1995-2014 by ISV Foundation. All rights reserved internationally. Used by permission of Davidson Press, LLC | Scripture quotations marked KJV are taken from the King James Version of the Bible. Public domain. | Scripture quotations marked LEB are taken from the Lexham English Bible, Copyright © 2012 by Logos Bible Software. Lexham is a registered trademark of Logos Bible Software. | Scripture quotations marked LSB are taken from the Legacy Standard Bible, Copyright © 2021 by The Lockman Foundation. All rights reserved. Managed in partnership with Three Sixteen Publishing Inc. LSBible.org. | Scripture quotations marked MEV are taken from The Holy Bible, Modern English Version, Copyright © 2014 by Military Bible Association. Published and distributed by Charisma House | Scripture quotations marked NASB are taken from the (NASB®) New American Standard Bible®, Copyright © 1960, 1971, 1977, 1995, 2020 by The Lockman Foundation. Used by permission. All rights reserved. www.lockman.org | Scripture quotations marked NIV are taken from the Holy Bible, New International Version®, NIV®. Copyright © 1973, 1978, 1984, 2011 by Biblica, Inc.™ Used by permission of Zondervan. All rights reserved worldwide. www.zondervan.com. The "NIV" and "New International Version" are trademarks registered in the United States Patent and Trademark Office by Biblica, Inc.™ | Scripture quotations marked NKJV are taken from the New King James Version®. Copyright © 1982 by Thomas Nelson. Used by permission. All rights reserved. | Scripture quotations marked NLT are taken from the Holy Bible, New Living Translation, copyright © 1996, 2004, 2015 by Tyndale House Foundation. Used by permission of Tyndale House Publishers, Inc., Carol Stream, Illinois 60188. All rights reserved. | Scripture quotations marked NLV are taken from the New Life Version Bible, Copyright ©1969, 2003 by Barbour Publishing, Inc. | Scripture quotations marked RSV are taken from the Revised Standard Version of the Bible, Copyright © 1946, 1952, and 1971 by the Division of Christian Education of the National Council of the Churches of Christ in the United States of America. Used by permission. All rights reserved.

For foreign and subsidiary rights, contact the author.

Cover design by Sara Young
Cover photo by Naomi Steel

ISBN: 978-1-960678-19-5   1 2 3 4 5 6 7 8 9 10

Printed in the United States of America

IAN MILLAR

THE JESUS ADVENTURE

JOURNEY TO SPIRITUAL FREEDOM

CONTENTS

ACKNOWLEDGMENTS .... **VII**

WELCOME TO THE JESUS ADVENTURE 9

PART 1. STARTING IN THE WAY OF JESUS 13

    CHAPTER 1. **SCOUTING THE WAY** 15

    CHAPTER 2. **COMMENCING THE ADVENTURE** 21

    CHAPTER 3. **THE ADVENTURE WAY** 41

PART 2. WALKING THE WAY OF JESUS 53

    CHAPTER 4. **THE VITAL CURE** 55

    CHAPTER 5. **THE VOYAGE CHARTS OF PROVIDENCE** 97

    CHAPTER 6. **CROSSING OVER BY FAITH** 119

PART 3. STANDING FIRM WITH JESUS 149

    CHAPTER 7. **REST AND REFRESHMENT (ON THE WAY)** 151

    CHAPTER 8. **ADVENTURE OUTWARD: THE PRIME DIRECTIVE** 169

    CHAPTER 9. **EQUIPPED WITH SPIRITUAL WEAPONS** 197

PART 4. SEATED WITH JESUS 219

    CHAPTER 10. **SUPPLYING EARTH'S NEEDS FROM HEAVEN'S RESOURCES** 221

    CHAPTER 11. **CROSS WALKERS OF A NEW IDENTITY** 233

    CHAPTER 12. **THE TREASURE CHEST OF CHRIST** 259

ACKNOWLEDGMENTS

Early in my walk with Jesus, I asked the Lord to send me a mentor. I was disappointed when no one stood up for the role. Then, years later I looked back and realized that I did not have one, but many. Thank you to the many men whose steadfast friendship, counsel, and mentoring have helped my walk and ministry: Dale, Ed, Bob, Malcom, Ron, Dave, Dan, John, Steve, Art, Tom and so many more. So many of you have already gone on to be with the Lord, but life has even separated those of us still here. I appreciate and miss each of you.

SPECIAL ACKNOWLEDGMENTS

Nik and Andy, are two faithful brothers who don't know each other, but each made this project possible in more ways than they can ever understand – just by walking the walk of faith. Thank you for your encouragement, prayers, contributions, and integrity.

Tom C. is an unsung hero and one of the greatest friends a man could ever have. His encouragement, prayers, and brotherhood sustained me through times of great trials. He left this realm too early for so many of us. You are missed, brother.

To my wife, daughters, and sons: you are all amazing. Thank you for following Jesus with me, and for traveling with me on amazing adventures of faith. Thank you for enduring ten thousand nights of research, writing, praying through this project. Thank you especially to my faithful wife for being a helpmate suitable to me, who encouraged me when I didn't believe in myself; and for faithfully praying through it all without quitting.

The prophet Isaiah said:

"The 'I Am' will travel before you."
—Isaiah 52:12 (author paraphrase)

WELCOME TO THE JESUS ADVENTURE

This book is a guide to travelers on the Jesus Adventure. Some think His adventure is only a myth. Others believe it was once true, long ago. Some are satisfied just reading about others who lived the Jesus Adventure long ago.

Yet there are others today—ordinary people like you and me—who are boldly living the Jesus Adventure and experiencing greater joy. Regular people discovering that it is still real, powerful, and amazing. We have found the true adventure of Jesus, and we are on a marvelous journey!

THE OBVIOUS MYSTERY

Hidden in plain sight, the epic adventure from Jesus is the climax of the vast mystery of God. Often missed, the adventure transforms anyone who sincerely takes the journey. As we go, life is refreshed and brightened in ways we have never known before.

This is a challenge to re-discover the philosophy, spirituality, and guidance of Jesus of Nazareth; to find the true power of God while we explore the adventure that He intended for everyone. Along the way, we discover our soul and experience life in a fresh way that Jesus intended.

WORDS THAT QUENCH

When discovering Jesus in His own words, at face value, something interesting emerges: There is a clear, cool, and refreshing flavor that refreshes every thirsty soul.

There is passion, energy, and appeal in Jesus's teachings that transcends what religion tells us. The more we understand Jesus, the more refreshing His teachings and life become.

WORDS OF HOPE

The New Testament was not written in arcane or sophisticated language. People forget that today. His followers wrote and taught His words in the common lingo of their world. My goal is the same. I have primarily used the Contemporary English Version of the Bible because it reads like a conversation. I have also used other versions where the meaning comes out more clearly. The goal is to start a conversation with you in this book.

Scholars want to impress us with complexity (especially with religion). But Jesus challenges us with simplicity. His clear confrontation is what makes Jesus so interesting. He could be understood by common people and yet challenged the great intellectuals.

OPPOSITION TO THE LIGHT

Jesus did not accept the authority of mortal men. He defied powerful leaders, who insisted that He explain everything. Instead, He challenged them and demonstrated the life-transforming power of God. Jesus refused to be held captive by the expectations of fools or scholars.

There are those who claim to have knowledge about God but fail to follow what Jesus instructed. In the same way, I expect people will say this book is too simple.

There are many people who think that Jesus has to be complicated. When we really learn <u>and do</u> what Jesus said, there is transformative power for our lives and our world. Nothing else comes close! The goal is to take a journey that is truly life-altering, the way Jesus did with his original followers.

Jesus said:

> **"I came so everyone would have life, and have it fully."**
> **—John 10:10**

This is the way of Jesus!

Note to reader: I encourage you to pay special attention to any underlined or bolded words and phrases throughout the scriptures in this book, as they are there to solidify and reinforce the themes demonstrated in their respective contexts.

PART 1

STARTING IN THE WAY OF JESUS

About 400 years before Jesus arrived, the prophet Isaiah spoke of Messiah saying:

> "He won't break off a bent reed
> or put out a dying flame,
> but he will make sure
> that justice is done."
> —Isaiah 42:3

CHAPTER 1

SCOUTING THE WAY

You are invited into a spiritual journey to travel across a wide blue ocean of things you may not believe. You need not be afraid because this is a journey that Jesus will lead—He has already walked ahead of you. Others have fantastic reports of things that are hard to imagine in places you may not have seen. Sometimes those places are just around the corner.

Jesus Himself pronounced a special blessing on those who take on the adventure today.

THE SCOUT'S REPORT

Consider this a course on the supernatural, following Jesus, the one who is called Messiah and Christ. So, who is this Jesus? To begin the Jesus Adventure, we first consider our faithful Scout who went before us.

Until He began His ministry, Jesus of Nazareth was known only as the son of Joseph, a carpenter. Then He became known as Jesus the Rabbi/teacher, and later as Jesus the Master and Lord. Some people declared Him a prophet; some called Him the Son of David (the shepherd who became king).

He called Himself the Son of Man (referring to the prophecies foretelling His ministry). The authorities called him a deceiver; some even called Him the son of the devil. At the end of His ministry, His followers called Jesus the Messiah and the Son of God. What can we learn from Him?

Both New and Old Testaments speak of a **peerless Messiah**, a man who was promised thousands of years ago to be King over all the earth. Jesus's friends told us that He fulfilled over 300 prophecies from the Old Testament, proving He is the long-promised Messiah of Israel, destined to be their king, indeed, the King over all Kings.

He came from the Father's throne in Heaven to the womb of a poor woman. He put on humanity and became the Son of Man so that we might become children of God. He was born supernaturally, yet raised in poverty and obscurity in a small town of an oppressed nation.

He never had wealth or political influence, yet kings and authorities have sought Him. The understandings of all of mankind have never matched His wisdom, and no one has ever spoken like Him.

As a boy, Jesus challenged religious teachers with His understanding because He was taught by God. As an adult, He miraculously quieted storming seas. He healed crowds of people without medicines and fed thousands from a boy's lunch. He gave life back to the dead, and demons obeyed Him.

He never wrote a single book, yet no library can contain every book ever written about Him. He never wrote a song, yet He is the theme of more songs than all the songwriters in the world. He never founded a school, yet all the colleges cannot brag about having as many students as He has. He never formed an army, yet no leader ever had more volunteers.

Great men have come and been forgotten, yet Jesus remains. The devil could not tempt Him, fear could not restrain Him, and the grave could not keep Him down.

He laid aside royal robes of colored light for a peasant's drab garment. He was rich, yet for our sakes, He became poor. He was born in another's barn, He rode on another's donkey, He was buried in another's grave, yet

He conquered death and rose on the third day (as He said he would). He ascended into Heaven and is now at the right hand of God.

One day He will return with immense power and blazing glory to judge the world, and every knee will bow to Him, and every tongue will confess Him as Lord over all Lords. His friends will do it gladly, but His enemies will tremble and bow before His face. He is the perfect one, the only one who can satisfy the thirsty soul. He gives everlasting life to those who love Him and calls us His friends.

The Bible boldly says that your eternal destiny, as well as your soul's current substance and peace, depends on your relationship with Jesus, whom it presents as the Son of God, the Messiah and ultimate King over Earth.

MODERN ADVENTURER CHRONICLES

Have you ever felt a deep inner hunger that nothing could satisfy? That's how it was with many of us. Jesus fills the soul's hunger and gives confidence where there has been doubt and fear. As Jesus guides us, He calls us close to Himself. When we tend to wander off the path, He calls us back.

WHERE YA GOIN'?

Jesus promises a hope and a future. Not because we're good but because He is good. My life seemed like a dead-end routine of impossible situations for years until Jesus changed everything. He doesn't just ask us where we're going; He helps us figure out where it is worth going and how to get there.

Jesus still transforms ordinary people from creatures of darkness, distress, rage, and shame to creatures of His light. Along the way, we find transforming strength. There's hope, joy, peace, and an incredible experience for all who take on the Jesus Adventure.

ADVENTURE BOOTS

Why should we go on His adventure? Because we are hunting everlasting treasure! There are clues, perils, resources, skills, and danger. Jesus gives us everything we need as we go. And getting there is exciting.

When we do what Jesus taught, something powerful happens: life changes! Miracles occur! We begin a life adventure that transforms ordinary people from the inside out. When you take the first step, Jesus gets you going.

Doing what Jesus taught is always challenging and fun. Once we commit and start, it is rewarding. The things we once feared become the things we love the most!

So, this is a guide to the spirituality of Jesus. But don't think of Jesus like some soft-handed guru who sits alone chanting. There's action involved. Jesus is a hands-on guy who got His hands and feet dirty doing things.

After all, He started as an apprentice in a carpenter's shop! The Jesus Adventure is about becoming one of Jesus's apprentices in His greater work: life transformation. It's about walking a spiritual journey with Jesus and learning what He taught.

FRESH AGAIN

Start fresh, even if you have read the Bible before. You may be tempted to skip past or rush through parts. But let each section speak to you in a fresh way. Jesus always has something new and fulfilling when we trust Him.

When people take on the Jesus Adventure, the same thing happens: God begins working amazing things in their lives in unexpected ways, whether they are new followers just checking it out or are lifelong church people.

My wife and I started a small home-based group to pray and study Jesus many years ago. When we studied Jesus's spirituality this way, the results were amazing. God's Spirit showed up and changed the lives of everyone there.

That little group grew until it became many. Incredible things happened. It still seems amazing to me: God was truly at work there changing lives. Amazing things happen when people do what Jesus says.

ORIGINAL ADVENTURERS

After Jesus left this world, His original followers began teaching what He had taught and doing the things He had done. They did exactly as He instructed them. The one who lived longest was John. Late in his life, John became concerned that some people were forgetting what Jesus had taught. So John wrote a letter to all of the followers of Jesus to remind them, saying:

> **"We will know that we have come to know Jesus if we do His teachings."**
> **—1 John 2:3 (author paraphrase)**

It's the same with whatever discipline you study; Knowing **about** something is not the same as **knowing by doing** it. The best trainers make you do the work first, then study it. You come to know a thing intimately when you do it. This is how Jesus taught, and many have forgotten that, but Jesus repeatedly instructed His apprentices to be doers of His Word (see Matthew 7:24).

We have true intimate spiritual growth and intimate knowledge of Jesus when we do what He teaches. Jesus empowers us to do what He did in His life on earth. When you take a step at a time and do it, you come to know Him intimately. Then you master the details later.

Meditating on the Report: Jesus's apprentice taught that we could **know Jesus** by doing what He taught. Could this be true? Let's find out!

CHAPTER 2

COMMENCING THE ADVENTURE

*"Call to me and I will answer you and tell you great
and unsearchable things you do not know."*
—Jeremiah 33:3 (NIV)

STRAIGHTENING THE MAP

When Jesus came, one of the first things we notice is that **He made friends with ordinary people**, including some rough characters and some very messed up people. Religious people didn't like Him because He was a friend of corrupt businessmen, prostitutes, and foul-mouthed manual laborers. That's not how most folks think of Jesus!

Jesus went through the towns and villages, urgently inviting ordinary people to turn to God, saying that a great opportunity had come to them. Jesus put God first in all of His teachings. He said, *"The time has come! God's kingdom will soon be here. Turn back to God and believe the good news!"* (Mark 1:15)

If we start anywhere else, then we start with confusion. It's like having a map turned in the wrong direction. This is where Jesus started developing His apprentices. In the same way that a map starts with a marking for True North, we have to start with the one point in life that is permanent and unwavering. Jesus invited people like us to **turn to God** before He said anything else. That is what Jesus is still inviting people to do now.

Many religious leaders say you can only approach God through their organization or leader. But Jesus Himself is the connection point to God, not any organization. **Jesus openly invites everyone to come to God through Him!** (see John 1:39; John 6:37; John 5:21-22; John 10:27; Matthew 11:27-29).

Jesus came with a direct, specific invitation, and it's still true today. There is a great opportunity at this time to turn to God, who **welcomes you through Jesus**. It is just this simple: Ask God to help you turn to Him through Jesus. He gives you an open door to do that (see John 14:6).

UNLOADING OLD GEAR

Many people grew up in large organized religious movements and were taught that you have to be really religious and good to be accepted by God. Some folks believe that you have to keep many rituals to be accepted by God.

Other groups start by telling us all the things we must <u>turn away from</u>. They create lists of things we should not do that will make us unworthy of knowing God. This is also completely wrong. **Jesus has good news!** His plan is generous beyond comprehension.

CLARIFYING HIS CALL

The right focus, from Jesus's point of view, is to turn to God—not away from something. If we turn away from bad habits or false beliefs, we may choose another false way and still wander. Many religious people find exactly that. This is a testimony I have often heard: they had replaced addiction with religion but didn't really follow Jesus until much later.

Jesus says to start by **turning to God** first. Any other focus is as misleading as turning to a myth. Let's align where Jesus says to begin.

TRUE NORTH: OUR EXPEDITION'S OWNER

Before traveling into unknown territory, it is important to find True North. Without finding and aligning with it, you can never use the map.

At the beginning of His ministry, Jesus aligns Himself for us to properly understand the adventure. He makes it clear that He did not come in His own name. He came **in the name of His Father**, God Almighty.

Jesus claims that His Father is the one who spoke to Abraham and Moses. Jesus quotes the Old Testament Bible: the prophets, King David, King Solomon, and especially Moses, demonstrating that He is in accord with Almighty God, the Creator.

Jesus demonstrated that His Father is the Holy God of Israel, who led the people out of Egypt by great miracles to a sacred mountain in the middle of a vast desert. He gave them a covenant (agreement) and commandments through Moses, which the people accepted and promised to obey.

Then God told Moses that if the people rejected that agreement and continually broke the covenant, He would have to curse them. Through many centuries, that is exactly what the people did. They kept rejecting the covenant. It was to those people that Jesus came, in a time when they were trying to prove that THIS time, they could do it right.

THE MOST FANTASTIC MAN

Jesus revealed the teachings of the prophets from the Hebrew Bible repeatedly by fulfilling exactly what they predicted hundreds of years before He came. Jesus's entire life was a marvelous stream of events that precisely fulfilled the predictions and promises of the prophets in the Jewish Bible/Old Testament. Jesus said, *"Do not think that I came to destroy the Law or the Prophets. I did not come to destroy but to fulfill"* (Matthew 5:17, NKJV).

We will learn later what Jesus meant by the last three words, *". . . but to fulfill."* Doing that requires understanding: He is not abolishing or destroying the teachings of Moses and the prophets. Jesus comes in fulfillment, that is to say, *"in completion"* of them as much as in *perfection*. This continuous stream of consciousness, His mystery, began with Abraham, to Moses, to the prophets, and is finally completed in Jesus.

Until Moses, the prophet who wrote the first five books of the Bible, the world was full of people who worshiped all sorts of false gods and idols; it was also full of violence, evil, and abuse.

Into that world, God called Abraham to trust Him so that He would bring forth the Messiah (the anointed deliverer also called Christ) through Abraham to reveal God's blessing of peace to the world by redeeming mankind to Himself (see Genesis 15:6).

Later, God called Moses to reveal the true God, who sets people free and shows His perfect nature. Moses is well-known for leading the Exodus of Israel from Egypt to freedom, demonstrating God's miraculous power. Moses said that ultimately a final redeemer would come to set people free in the Spirit, leading them out of the slavery of lies and death of this world. This is the great hunger of our souls: to be free from this death curse that came upon us.

Jesus is the fulfillment, the prince from God, who makes a way to God, His Father.

Jesus said: *"If the Son gives you freedom, you are free!"* (John 8:36).

HEAVEN'S AMNESTY PLAN

God gave laws to show people we cannot live perfectly on our own. His perfection is pure and absolute. Any violation of God's covenant makes us a debtor, a rebel. His commands were designed so that we would seek and hope for amnesty from Him because He is merciful and kind.

Yet, when Jesus came, the religious leaders who claimed to follow Moses had created a system that was just as lost as the pagans! They had changed the system from a way to understand how much we need God to a system where people thought they could be right without God. This was the opposite of God's plan.

Jesus came to show who God really is, to show what He wants for people, and to <u>open the door</u> to the heavenly realm for all people to know God and be known by Him. This was God's plan from the beginning: to open the door and grant us an incredible relationship with Him that transforms us from weak natural beings into His children with His spiritual nature.

Jesus came according to the Father's plan to proclaim amnesty to us, a hostile race of rebels. From God's objective point of view, this rebel race of humanity was already a failed project. But God sent Jesus to cure the failed project and proclaim amnesty, which is available to all who will accept it.

In the message of Jesus, we discover the offer of amnesty is **the only offer**. There is no other plan coming, no second option. When Jesus came, He made it clear that none of us had any hope of correcting the problem of our rebellion against God without Jesus's help (see John 7:19; Isaiah 64:6).

HIS AMAZING FATHER

Jesus reveals more about the vast mystery of God than all of the previous prophets combined. As we take a thorough look, we see that He never contradicts any of the prophets of the Jewish Old Testament in any way. Rather, He fulfills their predictions with every step. So, briefly, we will look at whom Jesus reveals His Father to be, the God:

- whose word gives life to humanity (see Matthew 4:4)
- who should never be dared (see Matthew 4:7)
- worthy of being honored (see Matthew 4:10)
- in Heaven who is perfect (see Matthew 5:48)
- who sees what happens in secret (see Matthew 6:4,6)
- we can pray to, who knows our needs (see Matthew 6:8)
- in Heaven whose name is sacred (see Matthew 6:9)
- whose kingdom will come to earth (see Matthew 6:10a)
- whose will is done in Heaven (see Matthew 6:10b)
- who we can ask to meet our needs (see Matthew 6:11)

- whom we can ask to forgive us (see Matthew 6:12)
- who can keep us from temptation (see Matthew 6:13a)
- whose kingdom, power, and glory are eternal (see Matthew 6:13b)
- who forgives the forgiving (see Matthew 6:14-15)
- who cares for you and knows your needs (see Matthew 6:25-32)
- who meets your needs when you seek Him (see Matthew 6:33)
- who gives good things to His children that ask (see Matthew 7:11)
- who is Jesus's Father in Heaven (see Matthew 7:21)
- who is to be feared, who can send you to hell (see Matthew 10:28)
- who knows if even a sparrow is harmed (see Matthew 10:29)
- to whom Jesus will mediate for His followers (see Matthew 10:32-33)
- who conceals and reveals truth as He chooses (see Matthew 11:25-27)
- whose kingdom has come, in the person of Jesus (see Matthew 12:28)
- who adopts those who do His will (see Matthew 12:50)
- who is far away from hypocrites (see Matthew 15:7-9)
- who uproots what has not been planted by Him (see Matthew 15:13)

THE TIMELY OPPORTUNITY

Jesus said: *"The time has come! God's kingdom will soon be here. Turn back to God and believe the good news!"* (Mark 1:15) Good news is hard to find lately. Are you ready for really good news?

Jesus came and immediately confronted our broken world with a simple message. Some Bibles translate that as *"Repent and believe the Gospel."* Few people understand what Jesus meant by *"Repent," "Believe,"* or *"Gospel"* anymore.

The phrase means that we acknowledge our inability before God, our reliance on Him, and that we turn to Him to be changed. The false religious systems of the world will tell you that you can and **must clean yourself up** (be good and live right) to be acceptable to God.

But there's one problem: no one can agree on what good is!! If they agree on "good," they don't agree on **how good**. What Jesus said was actually something else: ***"Turn to God and trust Him,"*** then your life will be transformed. That transformation creates "good" in us from Him.

That is what we desperately need. When Jesus said this, the word translated as "repent," means "turn around." It's the idea of making a decision to change your mind—to stop running **from** God and run **to** Him. The word "believe" means learning to trust and "rely on." The word for gospel means "good news." Therefore, Jesus is saying: *"Just turn to God and trust His very good news!"* **It's an invitation.**

An Old Testament prophet tells us that God said to the people, *"Come now, let us reason together"* (Isaiah 1:18, ESV). God wants you to turn to Him, reason with Him, and hear what He has to say. Hear and understand His heart. If you do that, it's not just good news, it's great news.

Adventure Principle: God is good, and we are not, but He has a plan to solve that problem, and that's great news for us.

THE TRAILHEAD

God sent Jesus to invite each of us to take the step of trusting His good plan. None of us can understand or correctly sort life out until we turn to God, who created our life. We can never be good enough; we can never sort it all out; we can never be "complete," until we turn to God and follow Jesus. That's the first great step of the Jesus Adventure.

Would you consider that you are reading this because God is calling you to take that important step? Would you consider that God Himself is asking you to trust Him? Consider accepting that and speak it in your heart.

Successful Adventurers call out to God directly and personally to receive His good news. God has a plan to prosper you and not harm you (see Jeremiah 29:11). Jesus revealed that God wants to give you a great future and a great hope in Him.

HEART OF THE MATTER

The natural mind is blinded spiritually; this tells us that we cannot be right with God even if we spend a lifetime on self-improvement efforts. Instead, Jesus says it is not with us, but with God, to make us complete; spiritual life begins the same way physical life begins. **You must be born into it.**

A very religious man named Nicodemus (Nick) once went to Jesus because he was troubled by all the miracles and teachings he saw Jesus doing. Nick knew that Jesus was doing miracles which the prophets said would be the works of the Messiah.

It was not the miracles themselves but what Jesus was teaching that bothered Nick. His heart was not right with God, and Nick knew that was a problem that Jesus's teachings revealed. So, he asked Jesus to explain it.

Jesus told Nick, *"I tell you the truth, no one can see the Royal Power and Authority of God unless he is born anew"* (John 3:3, author paraphrase). Nick struggled to see that his need was this simple. Religious people often resist the simplicity of Jesus. The problem is the heart. If you humble yourself to accept that God can change you, you are ready for His blessing.

But religious people are generally too proud of how hard they work, so they believe they have earned something. They have trouble believing that they have a debt to our Creator, which is impossible for them to solve. So, what can be done?

None of us did much of the work being born in the first place, right? Jesus is telling us that there is a dimension of life that we cannot perceive until we have a spiritual birth. Unlike our physical birth, each of us has a choice in this one.

We can respond to God and ask Him for spiritual birth. Just like our physical birth, this is a process. Don't expect to understand everything right away. Let God reveal it as He grows you on the journey.

So, what is the journey of spiritual birth? Jesus said to Nick:

> **Flesh gives birth to flesh, but the Spirit gives birth to spirit. You should not be surprised at my saying, "You must be born again." The wind blows wherever it pleases. You hear its sound, but you cannot tell where it comes from or where it is going. So it is with everyone born of the Spirit.**
> —John 3:6-8 (NIV)

Jesus is telling us that human eyes can't understand what God does in this spiritual birth process. In the same way, you could not be seen in your mother's belly, the working of God's Spirit is hidden—in a secret place.

ASK FOR HEAVEN'S OPEN DOOR

The Jesus Adventure offers an open door, but we have to ASK. Some people have difficulty with this idea of spiritual birth because they struggle to surrender their hearts. Many of us had the same struggle, and Jesus understood. That's why Jesus used the concept of birth.

Being born in this world is a great struggle! Some babies die in childbirth, and some mothers die giving birth. It takes all the passion and energy a woman has in her to give birth. The baby's body must relax and become flexible for birth. The days just before childbirth require a softening for the baby.

God understands this is a problem we have as people needing spiritual birth. It has been the problem with all people across all history—we don't want to yield to God! It is simple, yet it is a challenge to your soul. Many of us fear yielding to God more than we fear danger. So, it helps to really look at the character of God.

When you look to Jesus and recognize His heart—it makes all the difference. The heart of Jesus shows us that **God has great compassion for us.** The life of Jesus shows us that God has sent us His best and has given us more compassion than we can comprehend. Jesus said, *"God loved the people of this world so much that he gave his only Son"* (John 3:16).

Jesus also says His Father wants good things for you and has good plans for you. He said:

> **As bad as you are, you still know how to give good gifts to your children. But your heavenly Father is even more ready to give good things to <u>people who ask</u>.**
> **—Matthew 7:11 (author emphasis)**

As we look at Jesus, we see God's heart and it is trustworthy! In Jesus, we see that God is dependable. In Jesus, God's heart overflows with generosity and kindness. In Jesus, we see that God will not require anything of us that will ultimately destroy us.

Instead, He guides us to things that grow us, restore us, and make us alive with hope and joy. He leads us to Himself by kindness; He actually calls us to seek Him to **fulfill our needs**. All over the world, for twenty centuries, people have learned from Jesus that they can trust God. Jesus said, *"Ask, and it shall be given. Seek and you will find. Knock and it will be opened"* (author paraphrase).

What are we asking, seeking, and knocking for? That relationship with God through Jesus. He is not far. He does not ignore us if we simply follow this model. He is willing!

GOD'S LOVING COMPASSION

When I first began to follow Jesus, I thought I understood God. Then I had children. There was an instant and overflowing love for my children as a father. I would do anything for my kids, even give up my life. I love my kids with all my heart. This love is from God, the ultimate Father.

God repeatedly says that He is a Father who has compassion for His children. He loves His kids perfectly. Yet, we rebel against Him and reject Him. Our problem is that we don't love Him! Which is why we struggle to trust.

God has a plan for our best interests. God has more compassion than any human father has for his children. It is easier to trust God when we realize that He is for us, not against us; when we realize that His mercy for us is new every day; and that His forgiveness is so perfect that He throws our sins and evil deeds into the depths of the seas. So we can relax. We can release the fear and open our hearts to God.

TIME OF GOD'S FAVOR

At the start of His ministry, Jesus stood up in the middle of community worship, opened the Old Testament scroll of Isaiah, and read:

> **The Spirit of the Lord is on me, because he has anointed me to proclaim good news to the poor. He has sent me to proclaim freedom for the prisoners and recovery of sight for the blind, to set the oppressed free, to proclaim the year of the Lord's favor.**
> **—Luke 4:18-19**

Wow! **A Spirit of blessing, good news, freedom, vision, hope, and favor!** Hey, that's something to get excited about! Do you doubt God? Do you hate God? Do you hope that God is a fairy tale? Many of us who are now Jesus's followers had those same feelings. He has an answer for you, and it might surprise you! **He's reaching out to say: I welcome you!**

THE FRESH NEW SAYINGS

It is often missed by religious groups that Jesus did not say in any way that He was simply revising, renewing, reiterating, or repeating what God has already done. In fact, some of his most common phrases are *"Fresh," "New,"* and *"You have heard it said, but I say."*

Now, we know that the Bible is clear that God does not change. His perfection, His personality, and His standards are always the same. However, we cannot miss that Jesus is clearly saying in various ways that **the previous**

system is over. Therefore, the question becomes: what does that mean, and how does it affect us now? We discover this through the Adventure.

WAIT JUST A MINUTE

That God is unchanging is probably not what you have heard in the past. After all, doesn't religion teach that God is angry with us? Perhaps you're thinking, **"I thought God wanted to punish me."** There is indeed judgment coming on all people; every nation and every class of person must stand before God, but it is **not God's desire to punish us.**

God is actually looking for people that He can reward! The problem for us is that the standard of Heaven is too high for our rebel hearts. We have a problem at the core of our beings. While it's true that we have rebelled against God, it is also true that God wants everyone to turn to Him—because He has a cure. God goes to every length possible to win back to Himself every person who will turn and trust Him. This is **the heart of the Father.** He is calling us home, and Jesus makes it possible.

Maybe the idea of God being a good Father is hard to understand. Jesus knows that. So, He also tells us that He is like a shepherd. Shepherds are funny people, and usually shepherds love their animals like family.

I know a family who raised dairy goats. They named each one. One day, one of the goats pushed open a hole in the fence to escape, and a pair of vicious dogs from a nearby neighborhood got in and killed the goats.

Well, this is what happened in our spiritual world. **Our race has broken the boundaries.** We pushed open the fences. So now real evil stalks us. What was once a beautiful world has turned ugly.

God knows just how evil the world can get. He is calling us out from this corrupt anti-Christ, anti-God culture. His message is going out to the whole world, and Jesus has made a way for us to turn to God, trust Him, and receive blessings from Him. As the message says, in Jesus there is a Spirit of blessing, good news, freedom, vision, hope, and favor available to us! Wow! **This is the life-giving spirit of the Jesus Adventure.**

SHEPHERD OF THE HEART

There are surprising things we find upon simply turning to God—no matter who we are, where we come from, or how bad the things that we have done. **God surprises us!** He welcomes us with an invitation. Jesus said, *"I didn't come to invite good people to turn to God. I came to invite sinners"* (Mark 2:17).

Can you hear that call? Jesus is inviting the people who have messed up. He's inviting the ones who made foolish mistakes and those who are real rebels. **Each of us.** He's not inviting perfect people—because there are none.

Jesus has been seeking you already because He loves you with great compassion. Jesus said, *"The Son of Man came to look for and to save people who are lost"* (Luke 19:10).

Jesus is not expecting us to save ourselves. Some religious people grumbled about Jesus and said, "This man is friendly with sinners. He even eats with them." Then Jesus told them this story:

> **If any of you has 100 sheep, and one of them gets lost, what will you do? Won't you leave the 99 in the field and go look for the lost sheep until you find it? And when you find it, you will be so glad that you will put it on your shoulder and carry it home. Then you will call in your friends and neighbors and say, "Let's celebrate! I've found my lost sheep."**
> **—Luke 15:4-7**

He says **a good shepherd does the heavy lifting.** He does what we cannot do—and He's willing to do it for just one. The Shepherd empowers us to be much more than we are.

He understands we are born as rebel children in a rebel world. He wants to adopt us to make us His own kids—like you might do with a stray puppy, even if that puppy has been sprayed by a skunk.

Remember, Jesus also said:

> **God loved the people of this world so much that he gave his only Son, so that everyone who has faith in him will have eternal life and never really die.**
> **–John 3:16**

Our Great Shepherd came to rescue us and bring us into His flock to kindly lead us to good things. When Jesus said this, He was reminding His followers of Psalm 23, the memorable poem written by His ancestor David, the king who was once a shepherd boy:

> **The Lord is my shepherd, I lack nothing. He makes me lie down in green pastures, he leads me beside quiet waters, he refreshes my soul.**
> **He guides me along the right paths for his name's sake.**
> **–Psalm 23:3 (NIV)**

This tells us that God wants to bring us to good things, bless us, meet our needs, care for us, and comfort us in a harsh world of death and danger; God wants to give us blessings that overflow. But He can't lead us to blessings while we're running away.

THE GREAT INVITATION REPRISE

We have seen that Jesus invites us to turn to God and trust Him; Jesus welcomes us heartily to receive His love, to be empowered, and to be transformed. In doing this, He breaks down all the barriers that could possibly keep us from Him, except the one thing He leaves under our control: our own hearts.

Jesus is a gentleman. He doesn't force; He comes with a welcome, with open arms. He's never demanding. Jesus lets you respond because He wants willing, hopeful, and trusting followers.

This is why Jesus says to **turn to God and believe (trust)**: because that kind of believing comes from the heart, it's not blind faith! It's faith that relies on the character of God as He reveals Himself to us. If you want to have a relationship with God, Jesus offers the means to have it.

LOVING THROUGH PAIN

A sick child who needs painful injections may know that the doctors are trying to help. But it doesn't help the kid to accept it. But when the mother asks that child to trust her, her comfort encourages that child's heart to accept the doctors and their injections.

In the same way, Jesus says believe/trust Him. He offers comfort and leads you to trust that God intends the best for you. God's best is Jesus who proved that He cares for you because He came into our broken world and suffered the most desperate conditions any human has ever endured, for your sake. He said He did it because the Father loves you.

Trust the Shepherd, the Guide of the Adventure. Often when people are outwardly religious, they miss this call of Jesus to turn to God. They work so hard at being good, being better than others, that they lack understanding and humility.

So, they miss what Jesus meant when He said: *"Believe"* (see John 6:29; Mark 9:23; John 6:35). That word He used for "believe" is an appeal for us **to trust** God, whom we can know.

A friend of mine loved to climb high rock cliffs. He once climbed a cliff that was so high he had to sleep in a hammock overnight, suspended halfway up the cliff. He was held by ropes, more than a thousand feet off the ground. He did that because he believed his anchor would hold tight! That is the **idea of trust that Jesus gives us.** In the same way that Jesus trusted His Father, we can trust Jesus. He is the anchor.

We develop a dependency on Him. In a dangerous situation, we rest securely and sleep comfortably because the anchor is strong and reliable. Jesus showed us how to trust God and believe He will fulfill His promises.

How can we do that? It's possible when we learn God's promises and start acting on them. We can also see others who have come to trust God and had their trust rewarded. My friend learned he could trust the strength of the ropes and anchors, so he could sleep while hanging off a cliff. This is the way of Jesus's Adventure. Trust the anchor.

TRUSTING PROMISES FOR LIFE

Jesus is a Shepherd who makes and keeps promises.

Jesus said to His followers:

> **Don't be worried! Have faith [trust] in God and have faith [trust] in me. There are many rooms in my Father's house. I wouldn't tell you this, unless it was true. I am going there to prepare a place for each of you.**
> —John 14:2-3 (author additions)

Jesus is the only person who knew the exact hour and manner of His death. He also knew His death was not the end! On the night before His death, Jesus promised that they could trust Him to come back. So, three days later, He did!

Jesus has proven that we can trust Him. For three years, His apprentices watched Him keep His word <u>every time</u>. He was asking them to trust Him again, that this death would not be the end!

Here, Jesus said again, "believe" (or trust), as when He called them in the first place. Now, Jesus expects us to test and learn to trust Him according to His promises. Our belief is not a blind leap. Like my friend studied the reliability of the ropes on the cliff, we can learn and test the reliability of Jesus. It is a trust walk.

The interaction with God builds our confidence. Jesus did that from the beginning until the last day with His apprentices. He still does. He wasn't just speaking of coming back in three days. He will come back after the work of building His global fellowship is done.

Essentially, Jesus said, "Trust me, folks, I'm coming back." He wants us to learn to trust Him by the testimony of others who have found Him faithful, by the promises He makes, and by the way He does exactly what He says He is going to do. Jesus's apprentices found that He **did** come back, resurrected to their total amazement, three days later. This was the testimony of each of His apprentices.

So, the Jesus Adventure takes shape with Jesus guiding us to develop a trusting relationship with God based on the Great News that He offers. No one ever makes progress following Jesus until they enter through this passage.

The Great News is that **this door is open wide**. There is no other door available, but this one is completely open today, and no one can stop you from entering! Once we begin trusting God, we make headway. The light of God shines brighter on our path, and every new day offers us more opportunities to trust in God and see His awesome work.

ENTERING THE OPEN DOOR

As we close this chapter and move forward, it helps to note this moment. Some people on the journey take time to record the date and place. Personally, I can recall both the date and the place when I prayed to begin trusting Jesus.

Everyone who follows Jesus starts here: we humble ourselves and recognize that we need Him; we cannot do it on our own. Without Jesus, we have no standing with God.

We can't get spiritual life by ourselves, and we don't have to; it's the Life-Giving Spirit of Christ that births us into a new life. Just like a mother's love overflowing to give birth, the same is true of the Spirit of God! He is filled with love that comes from the Father! Jesus said it simply to Nick, the confused religious teacher, that night:

> **God loved the people of this world so much that He gave his only Son, so that everyone who has faith in him will have eternal life and never really die. <u>God did not send his Son into the world to condemn</u> its people. He sent him to save them! No one who has faith in God's Son will be condemned. But everyone who doesn't have faith in him has already been condemned for not having faith in God's only Son.**
> **—John 3:16-18**

Do you see the passion? It's love and desire to give life. For all human history, mothers have endured the pain of childbirth **to give life**. This is what Jesus shows us of God—that He is passionate about giving us life in the Spirit.

The spiritual life that God gives is so beautiful, joyful, and precious that people have been singing songs, writing poetry, painting pictures, and telling the story of God's love for thousands of years to pass it on! Faithful followers of Jesus have endured suffering and every discomfort, even giving up their lives to pass it on! Because this is what Jesus gave us! The greatest act of sacrificial love ever seen. This is the glory of God's spiritual life!

Jesus was so full of love for us to receive it that He went to a Roman cross and suffered the most brutal death to pass it on! No devil could tempt Him away from it. No man could talk Him out of it. No suffering could scare Him away from it; Jesus was so passionate to pass on this spiritual birth to the people of this world. He is still the same today.

Jesus is the door to heaven, which is open wide to those humble enough to receive Him. Enter and become part of God's eternal realm. We simply have to recognize that we cannot enter without God's Son. He takes anyone who humbles themselves.

SEEKING THE ADVENTURE'S GUIDE

If you have doubts, tell them to God.
If you have fears, tell them to God.
If you have hatred, tell it to God.
If you have a need, tell it to God.
If you have evil desires, tell them to God.
If you struggle to believe, tell it to God.
If you need assurance, ask God.

Jesus showed us how simple it is to move the heart of God when He quoted two men who prayed at the temple in Jerusalem. Two men went into the temple to pray. One was a Pharisee (a very religious man), and the other a tax collector (a cheating scoundrel). The Pharisee stood by himself and prayed:

> "God, I thank you that I am not greedy, dishonest, and unfaithful in marriage like other people. And I am really glad that I am not like that tax collector over there. I go without eating two days a week, and I give you one-tenth of all I earn. The tax collector stood off at a distance and did not think he was good enough even to look up toward heaven. He was so sorry for what he had done that he pounded his chest and prayed, "God, have pity on me! I am such a sinner." Then Jesus said, "When the two men went home, it was the tax collector and not the Pharisee who was pleasing to God. If you put yourself above others, you will be put down. But if you humble yourself, you will be honored."
> –Luke 8:11-15

One prayed pridefully, and God rejected his prayer; the other stood away at a distance and humbly said, *"God have mercy on me, a sinner."* Jesus said that man left with God's favor!

This is an example of what you could pray in a humble way that would please God: "Jesus, please show me the way. Father God, I struggle with trusting you; are you real? I am an unbelieving rebel at heart. But I want to turn to you and trust you. I want to find the Good News that Jesus taught. Will you accept me and lead me to receive spiritual life? Please forgive me for my rebellious heart and give me enough faith to trust you. Please change my life."

Praying like this will move the heart of God.

DISCOVERING THE TRUSTWORTHY HEART OF GOD

The prophet Jeremiah said that you can seek God and that you will find Him when you do it with a sincere heart (see Jeremiah 29:13). I have spoken to many people who have done this. It is not just the ancient people of the Bible who experienced this. The New Testament also says, *"God has done all this, so that we will look for him and reach out and find him"* (Acts 17:27). This is exactly what we have found: when people call to God through Jesus Christ (the Messiah), they really do find Him.

Adventure Principle: Even though we are not good, God accepts those humble and sincere enough to ask Him.

MEDITATION ON BEGINNING THE JESUS ADVENTURE

Consider how God shows us sacrificial love-filled living, like a mother giving birth to a newborn child. He yearns for you to receive His Life-Giving Spirit. This is just the beginning, so continue to the next chapter in the Jesus Adventure.

CHAPTER 3

THE ADVENTURE WAY

"Follow Me!"
–Matthew 4:19, Jesus calling His apprentices

INTRIGUING JOURNEY OF ACTION

If you have done what Jesus said this far, you are set for a great adventure! You are on your way to realizing and experiencing so many new things.

Jesus did so many astonishing things that are recorded in the four gospel accounts—it captures the imagination to consider them. Yet John, His youngest apprentice, said there wouldn't be enough books in the world to contain all that he saw Jesus do. Then, John and his friends went out and did more things that were amazing.

Although John was just a young fisherman when he met Jesus, he was eventually recognized for teaching all about the adventures of Jesus—everywhere he went for the rest of his life. A Roman Caesar tried several ways to stop John but couldn't kill him, so he had him marooned on a barren island. John survived and became even more enthusiastic about sharing Jesus.

John was an action guy like Jesus—he really enjoyed seeing God's power at work, so he didn't spend much time sitting around! This is what's so great about the Jesus Adventure. If you're willing to follow Jesus, very interesting things happen!

HEARING THE CALL

Is your heart hungry for this journey that Jesus is calling you to follow? I was, although I didn't understand Jesus at first. But I knew this life had to be about something deeper, higher, and bigger than I had known. I found the answer to that hunger in Jesus. Decades later, I'm still convinced.

Jesus is still calling us to continue on the adventure too! When John finally got around to writing about Jesus, he remembered and wrote that Jesus said:

> **The sheep know their shepherd's voice. He calls each of them by name and leads them out. When he has led out all of his sheep, he walks in front of them, and they follow, because they know his voice.**
> **—John 10:4-5 (author paraphrase)**

Originally, I didn't like being called a sheep, but I found comfort in knowing that I have a shepherd who calls to me. This is the way of Jesus: He calls quietly in the Spirit, almost imperceptibly, deep inside. He calls us to follow, and He keeps urging us. Will you listen to His voice and respond? "Yes, Sir, help me follow you, Jesus."

WHERE HE LEADS

Why did Jesus call people to follow Him? Some of us get weird ideas about what it means. We fear that He would want us to dress weirdly, walk around with weird haircuts, carry a big cross and a big garish Bible, shout at people, and pray out loud on the street corner. But Jesus **does not** want us to do that. Seriously. In fact, He said don't do that (see Matthew 6:5).

Jesus called ordinary people to come alongside Him. In fact, very few of His early followers were rich or powerful. Some used foul language; some were liars. One was an assassin. **Imagine that!**

They were laborers with calloused hands and sunburned necks. One guy was a cheating bureaucrat. Some were housewives and moms. Some were prostitutes and criminals.

The most remarkable thing about Jesus's followers is that they were mostly unremarkable. They were ordinary. Jesus made room for the scholar and the leader, but they were not His first choice.

As Jesus walked along the shore of Lake Galilee, He saw Simon and his brother, Andrew. They were fishermen, casting their nets into the lake. Jesus said to them, *"Follow me! I will teach you how to bring in people instead of fish"* (Matthew 4:19; Mark 1:17). The brothers dropped their nets and went with Him.

Jesus then saw James and John, the sons of Zebedee, in a boat mending their nets. At once Jesus asked them to come with Him. They left their father in the boat with the hired workers and went with Him (see Matthew 4:19-21).

Jesus called them to follow Him, but did you notice that He also made a promise? He said if they followed Him, they would become winsome enough to draw other people to Jesus. Following Jesus is interactive and attracts humble-hearted people.

As Jesus was leaving, He saw a tax collector named Matthew sitting at the place for paying taxes. Jesus said to him, *"Come with me."* Matthew got up and went with him (Matthew 9:9).

REQUIREMENTS FOR TAKING THE ADVENTURE

To truly follow Jesus, we must be willing to be guided. Peter, Andrew, James, and John (among His earliest followers) laid down their nets and left their businesses behind to follow Jesus. Matthew left his highly paid tax collector franchise. Mary Magdalene left her prostitution, Simon left his anarchy, Nathaniel left his lethargy, and eventually, Thomas left his doubting.

What would you need to leave behind to follow Jesus? Following Jesus is meant to change us, and that changes the world around us. To follow the Shepherd of our souls, everyone must become willing to be led. When Jesus leads, He always draws us away from lesser things.

What do you need to leave behind to follow Jesus? Don't miss out on what Jesus has in store for you.

Jesus had many more interesting things ahead for His followers. He promised them (and us) that we would gain more than we left behind. People still find that true today.

FOLLOWING THE WAY OF JESUS

There were many ways that Jesus could have called His followers. In the original Greek language of the Bible's New Testament, there are at least five different terms, each with a different meaning for how to "follow." The word Jesus used for *"Follow me"* is the word that means **"Work with me; let's partner together."**

Jesus invites us to join Him personally, to partner in His work, like apprentices. He wants to personally engage and train us. It's mutual, a joint venture. Jesus is relational, and He's calling you. I believe that's why you picked this book up and read this far—His Spirit is calling out for you to join as an apprentice in His work.

This is an invitation to actively join in the life-giving spiritual work of God. Come and see; you are welcomed. We start as what we were, however ordinary or special we may be, and begin learning from Him.

This makes us truly unique as Jesus develops apprentices, building His mastery into us. He calls us to turn to God, trust Him, and attentively follow His training. It's a spiritual training program for everyday people!

Adventure Principle: Following Jesus is about partnering in His adventure with Him as His apprentice.

RISKY INSPIRATION FROM THE MASTER

Have you ever wondered why so many people are drawn to Jesus? What motivated them thousands of years ago? What motivates them now? What keeps people coming? What makes them stay? Being a follower of Jesus is risky business.

Some say that fear is the motivator. But there was much more to fear in following Him; Jesus was not popular with the powerful people. **Their reason must have been deeper.**

Perhaps you have heard that Jesus did miracles and that His followers said He was the Christ, the Messiah, the Savior of the world. I heard that things were epic and magical about Him. But just hearing about Him doesn't satisfy us. His apprentices do more than listen—they take action and join in.

Following Jesus requires learning why He is worthy of being followed—and **then doing** what He says. It can't just be hearing epic stories about Him. **We want the real stuff, however risky it may be!**

There has to be more than tales! Taking action and following Jesus requires knowing that He is real, that He is alive, and that He is worthy of being followed. It requires knowing that His epic is true; it must be real. Well, the good news is that there is so much more to this man they call the Messiah, the Savior, the Christ.

He never carried a sword, yet tyrants have feared him since His birth. He never hurt a soul, but prideful people have hated Him and tried to destroy His words for nearly 2,000 years. People who knew Him were willing to leave everything to follow Him.

There has to be a good reason why. Those are just three of the many incredible things that compel us to learn more. His follower, Philip, said something to another at the beginning that gives us great insight. Philip became convinced he needed to get his closest friend to meet Jesus.

> **Philip then found Nathanael and said: "We have found the one that Moses and the Prophets wrote about. He is Jesus, the son of Joseph from Nazareth." Nathanael asked, "Can anything good come from Nazareth?" Philip answered, "Come and see."**
> **—John 1:45-46**

When I read that, I sense the excitement in Philip's voice. He really wants to be sure that Nathanael doesn't miss out. Philip promised Nathanael that Jesus would not disappoint him. Jesus was the very person that all the Old Testament prophets had spoken of. Despite concerns, Nathanael did come and see—and found what he was looking for.

When you research it, you find that numerous prophets foretold Jesus's entire life over a span of more than a thousand years. The greatest of them wrote more than 400 years before Jesus was born, and he was the most specific. The very details of Jesus's ancestry, His birth, His times, His childhood, His ministry, His miracles, His death, and ultimately His resurrection are foretold by multiple prophets.

Experts have documented more than 300 prophecies that Jesus fulfilled, but I will show you a few. As we meditate on the whole account of this fascinating humble teacher from Nazareth, we find every detail of His life leaps forward to fulfill prophecy, both directly and in amazing symbolic patterns. Every time I read the prophets of the Old Testament, I find something new that speaks of the man from Galilee.

HIS PROPHETIC ORIGIN

Many people are surprised to discover more evidence for Jesus in the Prophets than in the Gospels. The prophet Isaiah said He would have a miraculous birth (see Isaiah 7:14), and the prophet Micah said He would be born in Bethlehem (see Micah 5:2-4), the city of his ancestor, King David. This is the topic of Christmas celebrations around the world.

The prophet Hosea said He would leave His birthplace and return from Egypt as a child This was fulfilled when the tyrant King Herod put a death sentence on Jesus after He was born (see Hosea 11:1).

HIS TIMES

The prophets Isaiah and Malachi said that one last prophet preaching in the desert would come right before the Messiah (see Isaiah 40:3; Malachi 3:1). This happened exactly as promised. That man known as John the Baptist preached and baptized people in the desert to prepare them for Jesus. John the Baptist said Jesus was the one that he was sent to prepare people to meet.

Isaiah and David wrote that Messiah would be rejected by His own people (see Psalm 69:8; Isaiah 53:3). Less than 10 percent of the Jewish people were noted to be followers of Jesus in the first century, and still today, only a minority of descendants of Israel follow Him.

The prophet Daniel said the Jewish Messiah would be killed during a climactic time, and afterward the city of Jerusalem and its temple would be destroyed (see Daniel 9:26). Jesus came to Jerusalem at the **exact year and day specified** and was killed as a criminal. Jerusalem and the temple were completely destroyed thirty-eight years later, while many people who heard Him teach still lived, all of which precisely fulfilled what Daniel wrote.

HIS LIFE EVENTS

It was foretold that the Messiah:
- Would be known as a man from Galilee (see Isaiah 9:1-2)
- Would be known for bringing good news to the poor, healing brokenhearted people, and preaching God's liberty (see Isaiah 61:1-2)

- Would come suddenly to the temple in Jerusalem, bringing judgment on the corrupt leaders who exploited the people (see Malachi 3:1). Jesus went there on the day He was publicly recognized as Messiah the Prince and suddenly threw out people who were exploiting and profiting off the poor. He did this in the last week of His life, and this is one of the reasons they were eager to have Jesus put to death.
- Would bring a new covenant, which would explain a new relationship with God (see Jeremiah 31:31). Jesus said this referred to Himself, and He taught extensively about what this new relationship with God means. The details in these passages are right alongside other passages that speak of events during Jesus's life.
- Would be betrayed by one of His followers for thirty pieces of silver, which would be thrown into the temple and used to buy a potter's field (see Psalm 41:9; Zechariah 11:12-13).

This is just a short sample of the hundreds written by the Old Testament prophets. I recommend searching out this topic more fully later.

So, Jesus is no mere teacher. He is the most unique person who ever lived. Long before He was born, every major detail of His life was foretold by Bible prophets. Because of this and the works He did in His life, it is clear that God is calling us to trust and follow Jesus!

Adventure Principle: Jesus is no mere man. He is the only man who is the subject of the Bible from beginning to end.

WILL THE REAL JESUS PLEASE STAND UP!

One day, Jesus asked His followers who other people said He was.

> He asked them, "What do people say about the Son of Man?" The disciples answered, "Some people say you are John the Baptist or maybe Elijah or Jeremiah or some other prophet." Then Jesus asked them, "But who do you say I am?" Simon Peter spoke up, "You are the Messiah, the Son of the living God."
> –Luke 9:18-20 (author paraphrase)

> **Jesus told him: 'Simon, son of Jonah, you are blessed! You didn't discover this on your own. It was shown to you by my Father in heaven.'"**
> —Matthew 16:17-19

Afterward, Jesus told them not to tell anyone He was the Messiah (Christ). I believe that Jesus wants people to discover who He is by learning to follow Him and doing what He teaches—**not by popular consensus**. It is a discovery process.

It's much more enlightening to find out for yourself who Jesus is by reading the prophets and reading Jesus's own words. The Bible reveals much more than we can learn from being told by others. And it transforms you.

At one point, Jesus departed Israel into the land of the Samaritans and talked with a woman. From their conversation, she concluded and told others that Jesus was the long-awaited Messiah. Jesus did not correct her but acknowledged her discovery (see John 4). The people of Israel and Judah had long awaited this Messiah, knowing He would have authority from Heaven.

I encourage you to search out these Bible references and consider them. I am convinced these passages reveal who Jesus is and suggest you dig them out—it's more fascinating when you do it yourself.

There are a lot of discoveries to make while following Jesus. I made many while researching this book. Jesus fulfilled the qualifications of being the Savior, that is to say, "the one and only Messiah" described by those prophets.

Looking more carefully, we discover that God has hidden many treasures that reveal Jesus in every book of the Bible, both the Old and New Testaments. Jesus said that Moses specifically wrote about Him, and Jesus rebuked the religious scholars of His day for not recognizing that fact. Did Jesus claim to be God? Yes, because God said there is no other Savior. In Isaiah 43:11 (NIV), God says, *"Apart from me there is no savior."*

In Hosea 13:4 (author paraphrase), God says, *"I am . . . your God . . . You shall acknowledge no God but me, no Savior except me."*

So, who is Jesus? The prophets are telling us that there is no Savior but God. And when Jesus says that He is the Son of Man, then He is claiming to be the one whom the prophets Daniel and Micah claim **existed before time** itself (see Daniel 7:9-10; Micah 5:2).

In the Daniel passage, the *"Son of Man"* is referred to as being before time; that is what *"the Ancient of Days"* means in the original language. Daniel uses this phrase three times to refer to God. Micah says to the ancient people of Israel:

> **Out of you will come for me one who will be ruler over Israel, whose origins are from of old, from ancient times.**
> —Micah 5:2 (NIV)

Another peculiar phrase in the original language tells us the Messiah/Savior is literally from eternity, from outside time itself. So, you may say, "Yes, but how does that refer to Jesus?" Well, this is <u>the same prophecy</u> that was revealed to Herod, the tyrant king, when Jesus was born:

> **But you, Bethlehem Ephrathah, though you are small among the clans of Judah, out of you will come for me one who will be ruler over Israel, whose origins are from of old, from ancient times.**

The prophets are telling you who Jesus is. Can you perceive it? The Savior is the Shepherd and the Eternal King. This Shepherd of our souls is the Savior of the world, the Eternal Creator of the world.

To make this clear, Jesus revealed a mystery:

> **My sheep know my voice, and I know them. They follow me, <u>and I give them eternal life</u>, so that they will never be lost. No one can snatch them out of my hand.**
> **–John 10:27-28**

Do you see? Jesus shows Himself to be greater than the substance of time itself. He has **the power to offer eternity to us.** He is offering something that takes us on an adventure now and forever. It begins here and never ends. Eternal life is a quality of life, as well as a duration of life.

Well, what does He want us to do? What does it mean to follow Him? How do we find that eternal life from Jesus? Jesus is claiming authority and power here far beyond that of any mortal or created being. He is claiming supreme power, and He is promising to use that for our good. Okay, so we want to know: what is the way to get to that? Jesus is the way. He is not just offering to take us on an adventure; **He is the adventure.**

Adventure Principle: The King of Eternity is the Savior who offers the Eternal Adventure.

MEDITATIONS ON FOLLOWING THE GOOD SHEPHERD

In Matthew 5:3-12, Jesus makes amazing statements. He says that those who turn to God will overcome the worst circumstances. They will experience joy, happiness, and serenity; even when situations are opposite. He says anyone following Him will have blessings, joy, and happiness, even in poverty, mourning, or persecution.

LIGHTING OUR PATH

From here onward, we're exploring Jesus's instructions for His amazing adventure: to be empowered through His principle of trust and what He means by "faith" and "believe." We will explore how to receive His peace and power to overcome every difficulty. We will discover skillful listening and authoritative praying as confident explorers, able to take perilous journeys of faith. We will discover the heart of the loving Creator of life, who promises everything we need to discover the purpose we were created for. We investigate it all as we seek the epic Jesus Adventure.

> Examine me, O God, and know my mind;
> test me, and discover my thoughts.
> Find out if there is any evil in me
> and guide me in the everlasting way.
> —Psalm 139:23-24 (GNT)

PART 2

WALKING THE WAY OF JESUS

CHAPTER 4

THE VITAL CURE

E arly in Jesus's ministry, a man came to Him, and having heard of Him, the man believed that if Jesus was willing, He could heal him.

> **Moved with compassion, Jesus stretched out His hand and touched him, and said to him, "I am willing; be cleansed!"**
> –Luke 5:13 (author paraphrase)

Jesus spoke with power when healing diseased and broken people. The man was instantly healed.

POWER TO HEAL AND TRANSFORM

Living out this great adventure as an apprentice of Jesus is amazing. But it's not just about fun and fascination. The name of Jesus has power! There is power to overcome evil of every kind and to heal the most broken life—power over sickness and the things that cause it and power to heal souls sickened by rebellion against God.

This walk gives us joy, but it's a walk that challenges our natural minds. Getting there means we unlearn much of what we have learned in this broken world. We know there's something wrong with us, but we never seem to figure it out on our own. God says His ways are higher than our ways, and His thoughts are higher than our thoughts (see Isaiah 55:8-9), beyond our ability to understand.

We see this when we consider the history of the world before Jesus came, compared to our own times. Things that were normal then seem so wrong and alien to us now.

Jesus demonstrates that God's ways and plans work, even though our minds cannot understand how. God says give, and we will have more. God says trust Him and do, without knowing it all, and we succeed more than the person who tries to know it all. God says to depend on Him, and we become more independent than people who try so hard to control their own lives.

Everything God calls us to do seems wrong, yet it works. Everything that seems right ultimately fails. God teaches and empowers us to succeed in His ways. Living out this spiritual adventure requires power that only comes from Jesus. It's a power that we each greatly need.

HEALING AND HOPE

Discovering the spirituality of Jesus has a transforming effect and fills our hearts with joy. This adventure is a journey of healing, blessing, peace, and power **when we do it Jesus's way**. It's a gift of blessing for you, and it becomes a blessing to others through you. God wants to establish you in His love so that you become an agent of His love. This is the mission of Jesus.

Many sincere Christians do not realize that Jesus gives His loving power and authority to those He can work through to bless others. The power comes from Jesus to His apprentices to bring life into a dead world. That life transfers from each living person to bring life to the next person, like one candle lighting the next.

This lighted flame of God's Spirit gets shared from one soul to another without losing any flame from the first lit soul. Every lighted candle can light another candle, but unlit candles cannot.

We must receive and be carriers of that light to share it. Therefore, Jesus gave us a process so that we could become fully alive and become fully lit for Him.

CLEANSING THE VESSEL

On our mission, we are seeking promised treasures (see Matthew 6:20-21), discoveries, and great escapades—real adventures. He has prepared the way; we have promises, power, and purpose available to us. To get all of this, we must deal with something serious, and we need to do it now! Otherwise, we will never see the amazing and miraculous things ahead.

When Jesus said, *"I am willing,"* it means that He sees our need for true spiritual healing and offers it, just like healing a leper. We have **a very willing Savior who delights in us.** And this spiritual healing is vital for the journey.

A DISEASE OF TREASON

We all have a hidden illness of heart and soul that must be healed to succeed in the Jesus Adventure. The human race was made sick by the disease of spiritual treason from the beginning and works a lot like leprosy. Now all of us feel that it's normal to rebel against God. Even the best among us commit spiritual treason, resisting God—proving that we are all victims of this disease.

Jesus reveals to us that everyone has an infected soul, whether we know it or not. It makes us numb; it's progressive and destructive—like leprosy. Everyone needs healing. We are all carriers of this disease of spiritual rebellion, with the hearts of a spiritual traitor that rejects and resists God. The great news is that Jesus specializes in healing the spiritually sick. Jesus said:

> **People who have their health don't need to see a doctor. Only those who are sick do. I'm not here to call those already in good standing with God; I'm here to call sinners to turn back to Him.**
> –Mark 2:17; Luke 5:32 (author paraphrase)

Some of us are good at hiding it, but everyone has this condition that God wants to heal forever.

HEALER OF THE SOUL

Jesus began His ministry healing the physically sick, the blind, the lame, and those demon-possessed. Jesus healed so many people that the gospel writers use the word "multitudes" of people healed ten times.

GOD'S PROTECTION FOR HIS PEOPLE

Jesus is the perfect expression of God to us. As Jesus said, *"I and the Father are one"* (John 10:30, NIV). We see that Jesus had great compassion for people and came to heal both the physical and spiritual sicknesses He found. This is the heart of God! We must see God entirely through this lens, even if we don't understand it.

He desires to give us life, health, hope, and joy. Jesus said that with God, all things are possible.

As a result, we also can see how God sincerely desires to heal our inner sickness. Jesus began His work by quoting the prophet Isaiah to reveal His purpose:

> **The Lord's Spirit has come to me, because he has chosen me to tell the good news to the poor. The Lord has sent me to announce freedom for prisoners, to give sight to the blind, to free everyone who suffers, and to say, "This is the year the Lord has chosen."**
> **—Luke 4:18-19**

Just hearing that this was the mission of Jesus, we can conclude that God did not send Jesus to punish people but to bring great news of freedom, sight, healing, and comfort.

DECLARATION OF GOD'S AUTHORITY

When Jesus came, He proclaimed the Kingdom (ruling authority) of God had come among the people of Israel, the children of the Old Covenant. It revealed the redemption and completion of the Old Covenant. We see Jesus casting out demons, cleansing people of spiritual darkness that oppressed their minds, and miracles curing disabilities and diseases.

Physical healings were just the start of it. Even more amazing things happened. A confrontation with the spiritual powers of darkness is described:

> Suddenly a man with an evil spirit in him entered the synagogue and yelled, "Jesus from Nazareth, what do you want with us? Have you come to destroy us? I know who you are! You are God's Holy One." Jesus told the evil spirit, "Be quiet and come out of the man!" The spirit shook him. Then it gave a loud shout and left. Everyone was completely surprised and kept saying to each other, "What is this? It must be some new kind of powerful teaching! Even the evil spirits obey him."
> —Mark 1:23-27

Then shortly after that, Jesus healed this man with leprosy (see Mark 1:40-45; Luke 5:12-16).

Then, Jesus healed a crippled man who had been unable to walk. The man's friends were so convinced that Jesus could heal their friend that they tore open the roof of the house where Jesus was teaching, to get their friend in front of Him. What surprised everyone was that Jesus looked at the crippled man, who was completely paralyzed, and saw his biggest need: forgiveness for his rebellious heart. As it says in Luke's Gospel, *"When Jesus saw how much faith they had, he said to the man, "My friend, your sins are forgiven"* (Luke 5:20).

But why did He forgive sins when it was obvious that the man needed to be healed physically? I mean, he's crippled and lying there on the floor! Isn't that the most important thing? But Jesus sees what matters most; the man's deepest need was forgiveness and healing of his soul. Keep that in mind.

The religious guys totally freaked out. So, He said:

> **Which is easier, to say to the paralytic, "Your sins are forgiven," or to say, "Rise, take up your bed and walk'? But that you may know that the Son of Man has authority on earth to forgive sins"—he said to the paralytic— "I say to you, rise, pick up your bed, and go home." And he rose and immediately picked up his bed and went out before them all, so that they were all amazed and glorified God, saying, "We never saw anything like this!"**
> **–Mark 2:9-12 (ESV)**

Everyone was stunned by the miracle—<u>except the religious guys</u>. Jesus had just called their bluff, which bothered them too much to appreciate the miracle. They didn't have the power to heal or forgive! Jesus had just demonstrated the power to do both! This frustrated them out of their minds.

Just as when Jesus read from the prophet Isaiah at the beginning of His ministry, God is showing us parallels to our spiritual disease that needs healing. We must not overlook this. Spiritual paralysis is more common and more serious than physical paralysis. It's true of the worst of us and more so of the most religious.

These three healings had a purpose beyond the need of that specific person at the time. Healing the demon-possessed man shows us there are dark forces that attack our minds. Healing the leper shows us that we have spiritual rot making us numb to sin. Healing the crippled man was to show us that we are spiritually paralyzed, desperately in need of forgiveness—and Jesus reveals that God has power over all of this, so we can walk in truth, life, and strength—power from Heaven to overcome the worst things we face here in this world.

WITH A SINGLE COMMAND

Do you feel driven by darkness, shame, hatred, and unbelief? Jesus silences the voices of demons and casts them out without a battle.

Do you feel rotten and impure? Jesus heals and restores.

Do you feel powerless, and unable to change your situation? Jesus transforms.

Yes, Jesus can and does make sudden and remarkable changes in your life—when you're willing to receive it. Remember what He said first to the paralytic: *"Your sins are forgiven you."* Jesus isn't holding your past against you; He is offering new life. That's it. **You can have that if you're willing to humble yourself.** Whatever your situation, Jesus is still the answer.

Jesus promised to be with us to the end, and He is keeping His promise every day. Every changed life, experiencing His renewing presence, and every answered prayer is evidence that God is still with us, and still for us.

Jesus said He came *"to look for and to save people who are lost"* (Luke 19:10), and *"I came to invite sinners"* (Matthew 9:13).

That is such GREAT news! The Father in Heaven sent Jesus for this purpose. Not merely to teach people good ways to live. If that was all we needed, then Jesus didn't need to die. Jesus came seeking to save those who could not save themselves.

Jesus also wants us to learn to celebrate God's plan of bringing people back to fellowship with Him: *"We should be glad and celebrate! Your brother was dead, but he is now alive. He was lost and has now been found"* (Luke 15:32).

This is God's heart. We're called to join with Him, participate, and then celebrate Jesus restoring people. Our calling is to share it, join together, and celebrate His gracious kindness. We get the great privilege of coming to Him, and also to belong with others who come to Him. Jesus erases the boundaries between us when we're humble enough to come to Him.

We are all in this predicament together. We share in the madness or the adventure. Jesus brings us beyond brokenness, restoring us with the Father in Heaven and with each other.

Jesus promised that He would not give up on us before the end of this age. He has also promised to return to get us. He has promised to keep working in us and to be with us until then, in spirit.

> **If anyone loves me, he will keep my word, and my Father will love him, and we will come to him and make our home with him.**
> **—John 14:23 (ESV)**

Matthew 28:20 says, *"I will be with you always, even until the end."*

Those two promises are made to each and all of us. He's not going to leave anyone out who comes to Him. He welcomes you. Can you welcome Him?

TAKING STOCK OF THE INVENTORY

Each of us on the Jesus Adventure must take stock: Is my heart hungry for the life-giving spirit of Jesus? Am I seeking treasure that can't be stolen? Or, is my soul so dry and withered that I can't feel the thirst for the water of the refreshing Spirit? Do I despise my own behavior? Do I crave a true eternal life?

Realizing this truth is the point where God can really work in us. We are unsatisfied because we were created for greater things! We were created for purpose that requires an upgrade, and that upgrade comes both suddenly and progressively. True Adventurers are ready. Jesus calls us to seek earnestly so that we may receive it.

HEALING THE INNER DARKNESS

The shock comes in realizing we have a corrupted soul. Evil isn't just outside; it is within. Our hearts need healing at the deepest level. Many have decided to turn to God and follow Jesus. But bitterness destroys from within, so we need the complete healing of the Vital Cure. Something is wrong, and it has to be fixed.

Jesus reveals unforgiveness, hate, or bitterness can be as dark as any murder. God is very serious about the human condition because it is the nature of spiritual treason against God. So, He offers complete healing from it.

DEAD, DRY, AND DESPAIRING

The human heart is a barren desert. We don't love those who don't love us. We covet, lust, and curse. We hate those who reject or hurt us. We put on a good face for the public. We laugh and pretend. But inside, we all have rebellion toward God, saying, "I'll do it my way."

Even the most religious among us have this problem! Jesus told them, *"You Pharisees clean the outside of cups and dishes, but on the inside you are greedy and evil."* Jesus also said to them:

> **You are like tombs that are painted white. Outside they look fine, but inside they are full of dead people's bones and all kinds of filth.**
> —Matthew 23:26 (author paraphrase)

What? For anyone else it would be hypocritical. For Jesus, it was an observation that He was qualified to make.

Maybe you think you're a pretty good person, especially compared to others. You may think you don't really need much improvement. The problem is that the standard isn't other people—it is Jesus. It's Perfection.

Maybe you believe that you're doing okay. But Jesus knows. Jesus reveals there's something wrong at a level that we can't solve by self-improvement. He sees the heart; He knows every detail. Perhaps you can't pretend anymore, and you're seeking help. The answer is Jesus.

Let's remember what Jesus said:

> **Healthy people don't need a doctor, but sick people do. I didn't come to invite good people to be my followers. I came to invite sinners.**
> —Mark 2:17

And what did Jesus say was His personal assignment? *"The lost sheep of the house of Israel"* (Matthew 15:24, NKJV).

In other words, the people of Israel were/are lost, just like the pagans they despised. So, Jesus was sent to them first, before He sent His apprentices out to the pagan world.

Jesus came because we needed Him! Since He came, we have hope—there is a power to overcome the rebellious nature. Healing starts with the understanding that we need it; from God's point of view, none are healthy. <u>We need soul healing,</u> and Jesus is the cure.

BY THE KISS OF HEAVEN

When mommas give birth, we see tenderness and life-giving love. In movies, a baby gets a smack from the doctor to breathe its first breath. But in real life, most babies take a breath within seconds of being born.

I once saw the most beautiful thing: the new baby was not breathing, so the mother picked up the baby, cleared its throat, breathed its first gentle breath with a loving kiss, and looked at the baby, waiting. The baby breathed and opened its eyes to see momma lovingly looking into its eyes. The color came into the baby's face, and tears of joy filled the momma's eyes.

While God created many wonderful and beautiful things, He only created one face-to-face: humankind. We were given life by God breathing into Adam—Genesis says:

> **The LORD God formed man of the dust of the ground, and breathed into his nostrils the breath of life; and man became a living being.**
> –Genesis 2:7 (NKJV)

God created humanity with love! What a precious, personal, and loving way to start a new life!

In the face of every newborn, we see a creature with God's personal brand and creative heart imprinted right down into our DNA. We see in humanity a unique ability that is unlike any of God's other creations on this earth. And God gave us all that by giving us life, face-to-face with His very own breath, at the dawn of creation.

Scientists have discovered that every human being's DNA fuses together in a flash of light at the moment of conception. This means that God's energy is directly and personally involved in every person's formation.

Adventure Principle: God is directly and personally involved in our life from the beginning. He has loved humanity with a unique, tender, and personal love. He wants us to respond.

THE FIRST DILEMMA

As a species, humanity's first moral choice was to say to God: "I decided to go with the plan of your enemy instead of yours; I'm trusting him instead of You." That happened when the serpent said, *"In the day you eat of it . . . you will be like God"* (Genesis 3:5, NKJV). (The temptation was not the fruit's flavor.)

The issue is that Adam chose to usurp God's role; to replace God with self. This resulted in being enslaved by the tempter, Satan. Every one of us has done it ever since.

It's spiritual treason! This is the cruelest offense possible to an infinitely caring and kind Creator. We put a hand in the face that breathed life into us. Ever since, we each say, "I don't want you." We yield to a false god who hates us, hates everything we represent and every purpose we have. Our nature has been warped and has become sin-loving and God-hating ever since. We have grieved our Creator without remorse!

Yet, God has a heart more loving than we can imagine. He created love and compassion, then invested it in us. God created man and gifted man with His own talent and intellect—the capacity for all that God is and has. Then God put man in a world of beauty and gave man companionship with Himself and with each other. So, man rejected Him.

God had warned this would lead to death. It resulted in all of Adam's offspring having death and brokenness. A curse came on us all. This is the death curse of sin. This opened the door to spiritual darkness, not just a darkness on the outside but an incurable curse of darkness on the inside.

Separated from conscious contact with God, we experienced spiritual death, losing all but our flesh life—and then each of us must also die physically: the devil's plan for Adam, for Eve, and all of us. As their children, death has ruled over us ever since because death rules inside us.

Jesus told the people who were rejecting his message:

> **You are of your father the devil, and you want to do the desires of your father. He was a murderer from the beginning.**
> **–John 8:44-45 (LSB)**

The devil's plan for humanity is pride, selfishness, death, separation, suffering, and tragedy; the opposite of everything God gave. The devil convinced Adam and Eve to commit spiritual suicide. The result has perverted every good thing God gave us.

Our problem is deeper than we realize, being spiritually darkened and dead to God. All of humanity has a disorder: a devilish rebel nature has taken root. This is not trivial.

Yet, our holy Creator still loves us. He has not destroyed us. Our loving Creator has made a way for us to know Him and be given a perfect amnesty from His perfect justice—if we respond. He has made a way for total restoration, for life and love in fellowship with Him.

UNAWARE OF THE DEADLY SICKNESS

Bullfrogs don't know the swamp stinks; they just eat the flies. Likewise, we all exist in a world cursed by sin and evil. So, we do not understand the holiness of God! We can't because we are not like Him. Only when He has refreshed us with His living water and filled us with His holy light can we begin to know Him.

We see there are problems in our world. But we are naturally incapable of seeing that we are part of the problem. Our souls are born and nourished on prideful spiritual rebellion, and we can't dress it up.

God says we have all turned away. The good news is that Jesus offers us spiritual cleansing! He's giving it away so that we may follow Him! If we fail to deal with it now, we simply become shipwrecked later.

CURE FOR THE CURSE

This cure only comes from Jesus. He went to the cross and suffered in our place. To restore us to everything we were originally intended to be—and more. The real wonder and beauty of it opens up for us as we discover this mystery: Jesus restores everyone who takes His transformation challenge. So, press on with Him to receive all He has.

It's one thing to be forgiven of our rebellion; it's another thing to receive healing, restoration, and wholeness. The process begins inside, with truth. If we deal with this the way God has designed, we can walk in freedom and health from the inside out:

> "First clean the inside ... and then the outside will also be clean."
> —Matthew 23:26 (NIV)

> **So I confessed my sins and told them all to you. I said,**
> **"I'll tell the LORD each one of my sins."**
> **Then you forgave me and took away my guilt.**
> **We worship you, LORD. . . .**
> **You are my hiding place! You protect me from trouble, and**
> **you put songs in my heart because you have saved me.**
> —Psalm 32:5-8

God's purpose is to heal, restore, and cleanse us for a complete life transformation. This is why Jesus came; forgiveness of sins is the doorway to transformation: confessing our sins (our personal acts of rebellion) as God reveals them to us by His Word and His Spirit and then <u>confessing the healing and freedom of Christ that He promises</u>.

We acknowledge before God that we have a need and that we will accept His remedy. Christ did not come to make us religious. He came to set us free! Free from the penalty of sin and <u>the bondage of sin</u>, by making us new by His Spirit, as we practice truth.

Take this moment to privately confess your rebellious acts to God and accept His redemption in Jesus. Jesus is your Mediator to Holy God. Perhaps you think that the idea of private confession is strange. Well, it is! But Jesus brings you to the Father.

Confess that: "Lord Jesus, my rebel mind is resisting confession, but since God's Word promises new life and healing in Your name, I want your help!" Whatever ways you know you have rejected God, speak them plainly as rebellion before God.

Then thank Jesus, who came to take the penalty for our rebellion. The cross was a horrible thing for Jesus to endure, but it is a **powerful thing of healing for us.** Come to that cross and thank Jesus for His sacrifice. Receive that cure from Jesus, and you will find freedom.

Whenever we discover an area of bondage, the cure is the same: "Father in Heaven, I know this _____ is caused by my rebel nature, and it offends

You. I know that it has a hold on me, but I trust that Jesus came to set me free from bondage. Lord Jesus, I believe that Your suffering on the cross was enough. I thank You and I receive Your power to be set free from this!"

More times than I can count, I have known people who walked away completely free from addictions, terrible sins, darkened hearts, bitterness, resentments, and even illnesses this way. Yes, it is powerful.

Adventure Principle: Jesus is the cure that frees me from everything that keeps me in darkness; so that I can be free to praise, be faithful, and love the God who created me.

ULTIMATE CURE PENDING

We were created for harmony with God. So, God is reversing this curse, one person at a time! He remembers that we are the children He created with His own breath. But it's also a multi-step process. First, Jesus reversed the curse's authority. Second, He is reversing its hold on people. Finally, He will, one day, completely defeat the curse for all time.

So, here we are in that middle part, where God is reversing the hold the death curse has on people. So, the cure is still available to us now. One day, God will defeat it completely. As it says:

> **"No longer will there be any curse."**
> **–Revelation 22:3 (NIV)**

For now, we get freed from its authority by Jesus's vital cure to start our victory.

The only thing harder to accept than the fact that the whole world is cursed is to believe that the curse can finally be defeated. We spend our entire lives trying to overcome it. God promises that a time is coming when there will be no more curse.

SAVE ME FROM MY CIRCUMSTANCES

People often come to Jesus looking for a quick solution to their immediate problem. We come looking for a way out of bad circumstances. It's okay to do that! But we need to be careful not to treat Him like a butler.

Whatever our problems, Jesus is bigger. Jesus is greater. Jesus has the answer. Jesus is the answer.

Are you an addict? Jesus saves!

Are you full of anger? Jesus saves!

Are you depressed and have lost hope? Jesus saves!

Are you sick and facing death? Jesus saves!

Are you on the verge of bankruptcy? Jesus saves!

Are you facing jail time for committing a crime? Jesus saves!

Seriously, I have known many people with these exact problems, which Jesus saved.

> **"The LORD's people may suffer a lot, but He will always bring them safely through."**
> **—Psalm 34:19**

Whatever problem you have, your problem isn't the real problem. Your problem is a symptom of the real problem. The Bible tells us that the heart is spiritually diseased and desperately ungodly.

This is where many religious people go wrong. They think the solution to this rebellion curse is to stop doing rebellious things. If that were true, if it were possible, then Jesus did not need to come and die on a Roman cross.

Jesus takes away that rebel curse forever. When Jesus gives us the solution, then we enter into the spirituality of Jesus; we begin experiencing the dynamic energy of His heavenly nature.

THE DEATH CURSE EXCHANGE

Jesus did not come to teach us to be nicer rebels. The death curse has killed the light of our souls and left humanity in darkness. Jesus came to take our rebel natures and restore our connection with God. He takes our powerlessness, our anxiety, our rottenness, and ultimately our judgment of the second death. All of it: Jesus came to exchange it for His life, His love, His health, His honor, His light, and His truth. That's what He did on the cross.

Even though Jesus had never rebelled against God and had never considered being a rebel, God caused Him to be accused and convicted as a rebel in our place! He did this so that we could become faithful children of God, accepted and received as if we were Jesus himself.

THE GREAT DO-OVER

God offers a brand-new thing to us in Jesus: to become a completely new creation. He offers a complete do-over and, eventually, an upgrade beyond our imagination. For now, this new creation, this great upgrade, **is hidden**. No one can see it because God does the work on the inside.

This is the wonder of it, a total cure of the death curse. It's the only cure that God offers, and it is the only cure we need. God does not simply pardon people. God has justice and punishes evil. He gives no preferential treatment. But God knows no human can bear His perfect and pure justice.

So, He offers the cure on very simple terms. We must humbly turn to Him, which means we stop running and stop hiding from Him. We face our desperate need—and—we trust that His plan through Jesus is sufficient. We choose to believe it, trusting fully in His death, burial, and resurrection plan. Simple. God does the rest as we walk with Him.

Each of us has sinned, so we are worthy of His perfect justice. But, in His love and mercy for mankind, God offers a universal cure that anyone can take hold of, anywhere, no matter how high or low their position in this world. He offers this universal cure to all. God's love is so great that He will not withhold this offer from anyone.

> **God so loved the world that he gave his one and only Son, that whoever believes in him shall not perish but <u>have eternal life</u>.**
> **—John 3:16 (NIV)**

We receive it by turning to God, trusting in His plan completely—and letting go of all the effort to run our own program. It's an exchange. We give Him all that we were, and He gives us an entirely new life—a new gameplan, a new purpose, a new relationship, a new destiny. This is the Vital Cure of Jesus.

Jesus was betrayed by a friend, falsely accused by the religious authorities, punished severely by flogging then tortured to death on a Roman cross. Very few people realize that **this was God's exact plan**. This was not a defeat. It was a victory against the death curse that had held mankind captive. This is how God loves us: He came and took justice Himself.

A DESTINY OF DEFEAT

God always tells us what He is going to do in advance, but few understand it until it's done. Even then, many miss it. Speaking of the Old Testament, Jesus said,

> **"You study the Scriptures diligently.... These are the very Scriptures that testify about me."**
> **—John 5:39 (NIV)**

Jesus is making an incredible claim—that the Old Testament specifically spoke of Him. And that's what we find. As it says,

> **"But all this happened, so that what the prophets wrote would come true."**
> **—Matthew 26:56**

Jesus also said:

> **These are the words which I spoke to you while I was still with you, that all things must be fulfilled which were written in the Law of Moses and the Prophets and the Psalms concerning Me.**
> **—Luke 24:44 (NIV)**

How is that possible? Jesus is saying we can see Him fulfilling all the promises **in a single volume,** a single book as it were, which is what we now call the Bible. It says so in Psalm 40:7

> **"In the <u>volume of the book</u> it is written of me, I delight to do thy will, O my God."**
> **—Psalm 40:7-8 (author paraphrase)**

God is amazing. He knows the end from the beginning; He declared it before it happened.

THE PURE WATERS OF PROPHECY

There is a deep, cool, and refreshing well of promises that God has given us, which keep filling thirsty hearts in this dry and barren world—like oasis after oasis for weary travelers passing through a vast desert.

God says:

> **Declaring the end from the beginning, and from ancient times things not yet done, saying, "My counsel shall stand, and I will accomplish all my purpose."**
> **—Isaiah 46:10 (KJV)**

It's important to realize that Jesus came according to the plans and foreknowledge of His Father, the Architect of Creation and of Redemption. Jesus came to fulfill the epic plans that the Father set in motion from the beginning, to exchange His faithfulness for our unfaithfulness; He took our penalty and gave us His reward.

These truths are backed up by prophecy, history, and testimony of the Bible.

PERFECTLY BEARING EVERY BURDEN

To fulfill the call of the Jesus Adventure in our lives means we must recognize how Jesus paved the way by fulfilling the call on His life. He did what none of us could. He reversed the death curse by taking it upon Himself and rising to new life on the third day. The Bible tells us that He took the penalty as an innocent man. He did that by bearing every burden we may ever experience. As a result, He purchased for us what we could never obtain ourselves, far beyond forgiveness: He has made us royal family members.

The plot to kill Jesus was put in motion when one of His apprentices accepted a bribe to betray Him. As a result, Jesus was tried in three courts and was executed for capital crimes.

Yet, everyone declared His innocence, including Herod, the puppet king; Pilate, the Roman governor; Judas, His betrayer; and a thief who was crucified next to Him.

But most importantly, **God had already declared it by prophecy** in Isaiah 52:13, Isaiah 53:9, Isaiah 53:11, and Daniel 9:26. Jesus's death was **according to the foreknowledge and purposes of God!** The people acted out their evil plans, thinking they would get rid of Jesus forever. Instead, they merely put God's eternal plans into motion, making Jesus **a Savior who lives forever.** Because you can't kill the Son of God; death had no authority to hold Him. Therefore, **He had to rise from the dead.**

So now Jesus lives forever and intercedes for us in Heaven before the Throne of God the Father. This is another astonishing fact! When you trust Jesus as your Messiah-King, He makes your soul's success His priority in the Throne Room of God the Most High.

THE REPORTER WHO SAW THROUGH TIME

The second place that Jesus told us to look, after the books of Moses, is the Prophets. No place speaks so clearly as Isaiah's report. It's as if he was a witness to Jesus's crucifixion. Yet, Isaiah's book was written more than 700 years before Jesus's birth! We're going to look at a few excerpts, but I encourage you to read them in full.

In Isaiah 52:13-14 (NIV), it says:

> **See, my servant will act wisely;**
> **he will be raised and lifted up and highly exalted.**
> **Just as there were many who were appalled at him—**
> **his appearance was so disfigured beyond that of any human being.**

God really wants us to pay attention to this man who was raised up (on the cross).

> **Who has believed our message and to whom has**
> **the arm of the LORD been revealed?**
> **—Isaiah 53:1 (NIV)**

God is indicating that the message would be rejected.

> **He had no beauty or majesty to attract us to him, nothing in his appearance**
> **that we should desire him. He was despised and rejected by mankind.**
> **—Isaiah 53:2b-3a (NIV)**

God is showing that people saw Jesus as ordinary and therefore, not a regal king.

> **Yet we considered him punished by God, stricken by him, and afflicted.
> <u>But he was pierced for our transgressions</u>, he was crushed
> for our iniquities; the punishment that brought us peace
> was on him, and by his wounds we are healed.
> We all, like sheep, have gone astray, each of us has turned to our
> own way; <u>and the LORD has laid on him the iniquity of us all</u>.**
> **—Isaiah 53:4b-6 (NIV)**

Incredibly, God is telling us that His suffering had a precise purpose for our redemption; it was all put on Jesus.

> **Yet it was the LORD's will to crush him and cause him to suffer,
> and though the LORD makes his life an offering for sin ...**
> **—Isaiah 53:10 (NIV)**

God is telling us that Jesus was a substitutionary sacrifice for sin, just as lambs were under the Old Covenant. Verse 53:11 (NIV) says, *"After he has suffered, he will see the light of life and be satisfied."*

God says that Jesus would rise from the dead proving that God is satisfied with His sacrifice for our sins. Verse 11 (NIV) continues with, *"By his knowledge, my righteous servant <u>will justify</u> many."*

God is driving home the point that many will be justified by this offering for sin. Meaning there is nothing more to be done.

We have a dual perspective: what happened on earth and the heavenly perspective of God. It gives us all that we need to see that Jesus's suffering on the cross was <u>not an accident</u> but was God's plan.

The crime of humanity's rebellion has impacted all of creation; so, God has taken the punishment for it Himself, in the person of Jesus. And the amazing part is that God says He is *"satisfied"* (v. 11). This is the heart of it, friend!

When a legal debt is paid, you get a **"satisfaction of judgment"** recorded with the court because your debt has been paid. Our case has gone to the highest court and God says that Jesus accomplished the task—and God **is satisfied**.

Well, that is fantastic news! Unbelievable! Now, the only question is HOW do we take hold of that satisfaction of judgment? Because each of us will attend God's court of spiritual justice. We have been granted the right to claim this satisfaction, for God offers it to us through Jesus, who purchased it for us!

Well, verse 11 tells us that it is **by knowledge** of this perfect suffering servant that **we take hold of this satisfaction of judgment**. This concept is a dual knowledge. We have to know Jesus, and He has to know us. The meaning is a close, relational knowledge.

God wants you to know Jesus. It's a relational thing. God is really into relationships; they matter to Him. Jesus said that knowing Him gives us knowledge of the Father and that true trust in God will give us trust in Jesus (see John 14:1; John 10:30). Jesus has repaired our relationship with the Father, making a way for God's perfect judgment to be satisfied. Jesus said:

> **"I am the way and the truth and the life. No one comes to the Father <u>except through me</u>."**
> **–John 14:6 (NIV)**

That word "way" means passage or journey, in the original language. Jesus is calling us to join the quest; the adventure leads us to know the Father. So, this satisfaction of judgment is purely a wonderful gift from Jesus. This is the greatest of all the treasures we seek.

Adventure Principle: Jesus has already overcome and forgiven every kind of evil that we have ever committed, so we can overcome and live out our God-given purpose.

THE POETIC PLAN

Everything that we can ever encounter, every challenge, every victory, every joy, and every sorrow, has already been experienced and overcome by earlier travelers who went before us. The Book of Psalms is a book of incredible power and prophecy to enable us to overcome every challenge. It's an amazing spiritual revelation for us.

As you get to know Jesus's life and sayings, you realize that He knew the Psalms perfectly—because He didn't just quote them, He lived them out!

One passage, Psalm 22, gets our attention as the most phenomenal poetry ever written. You see, it was a prophecy written of Jesus on the cross as if Jesus dictated it from there.

Yet it was written by King David long before Jesus was born. Just so we don't miss it, Jesus quotes this from His cross while He suffered. Reading it, you get Jesus's perspective, His feelings—even His view on the spirit realm.

Jesus points people to read it and also showing His distress at the crucifixion:

> **"My God, my God, why have you forsaken me?"**
> **—Psalm 22:1 (NIV)**

Which is what Jesus cried out from the cross when God put our sins on Him.

Verse 16 tells us about this crucifixion, even though it was written about 500 years before Jesus lived: *"They pierce my hands and my feet"* (NIV).

And what is the final point?

> **"They will proclaim his righteousness, declaring to a people yet unborn: He has done it!"**
> —v. 31 (NIV)

Do you see that last line? He has done it! **It's done.** That is what Jesus's last words proclaimed: It is finished. The debt is paid. This reminds us of what Isaiah said: God is satisfied. There is nothing left to be done for sin, for those who have Jesus.

PLAN OF DESTINY AND IDENTITY

God gave us these clues to see how He planned Messiah/Christ to suffer for our sins. He planned a destiny for Jesus to defeat the death curse, and in doing that, He defeated death itself. Since Jesus rose from the dead on the third day, we are also promised to rise at the appointed time.

Since death has no hold on Jesus, He can free us from death. Jesus was able to look forward to today and know He was doing these things for us. The Father always reserves the best for last—so this last generation will see Him pouring out His best if we are on the Jesus adventure: incredible things for the final times before Jesus comes to take us home.

MORE POWERFUL PROMISES

At this stage, it is important to consider the power of God's promises. You may think, how can a promise have power? It's just a claim of something God will do later, right? With God, it's much more.

Since we are in the age of Jesus's authority, we CAN and DO receive the promises by taking possession of them. A vital part of the adventure is that we claim and apprehend God's promises. Our faith posture enables us to receive promises of God that were not available in the past nor to those outside of the Covenant of Messiah. The authority of Jesus lets us apprehend them by faith.

Many powerful promises—which we will cover extensively later—are given to us in the Bible. By some counts, there are over 300 prophecies that Jesus has fulfilled already. I share some of the most amazing ones at the end of the book.

Before we move forward here, let's look at one that's for His followers:

> **What God has planned for people who love him is more than eyes have seen or ears have heard. It has never even entered our minds!**
> **—1 Corinthians 2:9**

It's just a brief view of what Jesus plans for us! Jesus wants us to know that, in the coming ages, He has unmatchable riches of kindness for us. Promises now and forever—this is the way of Jesus.

REALIZING THE GREAT REDEMPTION PLAN

The Creator did all of this for us to discover. It was done before any of us even thought to ask. He gave us His best. That tells you who you are: loved and cherished **before you ever knew it**. On your worst day, God still wanted to bless you. This is the incredible privilege given to us by Jesus to bear His name.

Most of us spent too many years believing God hated us. So now we can accept the right perspective. The same Bible says that while we were still enemies of God, Jesus did all of this for us, even though we started with a heart of rebellion.

Can I urge you to stop right now and accept this offering? This spiritual cure God has given you is available now. Talk to God—choose to accept it right now.

God is spirit: He can hear and accept your request, even without speaking it. Talk to God in your spirit and humbly accept His amazing gift through Jesus—it's called prayer.

MEDITATIONS OF THE GREAT REDEMPTION PLAN

> "Not to us, O Lord, not to us,
> but to your name give glory,
> for the sake of your steadfast love
> and your faithfulness!"."
> —Psalm 115:1 (ESV)

> "In the time of my favor I will answer you, and in
> the day of salvation I will help you."
> —Isaiah 49:8 (NIV)

> "The debt is paid in full."
> —literal translation of John 20:14

THE ETERNAL FLOW OF LIFE

There are many messages in the world. But the message of Jesus is unique in that it offers a threefold promise, a triple guarantee of hope, backed by the name of God—uniquely great news promising eternal life in a place of total joy. At the same time, it fills this time with His joyful presence.

In other words, there is a joy-filled eternity that we call Heaven, which is also apprehended and experienced now, right here. Jesus brings this new life to those who faithfully accept it from Him. No other belief system can offer freedom from the death curse. Jesus's apprentices have testimonies of experiencing healing of soul, spirit, and often also of their physical body.

"LIFE—ABUNDANTLY"

That threefold promise is this: we take hold of the promises of Jesus today and are "saved." Meaning that Jesus opens the door to God for us now, here. We are redeemed from spiritual death, have access to God immediately and become justified by faith in Jesus.

The second part is that Jesus promises to be with each of us all the way to the end. Therefore, we are **"being saved"** as a continuous act of His kindness and commitment toward us—He does not cast us out.

Finally, Jesus gives us confidence that we **will be saved** in an ultimate final sense when we leave this corrupted body. Jesus grants us eternal inheritance.

But check this out: the promise of the now and future part comes from our eternal promise. In other words, because Jesus has put that satisfaction of judgment in place for us for all of eternity, we have access to claim it here and now! So that promise, and all its power, flows down to us from eternity and empowers us now.

In fact, it even heals our past. As we look at our past, all our hurts, all of our griefs, and all of our sorrows, we can know Jesus was enduring that with us. Jesus suffered that with us.

Therefore, we see that, through Jesus, our past has meaning; all sorrow is healed in the present. It has purpose since it brought us to the point where we now believe Jesus as the Author and Perfecter of our faith.

So, even though we did not know it then, we can experience its meaning today and heal our yesterdays. And because Jesus now lives, we can also live—in an eternal way. Now and forever is the way of Jesus.

CLAIMING OUR REDEMPTION TREASURE

This is a great birthright that Jesus purchased: a total redemption and more. It is a chest full of treasures. We have been offered something incredible, which we keep discovering. But we have to accept it and make our claim on it, putting these treasures to use.

Jesus wants us to get the whole treasure:

> **The kingdom of heaven is like what happens when someone finds a treasure hidden in a field and buries it again. A person like that is happy and goes and sells everything in order to buy that field.**
> —Matthew 13:44

Jesus left Heaven and gave up everything so that we could have everything He is. Do whatever it takes to receive Him.

Our purpose on this adventure is to discover it all. We are no longer beggars; we become owners, possessors. We want the treasure and the field it's held in!

We want the title to all of it. We want Jesus and all that He is, all that the Father has planned. Owning the whole treasure, we can bless others and share that inheritance, doing everything Jesus envisioned.

Let's consider a little more of what Jesus accomplished for us, from Isaiah's majestic prophecy (Isaiah 52:13-53:12):

> **"His form marred beyond human likeness."**
> —Isaiah 52:14 (NIV)

The Bible shows that because Jesus was so disfigured, <u>all</u> of our disabilities, scars, injuries, sicknesses, and deformities will be healed in the resurrection. Our resurrected bodies will be perfected beyond our comprehension.

> **"What they were not told, they will see, and what they have not heard, they will understand."**
> —Isaiah 52:15 (NIV)

Jesus died for the human family. His blood is enough for everyone to be saved. So, God is patiently giving power to those who will take this message around the world, to every nation.

Sometimes, we find that Jesus has already revealed Himself to people who have not yet heard the Bible. God is giving the people of this world the opportunity to know Him.

> **"He was despised and rejected by mankind, a man of suffering, and familiar with pain."**
> **–Isaiah 53:5 (NIV)**

Have you been left out? Despised? Rejected? Jesus knows, and He cares. He came to include you in God's Kingdom. Others may have drawn a circle that left you out, but God has a bigger circle, and He brings you in.

> **"Surely he took up our pain and bore our suffering."**
> **–Isaiah 53:4-5 (NIV)**

As we consider Jesus, it is astonishing to think that the Creator of the world allows Himself to experience actual pain and suffering. What could possibly be the purpose? Because He personally bore our suffering, He took what is the natural consequence of being rebels. This is so profound, and the fact is that there's more: He bore it in Himself, so that we can go to a place where there is <u>no suffering</u> (see Romans 3:21-26).

> **"We considered him punished by God, stricken by him, and afflicted."**
> **–Isaiah 53:4 (NIV)**

Maybe you have heard that your grief, suffering, loss, or sickness was a punishment from God. Jesus was also severely taunted by those who condemned him. Since He took that Himself, God gives us His approval when we trust Jesus. God says: *"I do not condemn you"* (John 8:11, GNT) because that punishment went to Jesus.

> **"He was pierced for our transgressions; he was crushed for our iniquities."**
> **—Isaiah 53:5a (ESV)**

When they put nails in Jesus's hands and feet, He paid for our transgressions. This means rebellious acts—every sinful thing we do with our hands, the sinful places we go with our feet.

Every crime we committed against God, now and in the future, was paid for by Jesus hanging from those nails—from the beatings He took from the fists of the soldiers hitting His face, to the scourging of His back, Jesus took the punishment for our acts of moral evil. Every one.

> **"The punishment that brought us peace was on him, and by his wounds we are healed."**
> **—Isaiah 53:5b (NIV)**

Here, the point is driven home. These acts of punishment, experienced by an innocent man, the perfect Son of God, **brought us peace**; those wounds brought us healing. What peace? Peace with God and peace with ourselves. What healing? Healing of our inner nature.

This is too big of a topic to fully cover here, but many people testify that God completely changed their hearts. I mean, people who were once evil people were utterly changed by God because they trusted Jesus.

> **He was oppressed and afflicted.... By oppression and judgment he was taken away. Yet who of his generation protested?**
> **—Isaiah 53:7-8 (NIV)**

Jesus so identified with the oppressed people of the world that He chose to be born to a poor family in an oppressed, occupied nation, then went to an oppressive judgment by His own people. To make matters worse, He saw to it that no one even protested His sentence! Many wept, **but no one said, "Stop He's innocent!!"**

Have you ever been falsely accused? Have you ever been stripped of your rights? Jesus understands, and He cares. Jesus deliberately endured this for us. Because of that, God declares you to be His own when you look to Jesus as your Savior.

When you declare Jesus to be yours, God declares you to be His (see Matthew 10:32; Romans 10:9-11). Your sentence has been forever commuted **because Jesus paid it already.** You have full and total amnesty because of His cross.

> **By his knowledge my righteous servant will justify many, and he will bear their iniquities. Therefore I will give him a portion among the great, and he will divide the spoils with the strong.**
> —Isaiah 53:11-2 (NIV)

I hope you are beginning to grasp how fully God makes this point. God has been preparing this truth for you to receive.

It is by **knowing Him and looking to Him as the one who took your place, and therefore being known by Him, that counts.** Jesus has carried our entire judgment on our behalf. So, God has given Him the title of King of Kings and Lord of Lords.

God gives Jesus the right to grant His apprentices shares in His inheritance. Those who trust in Jesus receive from His portion. He wants to share His inheritance with you.

POSSESSING PROMISES

These amazing things are offered to all, but only those who accept them by faith in Jesus can take possession. Why? Because the devil doesn't understand faith. So, it only takes the smallest amount of faith, trusting in Jesus—because of God's promises to us.

The world, our own rebel nature, and the devil all want to cheat us out of these promises. We have to resist ideas that keep us from receiving them.

How to Succeed

The Bible tells us that there are three things that hinder us from holding these treasures: the lust of the flesh, the lust of the eyes, and the pride of life; all of them are responses to unbelief.

So many people are so busy serving these three things they have no time to believe God. They forfeit the inheritance because they cannot withstand peer pressure, or their pride convinces them they do not need these promises.

When we decide to trust Jesus, believe, and do His Word, we win. God gives us victorious power to see the promises fulfilled—by faith. This is what it means to conquer and overcome.

This is not merely a reinstatement of what was lost by Adam. It's **much more . . . exponentially more.** Adam and his descendants <u>were only offered Earth</u>.

As the apprentices of Jesus in this special time of God's favor, we get an entirely **new inheritance that Adam never had.** Adam had earthly authority. But, when Jesus suffered, He did not just suffer as man; He also suffered as the Son of God. So, we are offered an eternal inheritance in the heavenly realms.

Because He was faithful, we are accepted by faith. Because He reigns, we will be given the right to sit with Him as family. Jesus says in Revelation 3:21:

> **Everyone who wins the victory will sit with me on my throne, just as I won the victory and sat with my Father on his throne.**

Such things were never contemplated before Jesus's resurrection.

People flippantly talk about Heaven, like it's just the next stop on a train ride. But Heaven is the realm of God Himself. It is the highest place of authority.

The Heaven that Jesus talks about is God's throne. That's one ride we don't want to miss. But **it is not promised to everyone.** It is exclusively for the fellowship of Jesus's apprentices, in the resurrection.

THE SUPERNATURAL CONDITION OF OWNERSHIP

Humans are a cursed species—a species that chose to serve God's enemy. We don't understand it because we can't see the problem objectively. God saw the problem and solved it. We must be purified of this curse, and Jesus is the only solution.

God will purify us with His Spirit, create a new heart in us, and lead us into a right path of life and blessing. To receive it, we come to Him completely apart from all that was once our worldly identity.

God isn't sharing His children with the devil. God is a consuming fire. He must deliver us completely from the curse, so we release ourselves fully into His hands.

When we do that, God declares us **a new creation.** He plants a new nature inside us; His Holy Spirit bonds with us at the core of our being—as we were created to be—joined with Him in the Spirit. We receive a new nature fused together inside, the very Spirit of God.

The new nature begins to actively heal the broken soul, similar to how computers operate. When you add a new operating system or a new antivirus software, all of the same programs exist, and all of the same hardware exists.

But the new virus-hunting software cleans out the bugs, the errors, and the malware. When it pops up with a warning saying, "This is a bad file," we're called to delete that and begin installing "new" healthy files.

In other words, we use the new nature to take old malware files "captive" so the new system can run correctly. How do we do that? Listen to the Spirit of God. Read the Word of God. Daily. Yes, daily! The Bible is our error-correcting malware-removing code-repairing administrative software tool, and the Holy Spirit is our new operating system.

This way we purge the bad programming. We still have outdated hardware for now, but we will one day get an upgrade with perfect hardware, a new resurrected body that never fades or gets old. If you're not computer savvy, this may seem complicated, but it's actually quite simple.

When we're tempted to doubt, lust, sin, grumble, complain, or quit, we confess that; then we confess our belief in God and His goodness; we choose to speak life-giving truths of confidence in Jesus and His providence.

Are you tempted to hate and condemn? Choose to confess that, and then confess that the person you despise was also created in God's image, whom Jesus died to save; pray for them to trust Jesus's salvation and find ways to be a blessing to show the love of God to that offending enemy.

If they reject it, you have lost nothing because God says He will store up treasures and crowns for everyone who does this for His name's sake.

In doing these things, we defeat the darkness and become carriers of light. This is how every great work of God began, how every nation that turned from idols was won, and how every heart has defeated the darkness within. This is the way of Jesus—an incredible adventure.

THE TRANSFORMING AGENTS

Taking hold of the ultimate cure is evidence of a change within. Trusting in the name and the work of Jesus on our behalf empowers us to become His agents! Like every one of the original apprentices. We learn to grow as New Creations that Jesus has called us to become. It's about exchanging the works of death for the power of walking in His light and life.

Look at the report His apprentices gave when they first discovered this. Jesus sent them out in pairs to share the news of the Kingdom in the villages and towns:

> **When the 72 followers returned, they were excited and said, "Lord, even the demons obeyed when we spoke in your name!"**
> —Luke 10:17

The excitement they felt is evident. They were amazed that they had authority over demons. So, Jesus revealed something far more exciting in His perspective: *"But don't be happy because evil spirits obey you. Be happy that your names are written in heaven!"* (Luke 10:20)

Rejoice that your names are written in Heaven. Say what?? Jesus makes a plain promise here. He gives us power to defeat Satan; but more importantly, access to Heaven.

Let's recall what we know: Jesus said He expects us to complete the mission until the very end. He said we're all to learn and teach the instructions He gave them (Matthew 28:20). Also, Jesus said He would build His gathering of faithful apprentices and that the *"gates of hell shall not prevail against it"* (Matthew 16:18, KJV). That phrase "not prevail" means that the prince of darkness can fight, but he can't win.

It also means that we will have difficulties, **but we can't lose**. I like those odds! Most of the time, I like underdog teams. But in this case, I want to back the winner. I've read the end of the book (Revelation 1-22). I know it says that **God wins**, and the devil is a loser. When we join with Jesus, we have power over the kingdom of darkness. He's stolen enough! Let's get in the fight and take back the high ground.

What is the cure? Getting healed from bondage to the prince of darkness. What gives us the victory? The answer is <u>not the gift</u> but the giver. Jesus said, *"I have given you"* (Luke 10:19). It is His power and authority. It was His from before the creation.

Now the power is available to us by the cross, sealed for us until the resurrection. This was done through His blood sacrifice. But much more important is that His apprentices' names are written in Heaven.

Remember the prophecy Jesus read at the beginning of his ministry:

> **The Spirit of the Lord God is upon me, because the Lord has anointed me to bring good news to the poor; he has sent me to bind up the brokenhearted, to proclaim liberty to the captives, and the opening of the prison to those who are bound; to proclaim the year of the Lord's favor.**
> —Luke 4:18-19 (author paraphrase)

God's favor comes through you when it is in you. We became agents of the vital cure; God's kids break bondages in this world. That power is the gift of God; God's favor is power and authority. More than that, this cure, this gift, is a person: Jesus Christ. We become united to the King of Heaven, the Son of the living God.

THE NATURE UPGRADE

Jesus also heals us of the curse's effects by His Spirit. Power is available to regain the paradise we lost. As we receive that inner healing of soul and spirit, He leads us on this adventure. He is our guide and forever soul companion.

It's a trade. We consider ourselves dead, so He gives new life by faith.

> **Bestow on them a crown of beauty instead of ashes, the oil of joy instead of mourning, and a garment of praise instead of a spirit of despair.**
> —Isaiah 61:3 (NIV)

The most amazing people to meet are elderly people filled with the Holy Spirit who have walked a faithful life trusting and depending on Jesus. Their eyes are full of light, their minds remain pure, their hope remains confident, and they inspire others with joy. They live as if Jesus is living out their lives in them.

Put on your new creation and your new rank with the gusto of a four-year-old kid in a superhero costume! Do not mourn; rather celebrate the death of your old self. Do not look back—look forward to the new life and all its benefits.

Welcome Jesus, sit with Him, listen to Him, and crave to understand all that He has! Be dead to the old rebel heart—because we want that new life-giving Spirit ruling our inner self. Embrace the grace of God every day with joy and gratitude. This is the way of Jesus, which we mark with baptism.

Adventure Principle: Because we died with Christ, we can now live with Him and for Him in a way that was never possible before.

GETTING UNDER WAY

Like a ship that has been loosed from the dock, we're now setting sail out of port. Everything was prepared for this moment, and we're in motion. God is already moving. Let's catch up!

Whether you are pulling out of the port of the old life for the first time or trying to get unstuck, there is a discipline that puts wind in your sails: confessing Truth. We often think of confession as admitting sins, which is only half of it. But there is an affirming side to confession that is about exercising faith.

This means we believe in God and His Word, so we're speaking it into our world and over ourselves, over our loved ones, and taking action on it with reverence for God. It's like speaking a prophecy over your life.

In doing this, God rewards us. His Spirit puts wind into our sails. So, we diligently seek out truth; as we discover it, we activate the rewards of God by speaking it, claiming it, and living according to it. As a young believer, I wrote verses on cards and put them in places where I could read them every day so that I could memorize them.

If God's Word says that God's judgment is satisfied by the death of Christ, then it would be <u>an offense to God to ignore that.</u> We confess that God is satisfied with the death of Christ; His blood is sufficient to cover our sins. No matter what the devil says and no matter how we feel, we speak the truth and say, "**God is satisfied.**"

Jesus told us, *"Every sin and blasphemy will be forgiven people, but the blasphemy against the Spirit will not be forgiven"* (Matthew 12:31, ESV).

We have been given the right to become children of God (see John 1:12). The more we confess the Word of God over ourselves, the more alive we become. We defeat the darkness by speaking the truths of the Kingdom.

What truth do you need to confess over your soul right now? Do you accept that God is satisfied with Jesus's death? Do you accept that God has offered you the right to become His child? **Say so.** Speak it with your own lips and break the curses that claim your life.

Reject the doubt. Speak the love of God over your soul. "God so loved **me** that He gave His only begotten Son that **I may believe** and not perish, so that **I may receive everlasting life.**" This is the way of Jesus; this is what God wants you to embrace.

CONFESSIONS THAT TRANSFORM AND EMPOWER

As we make this a regular practice, we discover freedom upon freedom, and the power of God liberates us. God's Word is power and light, and as we exercise His Word, quote His Word, and claim His Word, then God's truth breaks the bondage that haunts our souls. By confessing Jesus's perspective and speaking with the mind of Christ, we discover how to speak with authority from God Himself.

Even now, as you read this, there may be a call to doubt. But a deep, still, small voice is saying *"believe"* that "God is for you, not against you." God has made a way where there was no way.

Jesus began His ministry by confessing the Word of God as truth: *"Man shall not live by bread alone, but by every word that comes from the mouth of God"* (Matthew 4:4, ESV). We see that Jesus praises His apprentices when they speak or act with faith in the truth. He corrects them when they deny the truth or speak with doubt. Jesus even promises to intercede for us as we are in the process of confessing the truth of who He is. *"Whoever confesses Me before men, him I will also confess before My Father who is in heaven"* (Matthew 10:32, NKJV).

Jesus's confession before our Father is stated in the same tense as it is for us. (That's important.) In other words, Jesus will confess **us to the Father in Heaven as we confess Jesus** before others. It's not Jesus saying, "I'm going to someday," but rather Jesus saying, "I will be doing as you are doing." He will say "Dad! Look—that one is confessing me to others right now."

This is the testimony of those who have gone before us. Every adventurer faces challenges of unbelief, doubt, and despair. The voices of doubt even come from those who mean well but are unable to perceive His adventure.

Many of us, when we began, had friends, family, or leaders speak doubts or warnings to us as we confessed Jesus. So, we overcame that by reminding ourselves of the truths He shows us.

As we confess Jesus and His truth, He actively brings that truth into reality in the spiritual realm. The Father receives this and causes that truth to come to fruition.

As a new crew member, it is imperative to receive, believe, and confess the instructions of our Captain, Jesus. Shake off lies with the Word of God. Pray confessions of truth before God, even whisper them; in the spiritual realm, they will roar like a mighty wind, by the name of Jesus Christ, our Messiah King.

ADVENTURE DECLARATIONS

God loves me.

God made a way for me.

God sent His Son to die for me.

God is pleased with Jesus's sacrifice on my behalf.

Jesus has accepted me, and so God has accepted me.

God has freed me from the death curse of sin rebellion.

God gives me new life in Jesus.

God calls me on a real adventure as a true apprentice living out His purposes in this evil world.

Jesus the Messiah King guides me on this journey.

Jesus has overcome the darkness that held me captive, and I am free to follow Him. I am really free from the power of evil and sin and from fear of the second death.

All of these are biblical truths derived from the passages we've been reviewing in this section.

Peace. Trust in the way of Jesus.

MEDITATIONS FOR NEW LIFE: CLEANSING AND HEALING

God sent Jesus to give life, but His enemy comes to steal, kill, and destroy. We seek God's purpose for us and reject the devil's plans.

CHAPTER 5

THE VOYAGE CHARTS OF PROVIDENCE

Every quest for treasure requires a treasure map. It charts the way and indicates what you will find. The key for adventurers on this quest is to learn the messages, their symbols, and clues and discern the way. Avoiding hidden dangers on this journey requires studying the charts.

Jesus has mapped all the steps for our journey; with great foresight, He shows us how to avoid the perils, find the right passages, obtain the provisions, and win the prizes of the many treasures in a truly spiritual life. It's all available through His teachings.

Yes, we really are called to be pirates that capture loot from the enemy of God, setting free captives and ending the tyranny of the prince of darkness as we go. Doing that requires knowing the way, by the charts of providence. Our Captain knows everything we need and will experience along the way, so it's vital that we learn to listen to what His charts tell us.

"If you have ears, pay attention!"
—Mark 4:23

CALLING ALL ADVENTURERS: LISTEN CAREFULLY!

My Failed Wilderness Journey

As young men, my friends and I went on a journey into the mountains, far from our home. We were new at navigating, but we took a map, compass, and heavy packs full of gear. We planned a long hike to a high mountain lake deep in a wilderness area. The destination has pristinely beautiful views, and we were excited to hike to that high and beautiful place.

We planned everything carefully, but we made one crucial mistake—we were not paying attention and missed the plain markers at the trailhead. So, we missed the correct trail.

After wasting two hours in exhausting heat at high altitudes, wandering through obstacles in the wrong direction, we had to stop and reconsider what we had done wrong and then navigate correctly. What we took by mistake was a deer trail, a false path.

By the time we navigated across to the correct trail, we had exhausted ourselves and ruined some supplies. So, we lost the energy we needed to complete the journey.

We never saw that beautiful glacial lake, but instead spent the entire trip in lower places, far from the goal. We missed the destination due to a dumb mistake at the beginning.

Likewise, on the Jesus Adventure, we have an adventure map—the Holy Bible, our sacred Scriptures. We have this tool—a treasure map with clear and plain markings, which we need to use from the beginning. Many people miss the trail that Jesus already has planned because they ignore the map and miss the markings that Jesus has given us.

So, they exhaust themselves with wasted effort on false trails. We don't want to miss the journey by missing the markers in plain sight: the teachings of Jesus and His emissaries (commonly called the apostles). We call this the New Testament of the Bible.

Getting on the right trail at the beginning of the Jesus Adventure is not hard. We learn to be listeners by reading and staying close to Jesus, which sets us on the right trail and helps us to recognize that the **main** things are the **plain** things, and the **plain** things are the **main** things. We don't seek obscure messages—**the true message is clear.**

Like many treasure maps, there are hidden encryptions that reinforce the plain and clear point of the Bible; those will always clarify the guiding principles to make the essential things even more evident to us. Jesus made it easy for a traveler with a humble heart to find the truth.

For instance, we read how Jesus said He was the "Good Shepherd." He adopts imagery already plainly used of God Himself from the Old Testament, such as in Psalm 23:1, where it says, *"The Lord is my shepherd."* At another time, Jesus tells stories about a vineyard with unfaithful tenants (see Matthew 21; Luke 20). The prophet Isaiah uses this same imagery when God says that the ancient nation of Israel was *"my vineyard"* (Isaiah 5:3-5). Jesus is making obvious links. The messages align to show the same message from God more clearly.

HOW HUNGRY ARE YOU?

Travel makes us hungry. It's best to plan food for the trip and have a good meal before you leave. Starving travelers don't get very far. We need to eat daily. God knows this is also true for our spiritual journey. So, God has spiritual food for us to get started and keep us healthy.

Wise adventurers feast on God's spiritual food every day. We can also share a meal with other hungry travelers. So, find others on the Jesus Adventure and enjoy the company while feasting together on the bread of life, the Word of God.

FOOD FOR EMPOWERED LIVING

When Jesus was fasting alone in the desert, He was tempted by the devil himself to use His miraculous power selfishly to turn a stone into bread.

This was a real temptation to do something that we might not see as truly evil at first. But it was a temptation to misuse His power—in defiance of the Father's plan.

Fortunately, Jesus resisted saying, *"It is written, 'Man shall not live by bread alone, but by every word of God'"* (Luke 4:4, NKJV). In His response, Jesus shows us there is spiritual food that is more fulfilling than bread.

We are spiritual creatures housed in material bodies, blinded to our spiritual nature. So, we have a spiritual hunger that must be filled with spiritual food to truly live. **That spiritual food is the Word of God** which defines our identity. Jesus knew who He was and what the Father had declared about Him. Jesus was not defined by His hunger, His lack, or His loneliness.

Jesus knew He was the only begotten Son of God, who came into a rebellious world, and that God was with Him. Jesus was empowered by knowing that His Father was the one who defined Him.

This is what we crave; this is what is missing for us until we know Jesus. We are hungry in our souls and cannot fill that hunger with anything of this material world.

Until we are born of the Spirit, we are actually spiritually dead, without any of the life of God's Holy Spirit in us (see Ephesians 2:1-5). To begin spiritual birth, we need the spiritual food that comes from God: His Word. He declares who we are and to whom we belong.

Once we find that spiritual food that Jesus offers, we can be satisfied at any time. The nourishment that God gives truly satisfies. Are you hungry enough to eat the food that the Father gives? His food satisfies you where nothing else can.

THE BREAD OF LIFE IS LIVING BREAD

As successful spiritual listeners, we have to understand the messages given to God's people from the beginning to understand the Bible charts that Jesus provides, because Jesus came and taught in that context. In the beginning,

God led His people on the adventure across the sea and through the desert with Moses by giving them daily bread from Heaven, called "manna."

We discover that God was not just feeding His people's bodies, but also providing a model for how He leads us through the challenges of this life. In this way, Jesus spoke for us to learn and understand how to be led by God by knowing how **to be fed by God.**

In the next passage, people were chasing Jesus to find out what He was going to do next because, in a single day, He miraculously fed thousands of people with bread and fish from a small boy's lunch. Jesus told them they needed to seek out the real food, the real meat and bread (spiritually speaking). This was the point of why He did the miracle. But as often happens, the people weren't getting it.

Jesus taught how to find the spiritual food that God gives, saying: *"And the bread that God gives is the one who came down from heaven to give life to the world"* (John 6:33). They still didn't get it, so Jesus spoke more plainly:

> **I am the bread that gives life! No one who comes to me will ever be hungry. No one who has faith in me will ever be thirsty.**
> **—John 6:35**

Wow! Really? Yes. We can all experience that!

So, Jesus is telling us that He is the one who fills this deep spiritual hunger of humanity. Our inner cravings are satisfied when we have a true relationship with Jesus.

So, Jesus explains:

> **Here is the bread that comes down from heaven, which anyone may eat and not die. I am the living bread that came down from heaven. Whoever eats this bread will live forever. This bread is my flesh, which I will give for the life of the world.**
> **—John 6:51 (author paraphrase)**

Jesus explains a little later:

> **The Spirit is the one who gives life! Human strength can do nothing. The words that I have spoken to you are from that life-giving Spirit.**
> —John 6:33

The point emerges—Jesus Himself is the very Word of God given to us. Not merely as written letters, but He is a perfect living representation of the Father. He's the Living Word, speaking to us and showing us the way of spiritual life, giving His own body as an offering. Jesus receives anyone who listens and receives His Word, and He feeds our souls (see John 5:24).

We travel knowing that Jesus willingly and completely gives that to us who trust enough to follow Him. We learn to follow and do the works of God by listening to Jesus.

BACKING UP TO GO FORWARD

This may seem like a strange way for Jesus to speak. You may be struggling, especially if you have come from a very religious background where you were taught to earn a place with God or do rituals. You may question: does the Old Testament give us a precedent for this concept of Jesus as spiritual food for us? It certainly does.

Consider these passages from the Old Testament:

Psalms 34:8 (ESV) says, *"Oh, taste and see that the LORD is good! Blessed is the man who takes refuge in him!"*

Psalms 119:103 (ESV) says, *"How sweet are your words to my taste, sweeter than honey to my mouth!"*

Job 23:12 (ESV) says, *"I have treasured the words of his mouth more than my portion of food."*

And then we recall again how Jesus quoted Moses in Deuteronomy 8:3 (NIV), *"Man does not live on bread alone but on every word that comes from the mouth of the LORD."* God says that He feeds us with His Word. Jesus simply clarified it.

Recall Chapter 4, that it was ***"written in the volume of the book"*** about the Messiah. Jesus is now showing us, at a deeper level, how the Word of God is **spiritual food** and that **Jesus Himself is actually the living breathing Word of God** (made in human flesh).

THE NOURISHING MYSTERY OF LISTENING

God does something deeply satisfying in us when we develop the habit of carefully and regularly listening to Him. Now the Jesus Adventure is underway, and we want to be careful to listen. This kind of listening is like following the markings on a treasure map, where X marks the spot.

So, let's find that treasure!

Remember that Jesus is consistent with the Old Testament prophets, including the Psalms—His authority is established by them. Sometimes false teachers will twist the meaning to use Jesus as a way to advance their agenda. But we can check back to find the truth is consistent.

We faithfully follow His charts (the gospels in the New Testament) on this adventure. The Adventure has always been there, but many have missed it by skipping the trail map. We're not the first to find it, but it may seem like it sometimes!

Adventure Skill: Followers of Jesus develop a heart willing to hear God. We note where God tells us who we are, and we embed those words in our hearts to keep us secure.

MARKERS ON THE CHART

Jesus uses repetition to develop our skills. Each time Jesus repeats something or reiterates the same idea differently, He gives us a major clue. In this case, it's about how to listen more faithfully.

In the original language of the Bible, it becomes clearer: **Jesus wants us to know how to understand** and to listen correctly. In the Gospel of Mark 4:23, Jesus says: *"Now listen!"* He tells a story and says again, *"If you have ears, pay attention."* Then, Jesus tells several stories **about listening.** I think Jesus was teaching us how to focus on being good listeners who listen with understanding.

Maybe you were like I was as a kid in school. I could sit and watch the lips moving on the teacher's mouth and never really hear what she said.

On His adventure, Jesus helps us develop a lifestyle of listening—so that we can hear and **understand.**

LISTENING TO GOD, THE JESUS WAY

Jesus uses more than one means to speak to our hearts; sometimes, He speaks by His Holy Spirit (see John 14:16), and we hear Him deep in our own spirits. We call this the "still small voice."

Sometimes He also uses His people or even dreams and visions. Mostly He uses His Word, the Bible, to communicate with us. This is the only foolproof way to know the will of God; we can rely on it. Many of us find He will use all three, but He always starts and returns to the Word.

I often hear people say they don't hear from God. Well, God is always communicating, but most people aren't actively listening! We have to open the Bible and seek Him. The starting point is diligence in prayer, waiting for Him to speak. It helps if we're prepared to take notes. Becoming a listener is a skill like any other. But God is not silent!

Jesus prayed to the Father for His apprentices: *"I gave them the words you gave me and they accepted them"* (John 17:8, NIV). To do this, Jesus practiced a habit of listening (see Mark 4:24; John 15:15). We know that Jesus knew His Bible perfectly and had an exceptional prayer life—Jesus took time to listen to the Father, so that is what He's showing us to do by His example.

ADVENTURE PARABLE CHALLENGE

Jesus spoke to people in stories that illustrate, called parables. He did this so those with humble hearts would understand deeper truth and apply it well. The parables still work that way. But the stubborn hard-hearted were confounded and ignored Him.

Do you have a heart to receive from God? It just takes some humility to hear with understanding. If we ask God for supernatural wisdom and spiritual understanding, we can be confident that He gives it to us—by learning His Word.

ADVENTURE MAP: STORIES WITH GREATER TRUTH

Today most people live in cities. Maybe you work with computers or machinery. Most people get food from a store or a supermarket. But think back to a time when those things did not exist. Jesus used experiences that were common to the people of His day to reveal powerful spiritual skills.

His apprentices mostly worked with handmade tools and grew food at their homes to survive. That is foreign to us, but we can learn from the examples if we're willing.

THE SKILL OF SPIRITUAL LISTENING

Jesus gives us meaningful stories so we develop vital listening skills. The primary one is from Matthew 13. It's one of the most profound parables, which I encourage you to read. I want you to focus on what Jesus says in Matthew 13:11:

"*I have explained the secrets about the kingdom of heaven to you, but not to others.*" And just as you begin to wonder why Jesus would do that, He explains:

> Everyone who has will be given more. But people who don't have anything will lose even what little they have. I use stories when I speak to them because when they look, they cannot see, and when they listen, they cannot hear or understand. So God's promise came true, just as the prophet Isaiah had said,

> "These people will listen and listen, but never understand.
> They will look and look, but never see.
> All of them have stubborn minds! They refuse to listen; they cover their eyes.
> They cannot see or hear or understand. If they could,
> they would turn to me, and I would heal them."
> —Matthew 13:12-15

So, what we learn is that there were many, especially the religious leadership, who **refused to hear what God gave Jesus to say to them.** They refused to see the works Jesus did as validation of His teachings. They did not have humble hearts.

Jesus calls us to experience the power that gives life forever, and that power comes to us through the Word of God and prayer. So, we prepare ourselves with humility to actively listen and accept the message. In prayerfully hearing and accepting Jesus's authority, we grow like a good crop.

Sadly, some turn away, while others stay but don't let the message change them. True adventurers are those who want God's life-giving work to bring a great harvest in their lives. True adventurers humbly ask God to prepare our hearts. God will honor that prayer. We have to want to know Him, hear Him, and be determined to receive His Word!

PREPARING THE HEART

Jesus tells us: We have to become like a little child. The Bible tells us about the people who followed Jesus with real examples; they were ordinary people like us. Some were rough characters—people with messy backgrounds.

Consider the fishermen. Peter, Andrew, James, and John had a business together. They were tough guys! They worked on the sea, in the sun, hauling heavy rough nets full of fish out of the sea with bare hands. They left their work, which they knew and were confident doing, to follow Jesus and listen to Him. **They humbled themselves.**

Consider Matthew and his friends: they were rich tax collectors—guys who knew the numbers and calculated everything. Matthew left his Roman tax-collecting franchise. Another tax collector named Zacchaeus climbed a tree to see Jesus in person because he was too short to look through the crowd.

They were rich guys! **They became like little children, and with childlike faith, they trusted Jesus** for every need. They were not ashamed. Can you become like a child **and follow Jesus?**

Perhaps the best examples of Jesus's apprentices were the women. It would be a mistake to overlook them. We see one who took the most valuable thing she had and broke it to wash Jesus from His head to His toes with expensive fragrant oil. This was to honor Him on the night before He died. She gave her best.

Martha quietly served His team food, beverages, and lodging whenever they were in town. Others followed Him closely, sitting at His feet, listening to every word He said so they would know Jesus better and do whatever He asked.

These women had humble hearts, prepared to receive His Word. He rewarded the women with being the first ones He met after He was raised from the dead. God reveals the most amazing things to those who are humble enough to seek Him faithfully.

ONLY QUIT WHAT KEEPS YOU FROM GOD

I'm not suggesting that anyone should quit a job or sell a business to follow Jesus. But are you trusting God for your work? Are you honoring God in how you do your work? Are you seeking the work that God would ask you to do? Trusting Jesus and hearing God's Word means we become willing to follow where He leads.

Is there something that holds your soul hostage? Do you wonder what God would say to you if you could hear Him? Most people are unwilling to listen because they fear that God will make a change in their life. God only brings into our lives what is best for us from the eternal perspective. If we didn't need change, we wouldn't need God.

Adventure Principle: We ask, "God, what keeps me from listening to you?" Then we remove the things God reveals.

GOD'S SPIRIT BREAKS UP HARD GROUND

When we humble ourselves to God and admit that we have a heart problem, we can ask Jesus to prepare us, and He sends the Holy Spirit to come and help. Ask Jesus to reveal what is keeping you from having a heart for God and ask Him to make it ready for His Word to grow. He will do it.

Wait, listen humbly, and become quiet—God will answer. God delights to lead you on the Jesus Adventure. He is eagerly looking for travelers who take the journey seriously. Take time to seek Him right now. His Spirit will guide you.

ADVANCED LISTENING SKILLS FOR FOLLOWING JESUS

Jesus teaches us to develop advanced listening skills with this vital principle when Jesus said:

> **Pay attention to how you listen! Everyone who has something will be given more, but people who have nothing will lose what little they think they have.**
> —Luke 8:18

Notice that Jesus gives this promise with a warning. He is saying that if we are listening carefully with a heart for God, He will reward us with more—more understanding and more willingness, a greater heart for God.

But, if we do not listen to God, what little heart for God we have will wither away. It's grow spiritually or die. Your choice: abundant life or lose what has already been given.

There are eight Adventure Principles we get from Jesus for developing skills of listening to God.

Principle One: We discern truth by testing fruit. It seems hard, but we have everything we need if we do what He taught.

Principle Two: Big things start small. The small things you do today will have big results later.

Principle Three: Give the Word of God time to work. God does miraculous things with time and faithfulness. Don't quit the lifelong journey the first time the waves get high.

Principle Four: Let God teach you through parables. Why read an odd book about an adventure? God makes a point through a prophecy in the Psalms:

> **I will use stories to speak my message and to explain things hidden since the creation of the world.**
> **—Matthew 13:35**

Principle Five: Listening to God is like hunting treasure. When you know where the treasure is, you sacrifice everything to get it.

Principle Six: Let go of things that keep you hostage. If your current lifestyle keeps you from finding that treasure, let go of that lifestyle and get the treasure.

Principle Seven: Not everyone will hear and accept the instructions of God. Those who do are blessed with eternal life in God's Kingdom, but those who reject His Word are rejected.

Principle Eight: Discover things old and new. The Bible gives us a library of sixty-six books by forty authors, written on three continents over a period of more than 1,700 years—yet it's a perfect unity of revelation. The Old and New Testaments are an integrated message system that grows us every day.

REVIEWING WITH JESUS, OUR GUIDE

The Jesus Adventure is action. It's "doing" the Word, not just information. Jesus wants you to actively follow His instructions—that is the real adventure! His teachings give you spiritual life. This book is just a discovery guide to experience it.

In the first parable about the farmer scattering seed, Jesus focuses on four outcomes. We have seen these results happen with many people over decades, both good and bad.

Some hear the Word but never do anything because they don't take the time to understand it—they forget what they hear, and nothing changes.

Some hear the Word and get excited, but they quickly dry up and turn away because they have stubborn hearts.

Some hear the Word and grow, but lusts and riches choke their hearts with a love of temporary things. They never experience real transformation.

Some are different; some really are transformed. These are <u>the true adventurers</u>. God really changes their lives, and they really experience God's power, giving them joy and fruitful adventure. They never want to turn back; they don't want to miss seeing God do all the amazing things He promises.

Adventure Key: Jesus keeps transforming us as we do His teachings.

GOD KEEPS FULFILLING PROMISES

One of the fascinating Adventure Principles we get from the "listening stories" is that God is reminding us that He fulfills His promises even today. Jesus's teaching by parables is one of the signs that He is Messiah!

The more you see it, the more exciting it gets! To get the most out of this, write down every time you find a promise of God in the Bible. Write where you found it. Pray about it, and then watch. God will show you amazing things. Adventurers see things that others overlook.

Whether we meet in a church building or a small group—just two or three at a time—or even meet with Him alone in prayer, our purpose is to hear, communicate, and be empowered by Jesus for this journey. Our purpose is to actively live the Jesus Adventure daily, moment by moment in His presence. It is a daily experience everywhere we go.

THE ADVENTURERS WHO LISTENED AND SURVIVED A TRIBULATION

Jesus's final instruction to His apprentices was to go into the world far and wide, make apprentices of every tribe of people to follow Him; baptize them, **and teach them everything that Jesus instructed.** Those first apprentices went very far, across three continents. But thousands of His followers stayed right in Jerusalem. Even though their numbers grew into the tens of thousands, those followers of Jesus were always a minority group, and they didn't completely disperse until 66 AD.

You see, Jesus had warned that there was a day coming soon when a powerful army would capture Jerusalem. He warned:

> **When you see Jerusalem surrounded by soldiers, you will know that it will soon be destroyed. If you are living in Judea at this time, run to the mountains. If you are in the city, leave it. And if you are out in the country, don't go back into the city.**
> **—Luke 21:20-21**

His followers didn't forget. They reminded the younger ones that Jesus had said this would happen <u>in their generation</u>.

Sure enough, in 66 AD (about thirty-three years after Jesus's resurrection), an army from Rome came and surrounded the city. The city was under siege for several weeks, and then the Roman army just left unexpectedly. A few people returned. Jesus had not said to do that. His warning was to leave permanently. Most of Jesus's people did as He said.

The Romans returned less than two years later and brought a bigger army. For two years, they attacked the city. Ultimately, the people inside were so starved that some ate their children. Their temple was totally destroyed, and the remaining people were killed or taken as slaves. The entire city was sacked and plundered.

The people who failed to follow Jesus's instructions all suffered the same fate, whether they were the people who rejected Him in the first place or those who went back.

Jesus had warned that this was coming. Only those who listened and obeyed were saved! They formed a new community, and their children thrived for generations. They even built a church to commemorate God's protection from this disaster. It stands today, in the current nation of Jordan, at the top of a hill above the ancient city of Petra.

Today, many people claim to follow Jesus but don't follow His teachings. Then, they become frustrated and blame God. It is not God's fault when people refuse to hear. Rejecting His teachings leads people to suffer consequences. Only an arrogant person blames God for their rebellion.

LISTENING STRATEGIES

There are ways to improve your ability to understand as you follow Jesus.

Make a daily habit of reading God's Word. Take notes as you go. It keeps you from being distracted. Then research it.

Apply Jesus's teachings as you learn. He gives opportunities.

Pray about the things He says and ask Him to help.

Seek out wise teachers who are careful followers of Jesus and the Bible. Find a group that studies it chapter by chapter. Anyone who teaches primarily from other sources is not reliable. Make sure that you seek Bible teachers who openly live out the teachings of Jesus. God hates hypocrisy.

Always be careful to read the Bible passages that a teacher is using and check them out for yourself. **Good teachers will encourage this.** <u>False teachers will get upset.</u>

Always pray before any reading time, asking Jesus to guide and instruct you. He will. Pray for discernment and ask Him to transform you by the Word. He will.

Finally, <u>commit to do</u> what Jesus teaches. Choose to **do** God's Word by God's power. Real adventurers learn to practice faithfully every day. Jesus said, *"The people who are really blessed are the ones who hear and obey God's message!"* (Luke 11:29), and He also said, *"You are My friends if you do what I tell you"* (John 15:14, NLV).

Quiet Paths

As we develop the skillful habit of listening to God, we easily find our way on the journey. We realize that He is present at each step, making the journey more fun. Willingness to be silent is key.

"Truly my soul silently waits for God; From Him comes my salvation" (Psalm 62:1, NKJV).

Immature followers fear silence. They can't face the reminders of personal failures and faults. Jesus moves us past all of that, and His grace overcomes the anxiety. He says, *"Fear not!"* (appearing 103 times in the New Testament), showing that God is for us, not against us—**and waits for us in the quiet and stillness.**

Our hearts become eager to listen because the silence is no longer uncomfortable. We welcome it because we hear Him there.

God says to us, *"In returning and rest shall ye be saved; in quietness and in confidence shall be your strength"* (Isaiah 30:15, KJV).

God calls us to *"Be still, and know that I am God"* (Psalm 46:10, NIV). God is taking us along to accomplish His plans when we're quiet enough to hear Him.

FINDING THE WAY THROUGH THE CONFUSION

Discerning the right direction in a thick fog, blizzard, or wildfire is always difficult; it's easy to get confused. In those moments, you look for objective points of reality to help. Then keep your wits and find the right direction.

When it seems confusing on the journey, we look to Jesus. Jesus reminded us many times that He would be with us. We can rely on that. Jesus says, *"You <u>know</u> the way"* (John 14:4). Jesus is saying that the truth has already been given to us in Himself.

As you read this, you can look to Jesus. **He is always the way.** Perhaps you have been taught something that contradicts this; perhaps it's hard to understand how God really can love you. Whatever situation you are facing, look to Jesus. He is available.

Thomas, one of Jesus's apprentices, asked Jesus to show him the way. Thomas was confused about how to find this path Jesus promised. We don't need to wander as we seek it—**God brings it to us.** So, Jesus said to him, *"I am the way, the truth and the life; no one comes to the Father, but through me"* (John 14:6, author paraphrase).

When Jesus says, *"You <u>know</u> the way,"* the word "know" means to experience a personal interaction. It's not merely recognizing a fact by reading it, but rather that we come to intimately know Him by experience with Him.

At every point, Jesus is showing us an active journey—a living relationship, a dynamic life, this sacred journey and adventure.

Hearing God is not a spectator sport! We are participants; we know His voice by practicing as listeners who **do** His will. We learn how to discern it through the teachings of Jesus. If you have lost your way, ask yourself: what is the last thing you know God spoke to you? What did He call you to do? That is where He will meet you to go forward.

Are you ready to hear and obey God? He is ready to speak to you. He is ready to guide your life to the unspeakable joy and peace you crave. If you are ready, you will come to know the truth intimately and thoroughly.

Jesus was challenged by religious leaders who doubted that. How could Jesus have God's wisdom without being taught by them? They ignored what He was teaching. Jesus replied to them with a very significant truth:

> **I am not teaching something that I thought up. What I teach comes from the one who sent me. If you really <u>want</u> to obey God, you will know if what I teach comes from God or from me.**
> **—John 7:16-17 (author emphasis)**

If we **do** the truth of God, we come to know it confidently. Truth is an experience with God, not a lecture topic. This is our confidence to navigate in this dark world: God is with us. It's like when a little child learns to walk. Once the toddler realizes they can do it by experiencing it, you can't stop them from walking everywhere.

In the same way, when we experience the Jesus Adventure, we want to go everywhere He sends us and do everything He says. We know God is a good Father; we know He loves us. It becomes an exciting journey with Jesus.

Jesus said, *"If you keep on obeying what I have said, you truly are my disciples. You will know the truth, and the truth will set you free"* (John 7:16-17). Freedom is God's purpose for us. Jesus promises a freedom of spirit from above, which overcomes the rebel nature and this God-rejecting world.

It is the freedom that gives life, peace, and joy; it gives us full purpose and power in our lives. This freedom comes from knowing truth by experience and knowing God personally.

Adventure Key: God always leads us by relationship.

THE DIVINE PRESENCE OF GOD—THE COMFORTING GUIDE

The prophet Isaiah foretold that we would call Jesus *"Emmanuel"* (see Isaiah 7:14; Matthew 1:23). This name means "God present with us." For two thousand years, this is what His followers have called Jesus. **He is God who is present with us.** He was present with His apprentices physically in Galilee. He is present with us today by the Holy Spirit because He is God, who became man, and since Jesus was resurrected, He has had <u>perfect communion</u> with His people in the Spirit.

Not enough words are available in every language of the world to explain this completely. The core of our souls was created for the Spirit of the Creator to be alive in us. It is the deepest human need: the presence of God with us. Jesus was the real living and breathing presence of God with His people.

Jesus's apprentices understood Him as the presence of God with them in a physical body. Before Jesus left, He made it clear that He was sending His Spirit to remain in communion with us until He returns. Our *"Emmanuel"* is really "God with us"—in us.

The original meaning of this prophecy was that Jesus would be a real physical presence, and Jesus said His Spirit would be with us in the same way—a real and true presence for those who follow Him. Jesus used a few words to describe His Spirit who would be with us: "Counselor," "Helper," "Advocate," and "Comforter."

The Spirit of God is real and available—every moment. In fact, He is not only with us, but **He is present** in those who have turned to God, believed Jesus, and have been cleansed of darkness. Read the Gospel of John 14-15, where Jesus explains this in detail.

Yes, Jesus said that this is unique to **those who follow Him**: His Spirit is resident in us as our Guide. This is how we truly become listeners; we count on the Guide to lead and help us. We have His presence in us to open the ears of our souls.

The Guide, our comforting advocate, is pledged to us as the enduring light of life, which shines in the darkest places in our lives. He is the power of all of life itself residing in us. He was the life-giver that hovered over all creation at the beginning. The Guide helps us to stay connected to the Father while teaching us to trust in Jesus. He coaches us, encourages us, and reveals more about Jesus.

The Guide also empowers our prayers, helping us to know the Father's powerful design (will) for our lives. As the words of Jesus are like seeds, the Guide gives life to that seed within our hearts. He flows in us with new life, joy, and purpose.

Jesus said:

For my Father's will is that everyone who looks to the Son and believes in him shall have eternal life, and I will raise them up at the last day.
—John 6:40 (NIV)

So, Jesus connects us with life-giving power through listening and receiving His Good News. It is a living connection with God today, but it also is **a promise of the resurrection on the last day.** Jesus isn't just the bread of life to sustain us on the journey, but He sustains us through the final passage. Jesus promises it, and Jesus keeps His promises.

What about you? Are you willing to hear Him? Have you heard God tell you what He cares about? Do you know His plans? Are you willing to let God guide you? Listening to God is one of the greatest privileges we have on Jesus's adventure.

Meditations on hearing Jesus:
1) Find total peace and confidence from Jesus (see Colossians 1:20).
2) Jesus is our only true link to God (see John 17:3).
3) God uses His Word to establish our lives in ways that lead us to real, lasting life success (see Colossians 2:7; Isaiah 33:6; 1 Peter 5:10).

PROMISES FOR ADVENTURERS WHO LISTEN WELL

<u>Jesus will reveal Himself to you</u>.

> **He who has My commandments and keeps them, it is he who loves Me. And he who loves Me will be loved by my Father, and I will love him and manifest myself to him.**
> —John 14:21 (NKJV)

<u>You can be the most blessed of any people</u>.

Jesus said:

> **"The people who are really blessed are the ones that hear and obey God's message."**
> —Luke 11:28

<u>You can be unshakable</u>.

Jesus said:

> **Anyone who comes and listens to me and obeys me is like someone who dug down deep and built a house on solid rock. When a flood came and the river rushed against the house, it was built so well that it didn't even shake.**
> —Luke 6:47-49

CHAPTER 6

CROSSING OVER BY FAITH

Jesus said:

"Let us cross over to the other side."
—Mark 4:35 (LEB)

RIDING BOLDLY ON THE GREAT ADVENTURE

We are well on our way as we follow and explore the wide blue ocean of what Jesus teaches. This next stage of the adventure is where God takes us through challenges to do impossible things with us. Jesus has prepared the next steps, and His Father is setting the stage. This is where it really gets interesting.

We want to remember that everything we need for success on His adventure is available to us through our faith in Jesus and through His Word, the Holy Bible. We explore this in detail, so we can know how to get victory when we're challenged or tempted.

Unfortunately, this is exactly where many people quit. Yes, most people stop here and never discover what God has prepared. They struggle to go forward into the adventure because they get paralyzed by fear, frustrated when they face the impossible, or caught up in the superficial things of this godless world.

God has planned amazing things. Most people never see it, but we don't want to miss them! We're adventurers with hungry hearts, willing to dare God to do what He has promised! For this reason, it's important to pray now and ask God for the courage to go forward.

Take a moment: ask God to give you enough faith in Jesus, and **then trust Him for it**. With Jesus, admitting that you lack faith is enough evidence of faith for God to answer you.

THE GOD OF ALL POSSIBILITIES

Jesus taught that *"with God all things are possible"* (Matthew 19:26, KJV). He even prayed this on the last night before He was crucified. But most people only see limitations. By adulthood, we learn that this life is filled with impossible situations, and we feel powerless to change any of them. Many give up believing that the most difficult things won't change at all.

But as apprentices of Jesus, we see the ways of the Spirit, and we know from Jesus that *"with God all things are possible,"* so we are called to be world changers. With childlike faith, many have overcome incredible odds. So, we can face the impossible because we have a God greater than all things.

In the vast mystery of God, we discover His greater plans, and Jesus leads us to discover His power, which we experience when we abide in Him. We experience the impossible and He shows us that God will do it. Jesus gives us the faith to believe, and He gives us the answer to that faith when we do what He teaches. It is vital to learn and do what He teaches so that we can experience the adventure the Father has prepared.

God is good all the time. He is flowing with grace and gives all the time. The air we breathe? The world we live in? The rain that falls to water the land? All of it is sustained by the hand of God. We do not motivate God; God is always motivated! God is always love. He doesn't have love; He is Love (see 1 John 4:7-12).

As the prime mover of all creation and the prime motivator for all goodness, God wants us to trust Him. **He gives abundantly to those who live by faith in Him.** Remember that God always offers grace and peace, so He favors those who humble themselves to Him. He destroys the authority of chaos over our lives.

God knows we are mortal. Our acts of rebellion have consequences because we will harvest whatever seed we have planted, but that does not mean that God stops loving us. He plans good things in us and through us. If this was true of such people as Abraham, Jacob, Moses, and David—men who each had moments of failure—how much more is it true for us who have trusted in God's Son?

CROSSING OVER WITH TRUST

Jesus leads us out from the busy crowd. He calls us into journeys of faith and challenges us to trust in His promises and character. Sometimes that journey can look ordinary. But, with Jesus, nothing is ever ordinary for long. This simple boat ride across the little Sea of Galilee rocked His apprentices to their core:

> "That evening, Jesus said to his disciples, 'Let's cross to the east side.'"
> —Mark 4:35

Before that, men came claiming they wanted to follow and learn from Jesus.

> A teacher of the Law of Moses came up to him and said, "Teacher, I'll go anywhere with you!" Jesus replied, "Foxes have dens, and birds have nests. But the Son of Man doesn't have a place to call his own." Another disciple said to Jesus, "Lord, let me wait till I bury my father." Jesus answered, "Come with me, and let the dead bury their dead."
> —Matthew 8:19-22

But neither of them went with Jesus. Only those who were committed to the adventure went to the other side. We see here how it went.

> **After Jesus left in a boat with his disciples, a terrible storm suddenly struck the lake, and waves started splashing into their boat. Jesus was sound asleep, so the disciples went over to him and woke him up. They said, "Lord, save us! We're going to drown!" But Jesus replied, "Why are you so afraid? You surely don't have much faith." Then he got up and ordered the wind and the waves to calm down. And everything was calm. The men in the boat were amazed and said, "Who is this? Even the wind and the waves obey him."**
> **—Matthew 8:23-27**

Many people started to follow Jesus but gave up when it became uncomfortable or inconvenient. Others want to start, but **only if they can squeeze God into their plans.** Others do start but give up when storms arise. Some people doubt and question as soon as a challenge comes.

After starting on the adventure, others quit because of worry, doubt, or peer pressure. They miss what God has planned! They don't see the adventure, nor witness Jesus's incredible authority over nature. They also don't believe those who do see it.

The disciples were in a scary situation: the storm was severe, so even those experienced fishermen were afraid. The sea was coming into the boat faster than they could bail it out. But do you know what really bothered them? Jesus was asleep!

They forgot that Jesus said He was **going to the other side.** Jesus was confident and knew that His Father would not let Him drown. Jesus was at peace. His peace came from trusting that God was in control.

God will accomplish His purposes in us when we have committed to following His plans. We learn to trust in God's presence. Whatever we face, God is committed to taking us through. The Father favors those who favor His Son. He gives perfect peace and delivers you from chaos to design—this is the whole point.

You see, Jesus was teaching them to trust in His Word. He was **not trying** to cross the sea. He was crossing it! If they had trusted in God's Word, they would remember that it says:

"*Whenever I am afraid, I will trust in You*" (Psalm 56:3, NKJV).

If they had considered their worship psalms, they would have relied on prayers and thanksgiving because it says:

**Those who go down to the sea in ships, Who do business on great waters,
They see the works of the LORD, and His wonders in the deep.
<u>For He commands and raises the stormy wind,</u>
Which lifts up the waves of the sea....
<u>He calms the storm, so that its waves are still.</u>
–Psalm 107:23-25, 29 (NKJV)**

Jesus expected them to remember that Moses had parted the Red Sea and Joshua had parted the Jordan River so that the Israelites could cross on dry ground. They could have prayed and expected God's deliverance because one greater than Moses was with them. This is why Jesus said to them: *"Why were you afraid? Don't you have any faith?"*

What about us today? Do we trust God when things get rough? Or do we panic and get angry? If you are angry or panicked, it shows you have no faith—you're not trusting God. As we develop a relationship with God, learn His Word, and walk in His light, we will encounter challenges.

We will face fierce storms. That is the nature of living in a fallen world. In those times, we can be calm and remember that Jesus is with us. Jesus delivers us from harm when we praise and trust Him, and He will even give us the power to calm the storm. Yes. This is what Jesus is teaching!

That bothers many when you say that. But it's true. Most religious people, especially many strict Christian sects, would never believe God gives us authority to calm storms. Let's remember that it wasn't just once that Jesus sent His disciples into fierce storms, but twice. The second time, when Jesus was walking on water, Peter also walked on water.

Remember that it wasn't just the original twelve apprentices who had the authority to work miracles by God's power. There were others among the next generation of apprentices who also had faith and power from God to work miracles. This is the record of the early gathering of the apprentices of Jesus:

> **"And Stephen, full of faith and power, did great wonders and signs among the people."**
> **–Acts 6:8 (NKJV)**

Are miracles for us today? There's a lot of debate about that among people who follow Jesus. Some say emphatically, "Yes!" Others, just as emphatically, say, "No!" Before I answer that question, we need to look at how and when God does miracles.

Consider what Jesus said:

"Let's cross to the east side."

Jesus intended to cross to the other side because He had a mission planned. The apprentices were responding to a specific calling of God. So, Jesus intended them to respond with faith. Why did they have so little faith?

What about today? Many have heard of Jesus doing miracles and have heard of His original apprentices doing miracles. Many believe these were only for them, back then.

But what about Stephen, the first deacon? Was he an official emissary? No. He was an apprentice of theirs, one who came along later and was probably a child when Jesus taught in Galilee. There are even more amazing miracles done by Philip the Evangelist, who was also a later apprentice.

What about Paul, the emissary who came years later? He had his own apprentices who had never been to Galilee or Jerusalem. They also saw God do miracles through their prayers. Even later, apprentices received miracles among them.

And what about Barnabas, the associate of Paul? He also was given miraculous abilities. So, let's dispel this silly notion that God's power was only available for Peter and the other original apprentices. **The question is: by what criteria does God work miracles for His people?**

In each of these cases, they were faithfully doing the work Jesus gave them, as Jesus had taught, and God's power was there to do amazing things. Yet, most Christian people today do not have that power.

It seems that when people are "trying" to do something religious without being in His will, nothing miraculous happens. Worse, we sometimes see people making things up, which creates more confusion. Making things up is NOT the way of Jesus.

Are you following Jesus? He did not say that only a special group would have His authority. He said that those who live by His teachings, those who faithfully walk in His authority, and those who abide in Him would have the power to do the things He instructs.

Are you responding to His call? Are you living out the adventure He leads? Those taking the adventure receive power and authority from Him to do His Word by abiding in Jesus. This is the testimony of many people.

This is the missing key to the faith. God still does miraculous things as people faithfully trust Him to do what Jesus has called them to do! When we are following Jesus, God gives this authority and power to all who faithfully live out what He has instructed. This may be in a far-off country or with your rebellious teenagers in your own home—the mission is the same.

For those willing to trust Him and do His will, Jesus always has something new and amazing! He doesn't waste His wonders on hardened hearts, and He never does the same things twice in exactly the same way. When we believe in God, He shows up with fresh hope, and that is always exciting. We don't tell Him what to do; we submit to Him.

Some people talk about having great faith. Nonsense. God wants willingness. He wants humble hearts, not boasting. There's no power in our amount of faith; there's power in the God whom we trust. The real question is: are we willing to be used by God? He will ask us to do things requiring us to trust Him totally. The more consistently you trust Him, the more He works through you.

Adventure Principle: Jesus leads us to follow His instructions and fully trust that God will see it through miraculously.

THE GREAT ADVENTURE PLAN

The key to seeing God's miraculous adventure is confidence in Him. Confident faithfulness, doing God's plan as Jesus instructed and as the Holy Spirit leads, is how we see His mighty works. This confidence comes from learning God's plan and relying on the Holy Spirit's presence. Then, God does the impossible. I've seen it many times. Few people see His mighty works because they're busy doing anything but the will of God. So, God is not involved.

True apprentices follow the plans Jesus gave us, just like the original apprentices. We don't turn to myths, fables, or man-made ideas. We seek the truths that Jesus gave His emissaries, and we are careful not to be led astray by false teachings. So, what is God's plan? Remember that Jesus said:

> **All authority in heaven and on earth has been given to me. Therefore, as you go, disciple people in all nations, baptizing them in the name of the Father, and the Son, and the Holy Spirit, teaching them to obey everything that I've commanded you. And remember, I am with you each and every day until the end of the age.**
> **—Matthew 28:18-20 (ISV)**

Often called "The Great Commission," sometimes people get stuck there, as though this is some extra calling. But according to Jesus, this is the whole calling. As we say where I grew up, this is "the whole enchilada."

There are not two classes of apprentices. There are apprentices, and there are those who reject the call. The most normal instinct for a new apprentice is to share the "bread of life" with other starving travelers.

Let's break that out in today's language:

Jesus has full authority from God to fulfill the redemption plan; He is still focused on that. Redeeming people from the authority of the chaos is the priority. Nothing can be as important.

Jesus's game plan is teaching all people everywhere to become His apprentices, to make that the mark of their life, to start life anew, and to mark that new life through baptism—by the full authority of God.

It's a whole package, everything He has taught is for each apprentice, and the whole package is what He is guiding us in.

He is involved in this **until the very end of this age.**

Although some believe this instruction is just for His original twelve emissaries, Jesus doesn't give us that option! When He said, *"Teaching them to obey everything that I've commanded (instructed) you"* (Matthew 28:20, author paraphrase). He encapsulated the whole body of His teachings and said they are for all apprentices of all times until He returns. Because He said it's *"until the end of the age."*

This is a high calling, a grand adventure, a distinct privilege, for which we have been offered a role as participants who will be rewarded for the work.

EMPOWERMENT FOR THE ADVENTURE PLAN

Committing to becoming an apprentice of Jesus requires power from Heaven. None of us comes to faith except by a supernatural gift from God. The natural (rebellious) mind is completely against the things of God. So, He grants us faith.

We don't have to wear religious clothes, special hats, badges, or funny haircuts to be empowered for the Father's plan. We just need to be plugged into Jesus. Jesus came to give His power to the weak, so that we can be changed from captives of the rule of the evil one to being Royal Family empowered for Kingdom business!

Jesus is not a manipulator. The Father does not withhold any good thing from His children. It's according to His abundant riches of grace, not because we earn it.

God has a program that He wants us to join, and **He commits resources to those who willingly join** that program. I can't stress that enough. If your life following Jesus does not involve supernatural empowerment, perhaps you are not engaged in His program yet.

Jesus put it succinctly when He said:

> **And do not seek what you should eat or what you should drink, nor have an anxious mind. For all these things the nations of the world seek after, and your Father knows that you need these things. But seek the kingdom of God, and all these things shall be added to you.**
> —Luke 12:29-31 (NKJV)

So, there's good news because Jesus is committing Kingdom energy and provisions to those who come to Him in faith and take on the task of making apprentices. Don't let anyone tell you otherwise: there is nothing to keep you from having that in-filling blessing from God, except your willingness to be available.

This is the greatest epic of all history. Success requires the supernatural work of God the Holy Spirit in us to be transformed and to learn this confidence. No one comes to the point of trusting Jesus without the Holy Spirit convincing us. We all must receive God's Spirit to enter the Kingdom and keep being filled with His Spirit to accomplish Kingdom business.

God is willing to work His power into us and purify our hearts so that we can be effective agents of His blessing and peace. He gives us His favor and peace to become givers of His blessing and peace. It's that simple.

Jesus has given us His commitment that we can ask Him for things we need according to His will, and He commits to doing it, as Scripture reveals:

> **"Ask, and it will be given to you; seek, and you will find; knock, and it will be opened to you"**
> **—Matthew 7:7 (NASB)**

Also, Jesus said:

"If you ask anything in My name, I will do it" (John 14:14, NKJV).

We learn from Jesus that He puts the highest priority on the things that matter the most. That makes sense, right? Because Jesus says, *"Seek first His kingdom and His righteousness, and all these things will be provided to you"* (Matthew 6:33, NASB).

Jesus answers needs by priority without failing to meet our other needs on the way. He is also telling us that anyone who chooses sacrificial faithfulness *"for My name's sake, shall receive a hundredfold, and will inherit everlasting life"* (Matthew 19:29, KJV).

Millions of people have testified over the centuries that Jesus keeps these promises! All of His plans, purposes, and miraculous power are vested within that instruction which we call "The Great Commission." Perhaps just as important is to realize that He is <u>not committing to invest His miraculous power outside that program</u>. For Jesus said, on His final night of training His apprentices:

"Without Me you can do nothing. If anyone does not abide in Me, he is cast out . . . and is withered" (John 15:5-6, NKJV).

His promise, made here with the conditions laid out up front:

"If you abide in Me, and My words abide in you, you will ask what you desire, and it shall be done for you" (John 15:7, NKJV).

Notice that God is calling us to let our desires be shaped by His Word, specifically by Jesus's teachings. He is saying that when we conform ourselves to the plan, our faithful prayers will be answered. We will have much success in the spiritual realm, which will produce results in the natural realm because we work with His plan, purpose, Word, Spirit, and power.

Adventure Key: Jesus invests in His partners' work in the world. That work is done in us before it's done through us.

POSITIONED FOR PURE SPIRITUAL LIFE

Every person that I know who has been frustrated with prayer enough to quit has confided in me that they were focused on what they wanted, what they thought, and what they demanded God to do for their plans. That's a recipe for disaster. Jesus never gave us any reason to have such expectations.

That's the original temptation that got mankind in trouble in the first place: wanting to manipulate God for our purposes. It doesn't work. **"God opposes the proud but gives grace to the humble"** (James 4:6, ESV). So Jesus willingly invests in those committed to Him. He invests in those who are committed to Kingdom business. It only makes sense, right? For your prayers to be answered, you must focus on God's revealed will.

The beautiful thing is that God is lavish with granting requests, above and beyond what we ask when we participate in His plans. I've met many people who, while denying themselves and earnestly seeking God's power for His plans, have experienced joyful abundance in things they never asked for. God delights in giving abundance to those willing to faithfully trust Him and do His will.

It's never about how good you are, how deserving you are, how old you are, or how smart you are. It's about your willingness, which confounds religious people.

So, how do we position ourselves to receive this power? How do we orient ourselves for Kingdom business? Humility. It's a decision to willingly accept God's authority and submit to it. Humility is having childlike faith despite being the smartest person in the room. Humility is activated through confession.

God <u>resists the proud</u> and gives much favor to the humble (see James 4:6). Confession is when we agree with God's assessment of things, the world, and us. As Jesus said, the sinful man who prays, knowing he needs God's mercy, is closer to God than the religious man who thinks he doesn't. God is attracted to a humble heart.

Why is that? Because every one of us has a sin nature that draws us away from God. This is why Jesus says:

> **"The Spirit is the One who gives life. <u>The flesh doesn't help at all</u>.**
> **The words that I have spoken to you are spirit and are life."**
> **—John 6:63 (HCSB)**

Did you catch that? Our natural mind is "fleshly." The spiritual work in the mind is through the life-giving Spirit of God. When we humble ourselves under the amazing power of God, He lifts us up; He keeps us cruising no matter how challenging the storms. He commits Himself to do that with us, for us, and through us.

When we confess what God says about us is true, we become empowered.

There is an aspect to it that is about accepting and agreeing with God's way, according to the calling of Jesus. What is the life-giving way of Jesus? He demonstrated a willingness to joyfully do and believe whatever the Father said.

Doing the Father's will pleased Jesus. It filled Him with the joyful resolve to go to the cross. Jesus's life shows many examples of how to do the Father's will.

When we confess our sinful acts and thoughts, we may feel condemned and thus feel the weight of that burden. That is when the most powerful part of confession comes into play: confessing what God says about our rebellious acts.

When we bring our failures and sins to Him, God speaks <u>an absolute commitment</u> to forgive and forget. So, the positive side of confession is when we admit/confess what God says about the matter. He has forgiven us. He forgets our sins entirely, through Jesus.

<u>God says in the Old Testament:</u>

> **This is the Lord's declaration: "For I will forgive their wrongdoing and never again remember their sin."**
> **—Jeremiah 31:34 (HCSB)**

> **"You will hurl all our sins into the depths of the sea."**
> **—Micah 7:19 (CEB)**

> **"I am the one who wipes out your rebellious behavior for my sake. I won't remember your sin."**
> **—Isaiah 43:25 (CEB)**

<u>He says in the New Testament:</u>

> **The Father loves the Son and gives everything into his hands. Whoever believes in the Son has eternal life. Whoever doesn't believe in the Son won't see life, but the angry judgment of God remains on them.**
> **—John 3:35-36 (CEB)**

> **"I will be merciful.... their sins and their iniquities will I remember no more."**
> **—Hebrews 8:12 (KJV)**

Notice how God commits, every day, to welcome sinners. Jesus is not condemning us, but rather Jesus is committed to forgiving and restoring those who turn and trust in Him! He wants us to seek Him! When we confess our acts that offend God, we need not fear His anger. He wants us to confess His forgiveness in Jesus so that we can have open, loving fellowship with Him and receive His transforming Spirit power.

Once we confess that we offended Him, God actually wants us to also confess that <u>Jesus has paid that debt</u> and that we are forgiven (see Colossians 2:14; Acts 10:43). Yes, first we confess our sin, then we confess His perfect forgiveness through the cross of Jesus Christ. Doing this is incredibly empowering.

Jesus models a very powerful truth: when we are quick to forgive those who offend us, we become more like Christ. This empowers us to really draw closer and be filled with His power. The question is not whether God welcomes sinners but whether we welcome those who offend us. Are we able to forgive the person who offends us daily in our own lives?

Today, so many are cutting off friendships and rejecting family because people offend them. Let us be the incurably **unoffendable** people, even when serious offenses come.

That doesn't mean we tolerate evil; it means we forgive and forgive and forgive those who offend us—because we see the bigger picture.

Because we see that God has already forgiven our unforgivable offenses. Because we want to **operate in the supernatural power of grace** that comes by forgiving others, we must forgive quickly.

LIBERATION FOR GREATER THINGS

When we grasp the full commitment Jesus made to redeem us, it is life-changing. Our focus turns from our weak and simple desires of this world to God's grand desires. We join God's mission as the ones Jesus wants to reach, and we become part of the process of reaching others.

Jesus is granting us His favor to live a life of victory over spiritual darkness so that we can be joint participants with Him in reaching others like us.

This is the positive side of confession. It is liberating and empowering to be agents of Jesus, to be carriers of new life. So, we confess the truth of what He says about us and for us. He saves us from the spiritual darkness and, at the same moment, makes us active partners.

Life becomes biased in our favor to make us successful in carrying out His goal. Let me say that more clearly: Jesus has rigged the system in our favor if we will trust in Him and operate in His power of blessing others.

The passage in John 14, where Jesus gives His last instructions to His apprentices on the night He is betrayed, is actually a four-chapter message. He reveals to them the climax of all His teaching and mission plans.

In this final stream of thought, Jesus gives the great conclusion of everything He has taught and shown them for three years.

> **Most assuredly, I say to you, he who believes in Me, the works that I do he will do also; and greater works than these he will do, because I go to My Father. And whatever you ask in My name, that I will do, that the Father may be glorified in the Son. If you ask anything in My name, I will do it.**
> **—John 14:12-14 (NKJV)**

An incredible new kind of relationship was opened that few people fully grasp today! Before that moment, only Moses and a very select group of people like King David could even dream of such a promise. Yet we are invited to partake as we trust and abide in Jesus.

Jesus commits His presence and power to answer when we walk in His authority. Jesus summarizes the authority by saying whatever we ask in His Name. In Bible thinking, the name of a king is everything the king represents and everything the king stands for; the name is the essence of royal authority and purposes.

Jesus grants permission to use His name and authority. It's Kingdom authority for Kingdom business. We need to understand that. This is not about asking whatever pleases us. This is Jesus saying He gives us authority to be His apprentices, doing His work, with His authority and therefore with His power. Wow!

Let's see how this proclamation of faith reads in Psalms 20:

> The LORD will answer you in times of trouble. The name of the God of Jacob will protect you.
> [And so] Some rely on chariots and others on horses, but we will <u>boast</u> in <u>The Name</u> of the LORD our God.
> —Psalm 20:1, 7 (GW)

It's a resilient faith being summoned; a prayer of faith proclaiming victory over everything that opposes the work of God. Some people think that it's humble not to speak the name of God. The religious think it's best to stay quiet about His name.

Jesus and this psalm are **compelling us to speak and act with full confidence in His name, doing His work.** Summoning faith is the key. Remember that faith is an active trust in the character and promises of God.

Adventure Principle: The Savior wants us to walk with His authority and power!

THE RECORD OF GREATER THINGS

For three years, Jesus demonstrated that He has true authority from God. So, when He says we can ask anything <u>in His Name</u>, we are learning that we can leverage His authority if we belong to Him! If that doesn't astonish you, nothing will. Incredibly, He is saying that His apprentices will accomplish more than He did.

The apprentices of Jesus united people across divergent ethnicities and cultures, spanning many nations. Some groups of people were so touched by the faith, testimony, and power of those apprentices that their entire tribes or even entire nations turned to Jesus.

THE STANDARD OF ANSWERED PRAYERS

We see in the gospel accounts that Jesus answered requests in a variety of ways. He did this as an example for us today. Four answers to prayers are in His will:

No!

Go!

Sow!

Grow!

If we ask for something that is not in God's will, we should hope He says "No." When God says no, it is usually to protect us or someone else.

God knows what is good and best for us, and if He were to give us things that are against His will, then it would be a curse on us. So, we ought always to pray for His will to be done and for Him not to give us what is against His will, not to give us what would harm or wither us.

When we make requests that are in His will, and the timing is right, God will answer immediately and often miraculously. This always startles people—because many times you find out He had already started answering before you asked—and the answer is to send His Word forward to "Go."

Sometimes we ask for things that are in His will, but we have not invested in those things in the required way. We need to put something into it that builds our faith and activates the principle of sowing and reaping.

This is God's way of showing that we need more commitment and investment in the thing we hope for. It may be time, prayer, money, or other kinds of grace and blessings that cost us something. He wants us to stay resolved and invest prayer into that situation until the right time.

When we make requests that are in His will and it requires us to change personally, this is when He says, "Grow." It may be something that requires more maturity or something that requires more partners.

He may tell us to develop more of a plan or to study more. It may require more preparation, partners, or resources—or a change of direction. This request will be answered but requires some personal improvement first. In my experience, this is the most common kind of answer to prayer.

Many of us want an immediate yes answer. But we should really ask: "Father, what do you want in this situation?" God's will and timing are perfect. All His ways are right and true. If God is saying "No" or "Sow," then we can know that there is an important reason, even if we don't understand.

A faithful apprentice can accept "No." Unfaithful teachers will say that you can demand anything and that God will NOT say no. That's not true in any text or principle, and it's not really wise. If God is all-wise, then we <u>want</u> to know when the answer is no, even if we don't understand.

So, we learn to pray and ask Him: "Father, is this Your will for me?" We also study Scripture to know God's will. How do we know when He will say No?

Will it harm us, even if it seems good for us at the moment?

Will it harm others or fail to do good to others?

Will it harm the work of Christ in the world?

Will it violate the character of Christ?

These keys help us to get our prayers answered. First and foremost, we are seeking God's will and purposes. We want to know His mind because we can so easily deceive ourselves. Proverbs 3:5-8 (ESV) says:

> **Trust in the Lord with all your heart,**
> **and do not lean on your own understanding.**
> **In all your ways acknowledge him,**
> **and he will make straight your paths.**

> Be not wise in your own eyes;
> fear the Lord, and turn away from evil.
> It will be healing to your flesh and refreshment to your bones.

And in Proverbs 16:25 (ESV) it says:

> "There is a way that seems right to a man, but its end is the way to death."

Adventure Principle: When we do what Jesus instructs and pray according to how He teaches us, we can rely on Him to assume responsibility to answer those prayers according to the Father's will and timing.

ALL THE REWARDS OF SOWING AND REAPING

God created a connected world; all of nature is interdependent. And the Kingdom of God works that way also. One of the key factors to getting our prayers answered is the willingness to be the answer to someone else's prayer. Jesus tells us that even a cup of cold water given in the name of one of His disciples will be rewarded. This is the measure of commitment God has to this principle; everything we plant into that continuum of the Spirit will be rewarded.

As Jesus says:

> "Give, and it will be given to you. Good measure, pressed down, shaken together, running over."
> —Luke 6:38 (ESV)

It seems the opposite of what we want, but it's absolutely true. We invest in someone else to see our desires met. I cannot tell you how many times I have seen this proven. The more we give, the more God gives us so that we can give more. In contrast, the more that we hoard, the less God trusts us to share, so we have less, and then we want to hoard more. His goal is to change our thinking.

I'm not just talking about money. If you are discouraged, find a way to encourage someone else. If you are lonely, find someone more isolated and help them feel connected. If you need a miraculous answer to prayer, pray fervently for someone else who needs an amazing answer to prayer. If you lack confidence in God's provision, secretly help someone else with nowhere to turn.

Over and over, we find that God answers this kind of sowing (planting) with a harvest. We must do it with the right motive: not to get recognition from people, but to help someone without drawing any attention to ourselves so that God is the only one who sees—so that God gets the recognition.

God wants us to do things for His eyes only, whenever possible. He rewards us for it so that we know it is Him doing it, not just coincidence. God wants us to know that He sees. This is a reminder that there is a reward stored up for us in Heaven.

We often have selfish motives or the wrong timing for what we want, and when we do, we do not receive the life Jesus came to give us. This is why it's essential to seek God in all we do. Jesus says the Father understands all our needs.

This is the nature of adventurers: we accept that God is our source. Since we rely on Him, not ourselves, we learn that His provision is good, and we learn to expect that God will provide. This gives us the freedom to help others, to invest in the work of God, to be His source of blessing to others, for His name's sake.

Remember, the order of priorities sets the rest of it in motion:

> **"But seek first his kingdom and his righteousness, and all these things will be given to you as well."**
> **—Matthew 6:33 (NIV)**

This is the way God works. He guides us to put His blessings in motion by putting His priorities first. We can do that because He already put us first. You plant before the rains come, not after. Even if you're not a farmer, this makes sense.

In the spiritual realm, you put things in motion by getting the order right. Generosity in the name of Jesus brings the blessing of God.

PRAYER JAMMING BY THE ENEMY

In this spiritual conflict, hostile spiritual forces are working to stop us, aggressively trying to discourage or wreck us. They work like any enemy, jamming the communications between us and our supply lines. We don't see this with our eyes, but we can definitely experience it.

One of the ways they "jam" our communications, also known as "hindering our prayers," is by getting us to cherish sin. Even though we love Jesus, the enemy's agents can motivate us to commit secret rebellious acts so that we love that sin more than we love our God. When we forsake those passions and put the focus on God, He will deliver us from a whole lot of other spiritual obstructions.

One way our prayers get jammed is when we have broken relationships with a spouse or family member because we have done something to offend them. Our ability to be fruitful in God's Kingdom, hear God, or have prayers answered gets jammed. When this happens, many times people work with their natural talents to overcome this hindrance. That always ends badly.

The enemy knows the effective tools of distraction that draw our hearts away from God. We could be instantly freed from this "jamming," but we have to turn to God and confess these things so that they don't keep jamming the effectiveness of our prayer life.

> **"If I had cherished sin in my heart,
> the Lord would not have listened."**
> –Psalm 66:18 (NIV)

> *"Yet even when you do pray, your prayers are not answered, because you pray just for selfish reasons."*
> *—James 4:3*

The fact is that sin and selfishness are the natural bent of all people. We would not need to follow Jesus and depend on Him if we did not have this problem. So, how do we make sure that our prayers are answered? The answer is the mystery of abiding.

The answer is always the same: Go straight to God and confess our wrong motives, our wrong actions. Ask for forgiveness, ask for His healing and renewal of a clean heart (conscience), and if needed, go to the people you have offended and do whatever will make it right with them.

God is faithful and never wavering: He forgives and restores humble hearts that turn to Him by Jesus. You don't have to grovel before God. Jesus has already provided forgiveness, so we just need to admit the sin and realign with God's purposes. Jesus restores us faithfully, immediately. This is how Jesus operates.

THE MYSTERIOUS POWER OF ABIDING

Abiding in Jesus is about staying connected to Him and in fellowship with Him. It's about honesty and listening to Him. This is a relational connection of trust and devotion. We remind ourselves that the message of Jesus is ultimately that He came for us to have fellowship with Him, to know Him, and to be known by Him.

If He was willing to die on the cross for us, why would we think He would not forgive an offense after we have first believed? We take hold of that by confessing and believing His forgiveness.

The mysterious power of abiding with Jesus comes from discovering how Jesus gives us a privileged personal line of contact with the Father, which He tells us in John 12:25-26 (ESV):

Whoever loves his life loses it, and whoever hates his life in this world will keep it for eternal life. If anyone serves me, he must follow me; and where I am, there will my servant be also. If anyone serves me, the Father will honor him.

It's like any love relationship: if we are devoted to Him, then He will know it and honor those who make Him the focus of their lives. Love means we stay in touch, pursuing what matters to the other person, and we trust our hearts to them.

We learn to keep His Word close, to read it regularly, to study it to understand. Like lovers, we want to know Him and hear His voice. We want to understand what matters to Him.

Part of this abiding power is meditating on God's Word, comparing one passage to another, and hearing the mind of God. Another part is establishing a prayer life with Jesus that is honest, personal, and faithful. We seek His mind to do His will.

Walking in the Spirit of God leads us to experience His power. Praise-filled worship is another part of that abiding. Singing in our hearts with thankfulness to God brings us closer to Him. This is the way of Jesus—a love affair that ends with us joined forever in His Father's house (see John 14:2).

We develop the habit of faithfully doing what He says. Because the Father seeks active doers of His Word, He seeks us out, calling us to be apprentices who live by faith—as agents of Jesus. Faithfully doing one thing is far better than knowing a hundred things we don't do. As Jesus said: *"If you live by what I say, you are truly my disciples"* (John 8:31, GW).

Adventure Principle: We activate the results that God promises by faithfully sowing the good seed of faithfulness.

HARVESTING WHAT WE'VE PLANTED

There is a law in the spiritual dimension that governs our spiritual adventure, just like the law of gravity is in the physical world. **Worldly people can sometimes be wiser about this**, in a way, than people who follow Jesus.

The worldly people will tell you, "What goes around comes around." This is a Law of Judgment based on how you judge. It's tied to the Law of Harvesting which says that what you send out is ultimately what you receive.

People who condemn will harvest condemnation; generous people harvest generosity. Kind people harvest kindness; hateful people harvest hate. Jesus said,

> **For in the same way you judge others, you will be judged, and with the measure you use, it will be measured to you.**
> **—Matthew 7:2 (NIV)**

This is why Jesus repeatedly warned His apprentices not to seek judgment against their adversaries. He demonstrated how to warn but not condemn. Because this is a law of judgment that's like gravity, it is unyielding.

You are judged by your own judgment. You are measured by your own measurement. You harvest what you plant. You receive these things in this life as evidence that it will be more so in the judgment to come.

The wonderful thing about this is that **in Christ**, we can turn completely from judgment to blessing, from adversity to favor, and from darkness to light. This is a gift of His grace, in which **He transforms life for us by faith.** Yes, what we experience can be changed by what we sow into the world. **This is why following Jesus must be a practice, not a theory.**

Jesus warned us about this, but He also promised us there is a very positive side to this law, and He demonstrated that we could use this law in our favor. In other words, Jesus wants us to know how to make this law work for our good and for His Kingdom. He wants us to know that **the Father sees what we do secretly, and He will reward us for it.**

The key is to plant the good and faith-filled things of His Kingdom everywhere we go. In this way, we will ultimately reap a good harvest. Here are a few of the key promises Jesus gave us about this:

> **Give, and it will be given to you. A good portion... overflowing... The portion you give will determine the portion you receive.**
> —Luke 6:38 (author paraphrase)

> **I assure you that everybody who gives even a cup of cold water to these little ones because they are my disciples will certainly be rewarded.**
> —Matthew 10:42 (author paraphrase)

> **And whenever you stand up to pray, if you have something against anyone, forgive so that your Father in heaven may forgive you your wrongdoings.**
> —Mark 11:25 (CEB)

This law of planting and harvesting is one of the most important tools for "crossing over" in faith. God has different economics than the world. It takes confident faith to live this way. When you apply that faith, God gives you more! Here we have four examples from Jesus of how God works to redeem life in our daily practice for those who trust Him:

Giving to others increases, rather than decreases, our own supply.

God sees the smallest acts of kindness and faith, rewarding us for them—especially when we do them in secret and for His recognition, not ours.

The way we hear and evaluate others is how God will hear and evaluate us.

We receive forgiveness and become accepted to the same degree we forgive others and accept them.

Jesus is calling us to develop a new living paradigm. He knows this takes miraculous faith. As we apply these principles, we begin to walk in His miraculous power. The fleshly mind rejects this. But the Spirit of God gives us grace to develop this powerful new way.

Do you want God to supply your needs at all times? Be generous, even to strangers. Do you want confidence that God is watching over you? Then watch over those who cannot do anything for you. Do you want confidence that God will trust your sincere intentions? Be willing to believe the best intentions of others. Do you want confidence in God's forgiveness for your mistakes and acts of rebellion? Choose to forgive those who negligently or deliberately offend you. Operating in this way activates God's blessings.

"Crossing over" develops our faithfulness in small things, and then God responds with abundance for bigger things. He gives us the power to live **in abundance** through miraculous faithfulness. The more we exercise faith, the more God gives faith for greater things.

This habit becomes skill; the skill becomes a lifestyle that gives us the confidence to overcome every obstacle. Our faith in God becomes unshakable. Our confidence increases no matter how challenging things get.

We will harvest blessings when we do not give up and don't lose heart. So, we press on, with all of our faith in God, even if we don't "see" immediate results, because the longer the wait, the better the blessings.

That's right! The more time we are required to wait, the greater the result we receive if we don't lose heart. I've seen this demonstrated many times. So, it gives us confidence for the resurrection because we know He has promised much more in the next life.

THE SECOND BLESSING OF THE SECOND CROSSING

There's a lot of discussion among Christians about a "second blessing." I do believe in a second blessing, but it is not what is often discussed. The initial crossing of the lake in a storm was apparently just a primer course into walking by faith through storms because Jesus sends them into another storm later. On that later journey, He sent them by themselves; then, a storm arose and terrified them. The second time, Jesus performed an even more amazing miracle when He came out of the storm and walked on water (see Matthew 14:25; Mark 6:48).

God never does the exact same thing twice, but He guides us during greater challenges to remember earlier encounters when He answered us. Therefore, the second blessing comes when we just go forward in faith, trusting in our Savior—because we have learned how to follow Him and **expect His intervention.**

As before, Jesus challenged the apprentices to take courage, to trust God. He asked, *"Where is your faith? Why did you doubt?"* I believe this is the most important thing we can do on the Jesus Adventure—look inside and ask why we're fearful or doubtful.

Why do we think God will not see our needs? If a person has no faith, then it's understandable. They think they are alone, without any hope of help. But the point Jesus is making to us is that we are not alone! We have God to help us! God delights in delivering His people.

When we hear Jesus and answer His call, we know that He is leading us to deliver us. He wants us to abide in Him so that we may have confidence in facing all kinds of storms. There are always challenges for people to face, and we are offered the opportunity to help others hear His voice so that they can survive their own storms.

Adventure Principle: As He has been before, He will be with us again through any trial or adversity.

ADVENTURER'S MEDITATIONS

> "The LORD was my support. He brought me out into a broad place; he rescued me, because he delighted in me."
> —Psalm 18:18-19 (ESV)

PART 3

STANDING FIRM WITH JESUS

CHAPTER 7

REST AND REFRESHMENT (ON THE WAY)

"Come aside . . . and rest."
Mark 6:31 (NKJV), Jesus speaking to His apprentices at the height of a tense time of ministry.

STRENGTH FROM HEAVEN

We must understand that Jesus wants us to be steadfast in this calling, walking this journey with Him, ready and able to stand firm for the long haul. This is not a sprint; it's a race that we run with endurance. Even though we are much closer to His return now than when this all began, we cannot defeat the forces of darkness in a frenzy. We will defeat them on God's terms, with His power. As we go forward, we want to remember what Jesus said:

> "Learn from me, for I am gentle and lowly in heart,
> and you will find <u>rest for your souls</u>."
> —Matthew 11:29 (ESV)

RESTING IN FULL ASSURANCE OF RESTORATION

No part of the apprentice training for Jesus's adventure is more vital to sustaining the power of God than catching this powerful truth of being refreshed and strengthened from Heaven. The rest is the design of the Father and the passion of Jesus to give us rest for our souls. Consider how God has given the principle of rest for His people from the very beginning of time.

God gave us a potent energizing tool that keeps us refreshed, empowered, and restored. This single principle spans all time, and it reaches deep into gaining the spirituality of Jesus. Receiving and holding this sacred principle from start to finish, we will have an unstoppable faith that overcomes all forces trying to defeat us.

This is the sacred adventure principle of rest in Jesus. As I said in the beginning, there is a vast mystery in this life that confounds us all until we discover its power. We are naturally tempted in every wrong direction on the compass, toward every wrong destination, and tempted with every wrong method until we discover the call of God in Jesus.

Discovering these sacred adventure principles of Jesus means finding all the ways, means, and skills that are often missed to succeed on the adventure that the Father has planned. It means exploring the meaning of His mystery and discovering the God who designed and created us with purpose.

This is one of the deepest and most sacred parts of the adventure with layers of truth and powerful significance. It is what Jesus wants us all to receive; it is what He prayed for us to receive on the night He was betrayed, and it is the deepest hunger of our souls. See John 17 for the full prayer He prayed over us all; consider memorizing it!

For the purpose of this chapter, we will look at three key things Jesus prayed for us:

> "So my followers will have the same complete joy that I do."
> —John 17:13

> I am not praying just for these followers. I am also praying for everyone else who will have faith because of what my followers will say about me.
> —John 17:20

> "They will know that you love my followers as much as you love me."
> —John 17:23

In these excerpts, Jesus is telling us that He wants us to be filled with His full measure of everlasting joy and that He specifically includes us today in that prayer. This is so often misunderstood by the religious crowd! This is the incredible thing God has planned as the "foretaste of glory divine" that the holy people of God used to sing about.

So, be steadfast with Jesus to discover a powerful source of eternal renewal in the New Creation.

CONFUSING THE PURPOSE OF THE REST FOR OUR SOULS

This portion of the adventurous faith in Jesus may be the most misunderstood and argued aspect of this sacred journey. This is because our adversary, the devil, knows he must keep us from experiencing it to starve us of the spiritual nourishment that gives strength to complete the adventure.

This was God's plan from long before Jesus came. Isaiah, the prophet, foretells of Jesus having a sign that leads Gentiles to seek Him (the cross) and that will lead people to this rest for their souls that God told the prophet Isaiah:

> "And his rest shall be glorious."
> —Isaiah 11:10 (KJV)

Our goal as Jesus's apprentices is to discover this sacred success key for God's people: the rest of Jesus and the rest for our souls. This rest is the confidence of Jesus's total success in purchasing our redemption; it empowers those who believe. What we find here is that God gave us cycles for rest, but those cycles are not the goal! They are the shadow of the goal!

The rest of Jesus, this glorious rest, is not merely the rest of our bodies. It's a rest for our souls which extends far beyond physical rest. This glorious rest for our souls gives us healing into the depths of our whole person, spirit, soul, and body. It empowers us for spiritual battle against a relentless adversary, the enemy of our souls.

Adventure Key: God's plan for us is to be refreshed and empowered, undefeatable apprentices of Jesus.

God gave humanity a weekly rest from labor since the beginning. This principle of rest, called the Sabbath, was taught to humans from the beginning of creation. But we quickly forgot. Genesis says that God created for six days, and on the seventh day, God rested from all His works. It also says that He also made that day sacred, and He blessed it.

However, there is no record of mankind keeping a day of rest until the exodus. That is when God gave Moses the command in the Torah, which is called the Law of Moses. Think about that: thousands of years of toil without a day of rest. In fact, there is no record of a regular cycle of rest in human history, apart from the command of God through Moses. It's hard to imagine generations that never knew a weekly time of rest. And then, God gave rest to His people Israel by the Sabbath law. Yet the nature of man is so rebellious that they rejected it.

SPIRITUAL HEALTH IS SCIENCE

Science shows us that weekly rest is one of the most important tools for physical and mental health. It seems absurd, but we know that humans who rest one day a week are more productive than those who work every day. This blessing of resting makes life beautiful. For instance, a song without consistent cycles of rest is just run-on noise. But consistent rest cycles within a song, even a fast-tempo song, give that song poignant beauty.

There is something more profound, more beautiful to the rest of Jesus than just taking a day off; it's a sacred principle that has layers of mystery. Those mysteries are given to us who follow His adventure. Let's remember that the Bible says:

> "It is the glory of God to conceal things, but the glory of kings is to search things out"
> —Proverbs 25:2 (ESV)

and:

> "Call to me and I'll answer you, and will tell you about great and hidden things that you don't know."
> —Jeremiah 33:3 (ISV)

As we go forward contemplating these sacred adventure principles, we are being given insight into the things of Heaven. Yet, the real power of it is often missed by prideful religious people.

OLD COVENANT: A LAW OF CURSES AND BLESSINGS

We want to keep in mind that Jesus promises something that was not promised under the Old Covenant: *"Rest for your souls."* Moses commanded that the Sabbath was a time for rest for the body, a complete resting every week. Yet, some Sabbath feasts were a time to afflict their souls. Jesus promised something different: A New Covenant!

We want to keep that in mind: they are not the same. And this New Covenant promises not merely rest for the body but rest for the soul—not affliction, but restoration. Unlike the Old Covenant, this New Covenant of Jesus is not conditional or based on performance. Only admitted sinners qualify for it (see 1 John 1:8-9).

The Old Covenant was temporary, designed to be in effect until the Messiah came (see Galatians 3:19). The Old Covenant was a strict code of 613 laws, which the people were required to keep perfectly and were sentenced the death penalty for breaking them! Moses told the people they would fail as a people to keep the law, and when that happened, they would lose those blessings <u>and be cursed</u>.

This happened over and over throughout their long history You can find this record summarized in Psalms 106 and 107. In the Book of Nehemiah, we learn that an entire generation of Israelites had never heard the covenant in their entire lifetimes. When they finally read it together, the people wept severely for their national rebellion toward God.

In their history, one generation would keep the law and have great blessings, and the next generation would rebel and fail to keep the law, resulting in curses. Among those laws were the laws of rest, which are called the Sabbaths. There was a weekly Sabbath, seven annual holiday feast Sabbaths, and Sabbaths of rest from farming every seven years.

Moses explained the Sabbath commands this way:

> **Six days work shall be done, but on the seventh day you shall have a Sabbath of solemn rest, holy to the LORD. Whoever does any work on it shall be put to death. You shall kindle no fire in all your dwelling places on the Sabbath day.**
> **—Exodus 35:2-3 (ESV)**

And also:

> **You have six days when you can do your work, but the seventh day of the week belongs to me, your God. No one is to work on that day—not you, your children, your oxen or donkeys or any other animal, not even those foreigners who live in your towns. And don't make your slaves do any work..**
> —Deuteronomy 5:13-14 (ESV)

So, they were to rest the entire Sabbath day, from sundown to sundown, and do <u>no work at all, not even kindle a fire</u>! What's more, they could not even allow a servant or an animal to do any work. That was emphatic, and the penalty for failure was death!

This seems severe. Yet, we will learn that there are very sacred principles embodied here—profound truths concealed in this law—that are very essential to understanding the rest that Jesus gives: <u>rest for our souls</u>.

OLD CREATION VERSUS NEW CREATION

We learn from Jesus and His emissaries that He fulfilled all Old Covenant laws as the perfectly obedient Son that no mortal could be. He was the perfect embodiment of all that these laws required, so He became <u>the embodiment</u> of the blessings they offered.

In His sacrifice on the cross, Jesus took the death curse of rebellion against us all, and in His own body, He "nailed it to the cross." The perfect Son who had never known sin became the very offense of sin itself on our behalf, and He let the Father pour out all wrath and judgment on Him. It's astonishing.

And since Jesus is "the Word become flesh," He also nailed the Old Covenant to the cross. More astonishing.

On the cross, Jesus pronounced forgiveness of sins. Then, with His last breath, He pronounced that our debt was paid in full, and therefore the Old Covenant's requirements had been fulfilled.

This is another astonishing truth. Jesus's fulfillment of the law meant that He took <u>all the Old Covenant curses upon Himself</u> so that He could give its blessings to all who depend on Him by faith. But nowhere does this mystery become more vital to realize than with the Sabbath itself, the rest which God proclaims.

Because Jesus took the curse of death upon Himself, it is now impossible for the believers of Jesus to be cursed for violating the command of Sabbath. However, in giving us the blessings, Jesus Himself becomes the agent of those blessings to us.

So, Jesus Himself becomes the rest which Sabbath exemplifies. Sabbath is a shadow of a greater reality, and Jesus extends that reality into an eternal and spiritual dimension that the Old Covenant never could. The Old Covenant prophets hinted at this.

You see, the Old Covenant and its Sabbath were about the original creation, or what could rightly be called the "old creation"—the creation that became cursed through Adam's rebellion. We live in that cursed physical creation, although we are figuratively risen from the dead with Him as a "*new creation*" (see 2 Corinthians 5:17).

In Christ, we are the first fruits of this new creation, which is hidden for now, but will be manifested plainly for all to see when Jesus returns. God says that the old creation is passing away and is waiting for the revealing of the sons of the new creation. Wow! This truth excites me more and more as we see the day approaching.

For now, we live in this "hidden kingdom," which mortal eyes cannot see until it will be revealed—when *we* will be revealed! That glorious revealing day is the hope for all God's people when Jesus returns.

CHRIST OUR ETERNAL SABBATH—NEW CREATION'S REST

By fulfilling all the requirements of the Old Covenant in full to usher in a New Covenant and proclaiming total justification/forgiveness of our sins,

Jesus opened a whole new way of living. What, then, does that mean? How can we understand this?

Are we bound by old ceremonial requirements? Are we obligated to keep any weekly or annual days of rest? We should, but we're not obligated—because that was a mere shadow of a greater reality. We can rest on any day, without condemnation—as long as we live in the glorious rest of Jesus's salvation.

Jesus said a lot about rest, and it's all about the new relationship He gives. He says:

> **Come to me, all who labor and are heavy laden, and I will give you rest. Take my yoke upon you, and learn from me, for I am gentle and lowly in heart, and you will find rest for your souls.**
> **—Matthew 11:28-30 (NKJV)**

This rest for your souls <u>was never offered through the Old Covenant</u>. Do we notice that Jesus said, *"<u>I will give</u> you rest?"* We are meant to differentiate taking a day of rest from receiving this rest of Jesus. This is a clear "Messianic sign." In the Old Testament, the people of God had been promised a rest to come. Moses and Joshua did not give this ultimate rest; there was still a rest to come, as Isaiah said (see Isaiah 11:10; Isaiah 28:12).

More to the point, this is not merely rest for the body. Jesus said, *"You will find rest for your souls."* The Old Covenant offered refreshing for body, for the nation and for the land. It offered them a place in God's plan; the opportunity for Israel to inherit an earthly Kingdom with perpetual rights to land ownership in the Holy Land. <u>It did not, however, offer any rest for the soul</u>. It never offered a place in Heaven. It was only about the land of Israel on Earth.

The only time the Sabbath and the soul are mentioned in the Old Testament is when God says you must <u>afflict your soul</u>. The only time this spiritual rest is mentioned in the Old Testament (in a future prophetic sense) is when God prophesied to the unbelieving Israelites who refused to trust Him about their distant future through Messiah. He said, *"So I swore in my wrath they shall <u>never enter My rest</u>"* (Psalm 95:11, ESV; see also Hebrews 3:11).

This rest that Jesus offers is for now and forever available to us here and retained into and throughout eternity. This is why Jesus said we could *store up treasures in Heaven* (see Matthew 6:20). We're held by faith, transformed here and now, for eternity.

THE PRACTICAL REST OF AN APPRENTICE

When Jesus called His apprentices aside to rest that particular day of ministry, He gave them something real for their immediate need: physical refreshment and peaceful downtime. Yet, this also foreshadows what Jesus would give through the New Covenant. Let's look:

> **He said to them, "Come aside by yourselves to a deserted place and rest a while." For there were many coming and going, and they did not even have time to eat.**
> **—Mark 6:31 (NKJV)**

There had been a lot of stress on them, ministering and traveling around: demonic activity, sick people, needy people, and danger from the ruling authorities. All very stressful. Jesus gave an important principle: rest is not just for the Sabbath because this was an ordinary midweek day!

Downtime, quiet time, is key to keeping tuned into God's presence and staying sharp. Even with the miraculous presence of Jesus near, they needed rest. It reminds us that Jesus came to offer ultimate transcendent rest.

No matter who you are, you hear God better with rest, quiet, and in isolation. He wired us that way. The devil can use turmoil, activity, noise, entertainment, and busyness as tools just as much as he can idleness. The

Bible reveals times of rest often; Jesus withdrew to a quiet place many times. He even slept on the boat while they crossed the sea.

Why is that? Why did Jesus, the Son of God, need rest? Does God get tired? No, Jesus tells us that God is always at work. God is a source of inexhaustible power and is always active, holding together the fabric of the universe.

The answer is twofold: God wants us to stay in tune with Him more than the clamoring world. We were created with this need for refreshment, and Jesus subjected Himself to our limitations. By this, Jesus demonstrates this sacred principle, which He came to give us: Heaven's rest for our souls.

Quiet, rest, time for reflection, and deliberate peace are not just necessary but also powerful for the adventure of Jesus. The Psalm says:

> **"In vain you rise early and stay up late, toiling for food to eat—for He grants sleep to those He loves."**
> **—Psalm 127:2 (NIV)**

Sleeping can be an act of faith. This world system wants to drive us and deprive us of sleep, promising success, fun, or feats that all come at the cost of our wellness. That thinking wears down our ability to trust and live for God. Many people strive without sleep to achieve goals, yet end up spiritually bankrupt, sick, or both. Faith calls us to seek His energy and presence in rest.

Adventure Principle: God's purpose for His people is that we will have complete rest in Jesus, here and now, as if we have already awakened at home in Heaven.

RESTLESSNESS AS A WARNING SIGN

After decades of seeking out the spirituality of Jesus, I've come to realize how important rest is. Restlessness works against us. Rest empowers us, while restlessness depletes us. When we feel restless or overly drawn to busyness, the best way to break that cycle is to step away to somewhere quiet. It's like hitting a reset button and getting recharged.

When I consider how Mark focused on this call of Jesus in writing his gospel account, I can't help but think of Mark's own missionary work. He wound up quitting because the work was done at an intense pace. It was during this rest time that Mark connected with the emissary Peter and ultimately wrote his gospel account. I think God appointed Mark to that time of rest, and we benefit from the fruit of it (see Acts 15:39).

Restlessness can be a warning sign of needing time for reflection, gratitude, relationship, and renewal. God gives us rest as a gift, so we should gratefully use it. His powerful peace is then passed on through us. We connect with the people God has put in our lives, take time to enjoy them, and then invest in them to pass our peace into their lives. So take time to thank God for all He has done and reflect with the people in your life. Remind them of God's goodness and His glorious rest for our souls.

THE THUNDEROUS POWER OF QUIETUDE

In our journey as apprentices of Jesus, we discover that quiet is a tool for accessing great power. One of the most neglected aspects of walking with Jesus is the discipline of quiet. Modern people are clamoring and surrounded by noise all the time. People travel everywhere with earbuds playing something. Yet God calls us to know Him through the power of silence:

> "Our God says, 'Calm down, and learn that I am God!
> All nations on earth will honor me.'"
> —Psalm 46:10

> "Let all the world be silent—the LORD is present in his holy temple."
> —Habakkuk 2:20

> "In returning and rest you shall be saved; in quietness
> and in trust <u>shall be your strength</u>."
> —Isaiah 30:15 (ESV)

Quiet before God is a very powerful skill. It helps us evaluate ourselves more clearly. It helps us realize that God is dependable and near to us. He wants us to deliberately seek Him and know Him, to access the resources of Heaven by tuning out the clamor of this rebel system. We receive power when we practice quietude for drawing close to God. The more we practice, the better we get because Jesus invites us to experience His rest in every moment.

Many want to follow Jesus but have not discovered the transforming power of His rest. Everyone who was ever greatly used by God has developed a quietude. Every great work of God begins with this practice.

Jesus Himself left His baptism and went out into the desert for forty days of solitude. Moses spent forty years raising sheep on a mountainside. Elijah spent weeks of solitude in the desert.

Paul spent fourteen years alone with God before he began his ministry. John was exiled on an island before he received his visions of the Book of Revelation. Can you see how quietude and peace are power tools to grow stronger and be led by God's Spirit? This is the way of Jesus.

SHADOWS OF GREATER REALITY

In that earlier review of the Sabbath requirements (see Exodus 35), we found that there were inflexible requirements to keeping the Old Covenant Sabbath, and these are shadows of the greater reality in Jesus:

1) **It was solemn and serious**—Anyone who ignored the Sabbath was put to death. This tells us that there is nothing we can add to Jesus's rest for our souls; it is a gift from God and cannot be improved by human effort. Rejecting the rest for our souls brings a curse.

2) **It said you shall kindle no fire.** This tells us that human efforts cannot add to the warmth of the Spirit that comes from Jesus. The Spirit gives the fire, not man.

3) **No family, no servants, nor animals were to work, not even to kindle their fires.** This shows us that we cannot be their proxy facilitating their rest, nor can they be ours. This requires a direct relationship with Jesus, the rest for our souls. We also can't automate it. It must be direct, real, and personal.

The new creation's rest for our souls is much more than a day without work. This is about living by faith in the completed work of Jesus, an eternal kingdom from God that cannot be shaken nor earned. Jesus alone can be our proxy for the judgment due mankind.

Since Jesus, though innocent, took the curse upon Himself on the cross, He can now pass on the blessings to us who follow Him by faith. He became the curse on the cross Himself, so the New Covenant offers blessings with no curse so long as we live under it.

God says judgment is satisfied in Christ. God now receives us as His children again, in Christ. Blessings are granted as an inheritance in Jesus.

It also means that anyone who tries to justify themselves under the old system accrues only curses. The blessings do not belong to that system any longer, because it tells us that *"Cursed is the one who does not confirm all the words of this law"* (Deuteronomy 27:26, author paraphrase). So, if a person is putting themselves under that system, they are obligated to keep all of it (see Galatians 3:10). Yet, God has made sure that is no longer possible!

Adventure Key: Becoming quiet and still subdues restlessness and receives the calm confidence of Christ in us.

REST FOR WEARY SOULS

As apprentices of Jesus, we can confidently take hold of this rest for our souls by realizing that this is the goal of our Father in Heaven. This is why the Father sent Jesus to die for our sins. When we accept this fact, we have acceptance with the Father.

We may now come confidently to the Father at any time, in every circumstance, with confidence through Jesus. This gives rest to our weary souls. We do not stand before God in weak, imperfect righteousness; we stand before God in Jesus's flawless righteousness. Complete. Flawless. Jesus.

Through Jesus, the door to Heaven's throne is open wide to approach our Father by Jesus's blood.

"And I will give you rest."

A gift like that is too good to reject.

Likewise, our Father will not accept anyone who tries to come by any other means.

THE FATHER'S ACCEPTANCE OF HIS CHILD

Many of us who did not have a good relationship with our fathers cannot understand the heart of the Father in Heaven. Jesus didn't reveal His Father to us as a taskmaster. He didn't reveal His Father to us as a boss or a lord. He revealed Him to us as a generous Father, as Abba (Dad). A close, loving, and caring Father who loves His creation so much that He would sacrifice His very best to redeem us to be His family again!

The Father in Heaven is the architect of the universe and our redemption. He is a kind and gracious Father who will not fail to reach those who will receive Jesus. Our Father will never reject us.

We humans have a spiritual disorder that keeps us from believing God's love. In our disorder, we blame God for evil and credit the devil for good. We reject God's kindness. We hide from Him. We try to cheat to win, never knowing that our Father has purposed for us to win. The Father wants His children to win at everything that really matters. The Father is patient and kind, guiding us to constantly make progress. He eagerly wants us to trust His plan to make us family forever.

God adopts us as the kids we were meant to be. He wants to restore what we have lost. That is the message of the cross! (see 1 Corinthians 1:18) The rest for our souls is the humble acceptance of this inheritance that Jesus offers. We merely accept this by trusting Jesus in faith so that we may walk in His authority. The more we do that, the more we overcome the rebel system of this world.

The greatest fear is rejection. We run away rather than find we might be rejected. This is why Jesus pledges to us: *"Whoever comes to me I will never cast out"* (John 6:37, ESV). In the original language, this statement emphatically says, *"Never, no never, no never ever cast out"* (literal paraphrase). It is the strongest way to say that Jesus will not reject anyone who comes to Him. <u>That is the rest</u>. That is the confidence: a hope which does not disappoint.

REAL ADVENTURES: JESUS IS THE REST FOR OUR SOULS

After Jesus was crucified and buried, His enemies gloated and relaxed on the last Sabbath of Jesus's apprentices before the resurrection. Perhaps they even celebrated! They had finished Him off, right?

There's no way that Galilean preacher was causing any more concerns for them. Surely His followers would be no trouble. They were just common laborers, poor men and women, an uneducated rabble.

Meanwhile, Jesus's apprentices <u>did not rest</u>. For them, it was the most troubling Sabbath ever. They had seen powerful miracles; Jesus seemed invincible. But now everything had fallen apart. Shattered, weeping, and mourning—certainly, no rest or peace would ever come again.

Can you imagine their torment? Jesus had power over everything! Then, they saw Him surrender to fake trials and a humiliating death. How long until the authorities would arrest them? It was over.

Yet, both groups had it exactly wrong! The first day of that week would change everything forever for the apprentices, for the Jews, for

Rome, and eventually the whole world. Can you imagine the dismay of the women when they found an empty tomb? And then the elation when they saw Him alive?

Can you imagine the gasp of the men, hearing from the women that they had seen Jesus? Can you imagine the overflowing enthusiasm? What elation! They went from mournful sorrow to euphoric joy.

Seeing Jesus alive after witnessing His grisly death must have stunned their minds. How can it be? Nevertheless, there He was in their midst! Sharing the joy of His victory over the grave must have stunned their minds!

Now, they were wide-eyed with wonder. Can you imagine the peace that came over them when they saw that He truly was alive? It must have been awesome when He prayed and they felt His breath. Peace.

Have you ever been distressed and believed you would never find rest or peace again? Have you failed so badly that you thought you would never find hope again? Maybe you have felt like you lost Jesus, never to belong to Him again. If so, you are a candidate for God to amaze you with His rest for your soul. God wants to give you peace that exceeds all understanding, in Jesus.

Meanwhile, the men who condemned Jesus had a false sense of peace. It was the last day they could feel any confidence because they had crucified the Lord of Glory, the Son of God, and He had risen from the dead!

A PROMISE FOR ADVENTURERS WHO REST IN JESUS

Jesus told them in advance, and He's telling us in advance of our trials, to trust in His peace. A peace that can overcome all troubles:

> **I give you peace, the kind of peace only I can give. It isn't like the peace this world can give. So don't be worried or afraid.**
> —John 14:27

Adventure Principle: This is the way of Jesus: His glorious rest gives spiritual light and life that empowers the soul forever.

CHAPTER 8

ADVENTURE OUTWARD: THE PRIME DIRECTIVE

"You are like light for the whole world. A city built on top of a hill cannot be hidden."
—Matthew 5:14

Taking an adventure means going to new places and doing new things. If you had done it before, it would be routine, not adventure. So, it means taking risks and being uncomfortable, even though it may also be exciting. If there were nothing to lose, there would be nothing to gain.

We have no hope of changing life without the threat of discomfort. Most people fear adventure because they fear pain. But we're all experiencing pain already. The Jesus Adventure offers greater opportunity despite adversity.

Moving forward in this new phase, in partnership, we find Him calling us to do something that may seem uncomfortable, even though it is very easy. As we discovered before, adventures have storms and challenges. But, in this adventure, we are confident that Jesus has called us to an eternal destination, far beyond storms or struggles, if we persevere. Jesus is the captain who takes us on a journey far beyond earthly limitations.

Since He has gone ahead and is the master of eternity, Jesus gives us confidence and peace despite storms.

THE INAUGURAL MISSION: FREELY GIVE WHAT YOU GOT FREELY

Every one of us who decides to follow Jesus has a testimony, a story of God's work in our lives. What is yours? Think about it. Whether you have just begun or have been learning to follow Him for a long time, God has been at work in your life in many ways.

Something has happened in your heart; otherwise, you wouldn't have read this far. Consider writing this down, even if you have only just begun doing Jesus's teachings because Jesus has begun a powerful work in you. And if He has begun it, then He will continue to do that work to completion.

The next step is to give glory to God and actively join Him in His work. We know this change is real when we are willing to share our story with people who know us. Consider your situation: Can you say that the peace of God has come to you? Can you say that you have experienced God's forgiveness and redemption? Are you accepting His call to leave darkness and walk in the light of Jesus?

If so, then the most appropriate thing to do is tell people! Tell people who know you about what God has done. Who knows? Maybe they are hungry to hear of the hope and confidence in Jesus too.

As the adventure takes shape, we experience more of the Spirit of Christ. Part of continuing that powerful work is to go and tell others what God has done. As Jesus says, *"Freely you have received, freely give"* (Matthew 10:8, MEV). As we read in Chapter 6, Jesus led the apprentices to cross the Sea of Galilee through a ferocious storm. When they were near the other side, the storm suddenly ended at Jesus's command. And then a demon-possessed human storm breaks out.

> **When he [Jesus] was getting out of the boat, a man with an evil spirit quickly ran to him from the graveyard where he had been living. No one was able to tie the man up anymore, not even with a chain. He had often been put in chains and leg irons, but he broke the chains and smashed the leg irons. No one could control him. Night and day he was in the graveyard or on the hills, yelling and cutting himself with stones.**
> —Matthew 5:2-5

It's a terrifying thing to have a crazy man run at you. Especially after going through a wild storm. Can you imagine?

> **When the man saw Jesus in the distance, he ran up to him and knelt down. He shouted, "Jesus, Son of God in heaven, what do you want with me? Promise me in God's name that you won't torture me!" The man said this because Jesus had already told the evil spirits to come out of him.**
> —Mark 5:6-8

People often get focused on the many demons and what happened to them. I can't help but be focused on the demonized man and how Jesus treated him. To be clear: Jesus commanded the many demons to come out of the man, and they entered a herd of pigs which then ran into the sea and drowned themselves.

The people from the village came out to find out about all the clamor and what happened to the pigs. But that's not the important thing! What happened next is truly amazing.

> **When they came to Jesus, they saw the man who had once been full of demons. He was sitting there with his clothes on and in his right mind, and they were terrified. Everyone who had seen what had happened told about the man and the pigs. Then the people started begging Jesus to leave their part of the country.**
> —Mark 5:15-17

Luke's account (Luke 8:35) tells us that the man was <u>sitting at the feet of Jesus</u>. This tells us a lot about Jesus and His thoughts about that man, and it may not be what you think.

> **When Jesus was getting into the boat, the man begged to go with him. But Jesus would not let him. Instead, He said, "Go home to your family and tell them how much the Lord has done for you and how good He has been to you." The man went away into the region near the ten cities known as Decapolis and began telling everyone how much Jesus had done for him. Everyone who heard what had happened was amazed.**
> **—Mark 5:18-21**

He went to a major metro area and told everyone about what Jesus had done.

FELLOWSHIP OF THE REDEEMED

From these accounts, we learn that Jesus took time to help this man and show him personal care, including giving him some clothes. People ran to town to tell about it, and others came out to see. So, we know that Jesus was engaged with this man, who ended up sitting at His feet.

After having fellowship with the Gadarene man, Jesus sent him home as a message.

Notice that Jesus didn't just send him away! Luke says:

> **When they came to Jesus, they also found the man. The demons had gone out of him, and he was sitting there at the feet of Jesus. He had clothes on and was in his right mind.**
> **—Luke 8:35**

This tells us something important: Jesus acknowledged the worth that the Father places on every person, allowing the man to sit at His feet and have fellowship. The man had begged to follow along with Jesus and the apprentices. He wanted to stay close to Jesus. This is the natural experience with everyone born of the Spirit! We want to be with Jesus; we want to follow Him. But Jesus had a mission for the man: "Go and tell" —Jesus commissioned him!

When Jesus sent him home, He was saying three things: First, your testimony of deliverance is a powerful message. Second, your primary mission is to tell your people the good news. Leave your focus on death and go experience life! Third, Jesus also says that <u>God will be with you</u>. Jesus was not leaving this man; He was entrusting him, commissioning him to do His work without needing the training the rest were getting. God would guide him to grow in his faith.

This is the next progression of our journey, which begins with going to those who know us to demonstrate the message of what Jesus is doing. When we go to those who know us, the transformation will be more evident to them than to strangers. For the Gadarene man, just showing up at his home with clothes on would say that something amazing had happened.

SITTING AT JESUS'S FEET

This position of sitting at Jesus's feet confuses us today because modern culture is different. In that culture, the honored person sat and the people honoring him stood. Today, in our culture, we typically sit on comfortable chairs to hear a teacher who stands. But it was the opposite back then. Sitting at an important person's feet was a place of great honor. Jesus was honoring the Gadarene man, showing God's love and kindness to a broken man whom demons had terrorized.

The Gadarene man had done nothing to earn this position. He just showed up in a rage and was delivered from evil demons. Yet, Jesus wants the man to receive His grace fully. The same is true with us: Jesus wants to bless us with freedom and redemption; all He asks is that we receive it and then walk in it faithfully.

Adventure Principle: Jesus sees the image of God in us and will deliver those willing to receive Him. His compassion is greater than any evil that can torment us.

CALLING ALL ADVENTURERS: "GO AND TELL!"

This world is full of broken, rebellious people. We're a race of rebels. Some people do it by choosing everything God forbids. Others rebel by acting good and faithful while cultivating selfish hearts, determined to do everything for their own glory. Whatever form of rebellion we choose, it is a direct offense to God, who created us with gracious love.

The Most Powerful Message

Fortunately, God is extremely merciful and kind to us. Yet we don't like to hear it; we don't want to believe it. People who are the best at looking and acting good will look down on people who are broken and wounded. <u>Jesus hates that attitude</u>. They imagine that somehow because they are doing well on the surface that God loves them more, or that God is not real at all. They are blinded by their own pride and unaware that they, too, need saving.

People who know they are broken usually have a sense that God hates them because their lives aren't working out. Yet, we all have the same sickness: rebellion. Some are just better at hiding it. We all need to know: God is merciful, and God will heal us from the rebellion if we turn to Jesus. That is the message.

The most powerful message you have to share is your redeemed life. Like the Gadarene man, you are God's message to the other rebels. Whoever you were, wherever you are, the one fact that is undeniable in the eyes of another rebel is a changed life. You don't have to be clever, good-looking, or perfect. You just have to tell people what God has done. Jesus is not ashamed of us, so we should not be ashamed of Him.

Hungry Enough to Feed Another

People with a full plate are usually unable to see how hungry someone else is. But truly hungry people will share with other hungry people much faster than someone with plenty. Maybe you've seen it too: give a beggar a pizza, and he will share most of it with someone else.

Understanding hunger makes us want to help others who are hungry. This is also true of spiritual matters. Can we risk missing out to be sure that someone else gets a share?

It's a tough question. That's what Jesus was asking the Gadarene man! Sure, he could have come along and become an apprentice too, studying directly with the Master. His own life would have been drastically changed.

But no one in his hometown would hear about it or believe it unless he went back and showed them what God had done for him. The Gadarene man's witness of a changed life would be more impactful in his hometown than in a hundred city squares filled with strangers.

As we follow Jesus and believe His transforming Word, we become God's work in someone else. Someone you know may need to taste and see that the Lord is good by seeing His goodness in you first. Go and share your news; tell them the good things that God has done.

> **All who worship God,
> come here and listen;
> I will tell you everything
> God has done for me.**
> **—Psalm 66:16**

ORDINARY INVITATIONS FOR ORDINARY PEOPLE

Jesus once went to a bad neighborhood and met an outcast woman with a bad reputation to share with her the kindness and hope from God (see John 4:3-30). He spoke to her without any condemnation, even though He knew she was someone who had a really messed up her life. He ignored all of that and just shared the hope with her, letting her know that God's love was more than she needed for the thirst of her soul.

She was amazed at Jesus's kindness and how much he understood about her. Jesus simply welcomed her right where she was. The woman was stunned because people from Jesus's neighborhood didn't even talk with her people. When she realized that Jesus could be the Messiah, she quickly went into town, saying, *"Come and see a man who told me everything I have ever done! Could he be the Messiah?"* (John 4:29)

The woman didn't worry about what people would think. She realized that the kindness of God was available through Jesus, and she wanted others to know. Her message was simple, saying, "Check it out for yourself." Maybe you know someone who would check Jesus out for themselves if you invited them. You could be their lifeline.

Her people listened and went to meet Jesus. Who knows, but maybe God is going to reach other thirsty people in your world because you invite them to "check out Jesus." Those people were so impressed by Him that they invited Him to stay longer so they could learn more. Those people were transformed.

Are you willing to just invite people to check out Jesus, even if they might not like you for it? You never know; you could be the one person they will listen to.

SOME WILL, SOME WON'T, SO . . .

There are always people who won't listen, but it's not our job to pick and choose. We just tell the story.

> **"With all my heart, I praise the LORD."**
> **—Psalm 103:1**

Some will doubt. We don't force and we don't hold back from anyone. We love Jesus and what He has done for us, so we offer that to others to discover. Some people may reject the message, and some may be rude. That's okay; we just share the news and let God work in their hearts.

It may seem better to tell some but not others, like some don't deserve to hear. That's a mistake. We don't know how a person will respond or who will have hearts open to Jesus. We never know what is happening inside another person's heart.

Your personal experience with Jesus may be the one thing that gives a desperate person hope. One thing is sure: If you are genuine and just tell the story, you become the greatest evidence for the power of Jesus right in front of them, no matter how skeptical they are. Let God do the rest.

We never know who will be most affected. Telling the story, especially to people who know us, will give hope to hungry hearts. Some people are sure there is no answer, and it's tearing them apart inside. Some people are struggling secretly, yet deeply. When they see transformation take place in our lives, it gives them hope.

To most people, the Gadarene man was just obnoxious, violent, and crazy. When Jesus came, the real reason was revealed. Maybe you've had demons tormenting you, or maybe you just have a rebel nature like everyone else. Either way, Jesus loves you. And that is worth sharing.

Just like the Gadarene man, people who struggle the most will challenge us the most. They want to see if it's real. They may get angry about your decision but don't be offended because you can't see what they are experiencing inside.

Jesus came to heal us with kindness and comforting love, to give us the life-giving Spirit that puts us in our right minds. As the prophet Isaiah wrote:

> **"Do not be dismayed, for I am your God. I will strengthen you and help you; I will uphold you."**
> **−Isaiah 41:10 (NIV)**

Jesus Himself said,

> "Then I will ask the Father to send you the Holy Spirit who will help you and always be with you."
> —John 14:16

Jesus explained more about the Comforter a little later when He said,

> But the Counselor, the Holy Spirit, whom the Father will send in My name, will teach you everything and remind you of all that I told you.
> —John 14:26 (MEV)

Once we receive Jesus as our Savior King, the Holy Spirit will always be with us. We can rely on His care, guidance, and empowerment whenever we ask.

DOUBT NO LONGER

When we experience our own raging storms, we don't always consider that this may be the very thing bringing our rescue. Jesus comes to free us from raging torments and fears and release us from the bondage of fear itself. Who are we to deserve His care or be set free? The Gadarene man had nothing to offer Jesus! He was deranged, financially broke, naked, and outcast.

The story isn't about what the man had to offer or what others saw in him. It's about what Jesus saw. When Jesus sees value, then suddenly there is eternal value. Jesus valued him, and He values you.

As you share your story, people will doubt you; you may also doubt yourself. Remember that Jesus isn't ashamed to have you sitting before Him because Jesus values you completely. You have worth because Jesus says so. Can you receive that?

When you are valued by the Son of God, then your value is ultimate because of Him. Jesus paid the ultimate price for us all, and He cares beyond our understanding. When you realize that is *your story*, it doesn't really matter what other people think.

FRIENDS AND FAMILY FOREVER

Before we trust Jesus, our place and people form our original identity. But, when we come to Jesus, He accepts us as His friends and as His family. His greatness now defines us on the Jesus Adventure as we become united to Him.

The new identity extends beyond this world into eternal realms we can't see yet. This new identity links us to all the past, present, and future faithful adventurers.

One day all of us will be together with our great and kind Shepherd King who has led us on His journey. He promises to take us home to His Father's house. It's helpful to know that the Bible is clear: Jesus will boast of those who yearn to be with Him:

> **"God is not ashamed to be called their God."**
> **—Hebrews 11:16 (ESV)**

Wow. God is saying that He doesn't care what anyone thinks of it. God is staking a claim on us. Are you looking to the day when you meet Jesus in person? Are you eager to find all that God has planned for you? God enjoys people like that.

As a young father, I was surprised to see how excited my kids were for me to come home each night. They would celebrate my return with big smiles and a joyful outburst saying, "Daddy!!!" I love that so much. We are looking for a better place, a heavenly place where God is— we are looking forward to being with Him—where Jesus will call out: "Welcome Home!"

The bonus prize is that we gain forever friends and family among the other adventurers. God says:

> **What God has planned for people who love him is more**
> **than eyes have seen or ears have heard.**
> **It has never even entered our minds!"**
> **—1 Corinthians 2:9**

And Jesus also said:

> **There are many rooms in my Father's house. I wouldn't tell you this,**
> **unless it was true. I am going there to prepare a place for each of you.**
> **—John 14:2**

There is an amazing adventure ahead beyond this life for those who follow the Royal Shepherd of souls. The things He has prepared for us are too awesome to describe because we have never seen anything so good. This is truly the final frontier, the place that has been prepared for those who love Jesus.

The Bible describes it as a "great banquet" and a "wedding feast," a place where there is endless light with no sunburns. Life-giving trees and fruits in abundance, with rivers and a sea, but no storms or floods. It's a place where beauty and peace are in perfection, and life is in harmony.

Best of all, the Bible tells us we will know Jesus even as we are known by Him, the perfection of love and joy that we only get a glimpse of here. It's going to be the biggest party in the history of parties, and we get to be part of it! So, invite everyone you know. When you find something good, you pass it on!

STORING UP FOR THE PERMANENT DESTINY

It's hard to imagine a world where the rules are different. In this world, everything is temporary, no matter how good or bad or how hard we try to save it. This life is temporary and short. There are hardships and losses along with goodness and happiness. Nothing lasts long here. But Jesus's message is that there is a life beyond this to prepare for!

Jesus said repeatedly to store up treasures in Heaven—that nothing can destroy or steal. He's telling us that even though we can't see it, the next life is certain and permanent.

An eternal future is coming, and it cannot be restrained; it can only be prepared for. If you leave with amnesty, you have that amnesty forever! If you leave here with heavenly inheritance, that inheritance is permanent.

With all His heart, with all of His passion, with everything that He had to give, Jesus gave His best gift on the altar of that Roman cross. He gave Himself. Why would He do it? To prepare us for that future because the stakes are so high! There was no other way.

Many religious leaders are reluctant to talk about the next life. They want to put everything into the context of this world. Others speak only of the next world and nothing of this life. Jesus doesn't give us that option. He speaks of a place of eternity, unchanging and unending, permanent in quality and quantity. A place beyond our understanding—and it begins here, now. So, Jesus urges us to trust Him, act on His Word, and allow Him to prepare us.

The word eternity or eternal is stated forty-five times in the New Testament. We learn that God is eternal, His coming Kingdom is eternal, His salvation is eternal, and our fellowship and residence with Him are eternal. This is great news for those of us who are on the Jesus Adventure!

God is also warning us that the separation and judgment of those who hate God and reject Jesus are also permanent and irrevocable. This should grip our hearts. There is no middle ground. After this life, there is no place where repentance can be found. There is no way to change course. Psalms tells us of the atmosphere with God:

> **You cause me to know the path of life; in your presence is joyful abundance, at your right hand there are pleasures forever.**
> —Psalm 16:11 (ISV)

When we tell people of the good things that Jesus is doing for us, we invite them to experience the fullness of the joy that God gives. So, we who trust Him are not ashamed because we are convinced that He stores everything up for us that we have committed to Him. We do not see it now, but the Holy Spirit comforts us and reveals that we can surely trust Jesus's promises until that day.

WHO CAN TELL SUCH GOOD NEWS?

> **"Only the living can thank you, as I am doing today. Each generation tells the next about your faithfulness."**
> —Isaiah 38:19

Can you imagine the story Gadarene man had to tell? Can you imagine the joy in his heart? It must have softened the hardest heart and given hope to fearful people. No one could deny that a man who had been tormented and deranged was now in his right mind. The powers of darkness no longer had authority over him. His mind was healed. Like a broken bone that was suddenly healed, this man's life was set and healed: a powerful story.

Sharing with Respect

When we tell people of the good things that Jesus has done for us, we can touch their hearts and help them realize God has a salvation plan for them. It's not about what we know. The Gadarene man didn't know much about Jesus. It's not about how smart we are either. The man had been naked, after all. But now he had a testimony of dignity! Jesus valued that testimony and sent the man to share it.

Everyone who trusts and follows Him on the adventure has a story of how Jesus has changed our lives. The best place to share that testimony is with people who can see the change. He isn't sending angels to our friends and our families. He's sending us.

How do you start? Prepare in advance to answer anyone who asks you why you have changed and why you personally have hope in Jesus. Write down what Jesus has done for you. Keep your focus on Jesus. How did He get your attention? What captivated you? What about Jesus gives you hope? How has it changed you to trust Him? Decide in your mind, before you tell anyone, that you will share your story gently and respectfully, regardless of how rude they may be.

Plan ahead to be respectful and gentle, especially if they reject you. Plan how you will forgive them. That's just part of the process. This is the way of Jesus.

The Comfort of Hope

We often think that a personal testimonial has to be exciting with some gripping outcome for people to be interested. We tend to think that a simple story is not worthy of sharing. But that's not true. Struggles and sorrows are common to all of us.

The question is, what gives hope that endures? Is there a hope that won't disappoint? Is there a comfort for us when we have had real troubles? Even more: What can wash away the stain of rebellion that has polluted us and scarred our lives?

The Gadarene man's story was not pretty. There must have been deep anguish that drove him to the tombs. He would have to face people who may scoff at him, but he had a fantastic gift to share, even if it came in a messy package. Maybe you have a messy package. Maybe you have shame that colors your story. Jesus is not ashamed!

The sludge of shame is the fertilizer that grows great works for God as we trust Him.

Our own griefs may have come from a broken heart for a lost love, from an estranged relationship, or a terrible tragedy. Our grief and pain help us to rely on God's comfort, which builds our confidence. God often gives birth to the greatest works out of grief and sorrow.

Some people teach that believing in Jesus is about getting everything we want. That is not what Jesus taught, nor has it been the experience of believers through the centuries. The message of Jesus is that He has overcome this broken world, so we can also. He has prepared a new world for us, and that is the world we hunger for!

Are we willing to face grief and respond with hope? We're going to have grief regardless of how we respond. That's the nature of this world. We overcome grief by faith and hope. True hope comes from trusting God's promises and hope shared is hope expanded. The more we see Jesus change other people's lives, the more we are filled with hope in our own lives.

There is a hope, a confidence, and a comfort that endures and reinforces us through and beyond this life. There is a deep well of strength greater than the pain. Yes, God heals bodies, relationships, souls, and all manner of broken things. It's also true that some broken things never get fixed in this temporal world. Some things never heal until the next world.

For the first 300 years after Jesus, it was a death sentence to follow Him, and it still is in many countries. Does it mean someone is an inferior follower if they experience suffering, loss, or failure? No! The Bible tells us the opposite! Keeping our eyes on Jesus is what pleases God, and He has greater rewards for them. It's reasonable to say that a person who never experiences persecution has missed out!

Adventure Principle: Sorrows cannot defeat us when our home is Heaven.

THE "PROFESSIONALS" WENT LATER

One of those details you can easily miss: Jesus had trained His apprentices for over a year before He sent them out on their own in Mark 6. The Gadarene man's deliverance and commissioning story came before that in Mark 5. Jesus sent the apprentices in pairs but sent the Gadarene by himself. Others who had healings were told to keep the message to themselves. Yet, this man was instructed to go immediately and tell everyone.

Why? Apparently, Jesus wanted this man's story to be well-known. Jesus is not ashamed to let people know that this man's life was changed and that he was transformed by God. Jesus wanted him to make waves. Why? Because there's no way this man can take any credit! Jesus is willing to give graciously to undeserving sinners.

A healed and transformed rebel is a more potent message than a hundred well-groomed professionals. God wants to receive the broken; He works through the broken. Jesus was sent to restore the lost and broken. Believe that and draw close to Him.

The truth is that we're all messed up. We may not be living naked and screaming in a cemetery, but we all have a kind of spiritual insanity—as rebels against the Creator. Jesus wants us to know that we all can receive this restoration.

Understand this: not many worldly, wise, and well-dressed folks get chosen. Yet, Jesus accepts the broken and messy people every day. We tend to forget that because people often forget where they came from.

There's an account in Mark 9 where the apprentices tell Jesus:

> "Teacher, we saw a man using your name to force demons out of people. But he wasn't one of us, and we told him to stop."
> –Mark 9:38

You get the idea that they are very proud of themselves here, expecting to be commended for such wisdom. Instead, Jesus said to them:

> **Don't stop him! No one who works miracles in my name will soon turn and say something bad about me. Anyone who isn't against us is for us. And anyone who gives you a cup of water in my name, just because you belong to me, will surely be rewarded.**
> **—Mark 9:39-41**

Now, I can't prove it, but I suspect this was the Gadarene man. I think that he was so moved by the loving power of Christ that he had an urge inside to keep telling people. So, he kept going and going so that everywhere he went, he encountered more people who needed deliverance from demons. Since he already knew the authority and power of God, he just got busy doing what needed to be done.

Yet, the apprentices didn't quite understand the program yet. They thought it was about building some organization they could manage. Instead, Jesus has always been about building a gathering of people who report directly to Him, walk under His authority, and recognize Him as the one "in charge."

God isn't looking to build organizations of man-approved professionals. He transforms lives by His Word and Spirit. He uses amateurs to demonstrate His power. Each of us comes to Jesus broken, but we are changed by Him and receive His divine life.

If we have God's approval, that is all that's needed to be a vital player. We train together in community to master spiritual weapons to defeat darkness. We find purpose as community, but we don't need authoritarians to do that.

PREPARED MISSION OF POWER

Jesus wants us to study Him carefully, demonstrate faithfulness, and learn how to walk in His authority. In training His original apprentices, Jesus sends them on a first mission to the towns and villages of Judah (the remaining part of Israel). While the instructions do not apply to us directly, the principles are clear: go in faith and walk in His authority. That is the calling for all apprentices today.

> **Then he called together his twelve apostles and sent them out two by two with power over evil spirits. He told them, "You may take along a walking stick. But don't carry food or a traveling bag or any money. It's all right to wear sandals, but don't take along a change of clothes. When you are welcomed into a home, stay there until you leave that town. If any place won't welcome you or listen to your message, leave and shake the dust from your feet as a warning to them." The apostles left and started telling everyone to turn to God. They forced out many demons and healed a lot of sick people by putting olive oil on them.**
> **—Mark 6:7-13**

Remember that Jesus said He was given a specific ministry anointed with the Spirit of God:

> **The Spirit of the Lord is upon me, because he has anointed me to proclaim good news to the poor. He has sent me to proclaim liberty to the captives and recovering of sight to the blind, to set at liberty those who are oppressed, to proclaim the year of the Lord's favor.**
> **—Luke 4:18-19 (ESV)**

This five-fold ministry is still in effect! This is what apprentices do. The Holy Spirit came so all Jesus's apprentices can fulfill this work (see Acts 1:8).

This is what we are being called to do even now. Yes, it's okay to be an amateur! Go forth and share what God has done for you. That's the first step. Keep making progress, study to be capable workers who are prepared. It's not one or the other, but both.

CAN YOUR STORY MAKE A DIFFERENCE?

Maybe you have only just started, and you don't know how your story could make a difference. Maybe you're just beginning to see the things of God and how Jesus is changing you.

In this world, natural people are blind to the things of God until we see spiritually; then we can't unsee His presence in the world. The only way spiritually blind people can begin to see is by seeing what God does in us through Jesus.

Jesus once healed a man who was born blind so that the religious leaders of Jerusalem would realize they were spiritually blind. Jesus healed the man in a way that broke their made-up religious rules, and it really upset them. Jesus had compassion for the man and performed a miracle.

The blind man was well-known; people had seen him begging for years, and then he was no longer blind. This bothered the rule makers. They didn't accept that Jesus could do such an obvious miracle because that was something only Messiah could do.

They debated whether it was right or wrong for the man to claim that Jesus had healed him, and they demanded that the blind man give answers. The man said:

> "All I know is that I used to be blind, but now I can see!"
> –John 9:25

This is the attitude: I don't know everything, but I know what Jesus did for me.

Some people believed and some people just hardened their hearts, despite the evidence. When Jesus talked with the healed man later, he explained:

> **For judgment I have come into this world, that those who do not see may see, and that those who see may be made blind.**
> —John 9:39 (NKJV)

This means that Jesus will heal and change those who are willing to open their eyes and that some people just keep their eyes shut (spiritually speaking).

Those who take the adventure will be changed—eyes opened and hearts healed—regardless of whether others will see it. And what a joy it is when we see! What a joy it is when your heart is changed! Yes, your story makes a difference; it matters because it matters to Jesus! Some people will be touched, and some hearts will receive the message!

True adventurers celebrate when anyone joins our merry band, regardless of who they are or where they come from. We join the celebration God has in Heaven.

So, rejoice! Because some hearts will be renewed in faith by your story. Someone will see how you've changed and decide Jesus is real. Your adventure becomes forever bound together with theirs. Take courage in Jesus!

THE BOASTING SAVIOR

One thing that is often missed is how Jesus speaks about His (then) future apprentices, in the four gospels and the prophecies. He also rejoices in delivering us and brags about it. Check it out; in John 17:20, Jesus is wrapping up His ministry, giving His final instructions, and prays a detailed prayer that is meant for us today. He said:

> **I am not praying just for these followers. I am also praying for everyone else who will have faith because of what my followers will say about me.**
> —John 17:20

Okay, well, that's us! We believe this because His apprentices took this message to the world and wrote it in the New Testament. Right?

So, Jesus then says:

> **I have made you known to them, and will continue to make you known in order that the love you have for me may be in them and that I myself may be in them.**
> **—John 17:26 (NIV)**

Wow. He's making a huge promise there. Jesus wraps up His prayer, boasting to the Father that He has kept all but one (Judas Iscariot, His betrayer) for this purpose. Is there any other evidence to show that Jesus boasts about us who believe in these last days? Oh yes, lots of places:

> **"So every one who acknowledges me before men, I also will acknowledge before my Father who is in heaven."**
> **—Matthew 10:32 (RSV)**

Jesus presents a prophetic view of Himself to the Father with His people:

> **"Here am I, and the children the LORD has given me."**
> **—Isaiah 8:18**

Finally, we see a prophecy of Jesus leading all His apprentices and all He healed in body and spirit to trust in the Father.

> **I will declare your name to my people; in the assembly I will praise you....**
> **For he has not despised or scorned the suffering of the afflicted one; he has not hidden his face from him.**
> **—Psalm 22:22, 24 (NIV)**

I think the most important verse on this topic is when He revealed Himself after His resurrection (see John 20:29), where He spoke to Thomas, the doubter. You see, Thomas had seen Jesus crucified and scourged; He had seen the spear pierce His side. Thomas was certain that Jesus was dead. <u>This is the problem with seeing</u>. We place too much confidence in the natural world we can see and no confidence in the unseen God.

So, Jesus revealed Himself to Thomas, let Thomas see his wounds, and then said:

> **Do you have faith because you have seen me? The people who have faith in me without seeing me are the ones who are really blessed!**
> **—John 20:29**

That proclamation of Jesus speaks about all of us through time who would need to trust His Word without seeing Him. There is a greater impartation of His grace to those who live by faith rather than by sight. God wants us to know that there is a greater blessing and honor from Him for us who believe without seeing.

This is why Jesus reminds us to live by faith, to activate the work of the Spirit by trusting in Him through His Word. That's where the power is, and Jesus honors us who take hold of it! He honors us more than the original apprentices when we trust in Him. So, your story matters. Your ability to trust Him matters, and God will honor you.

Adventure Principle: Our restored souls are a trophy to Jesus. He is not ashamed to call us His own, even brothers, for our faith in Him.

WHO IS WORTHY OF OUR COMMITTED LOVE?

Following Jesus is possible because it is simple and because He is present with us who walk by faith. But it is an adventure because there are always challenges. Many of us who now love Jesus and are committed to

Him were once haters of God and haters of everyone who follows Him. We have been transformed by His great kindness. Yet, many who hate Jesus may come to trust Him. They need to hear the Great News of His mercy and salvation.

At this moment in history, no one comes to Jesus unless someone full of love for Jesus shares and lives the great news, despite the haters. Yet, many shrink back. Jesus said:

> **If you love your father or mother or even your sons and daughters more than me, you are not fit to be my disciples.**
> —Matthew 10:37

This truth is simple—and hard. Jesus is worthy, and He asks us to love Him more than anything or anyone. He wants true devotion because nothing less works.

THE FLIPSIDE OF CONFESSION

Recall that Jesus made us a great promise:

> **Therefore whoever confesses Me before men, him I will also confess before My Father who is in heaven.**
> —Matthew 10:32 (NKJV)

It's an amazing and wonderful promise. But there's a flipside to that promise.

> **"But whoever denies Me before men, him I will also deny before My Father who is in heaven."**
> —Matthew 10:33 (NKJV)

There was a time, not long ago, when it was possible to share your faith with people, and they would listen, if not out of interest, at least out of respect. <u>That time is over, at least in Western nations</u>. The modern attitude is open contempt for anyone who shares faith in Jesus.

Welcome to the real world. This is how it has been in most places in history and for most apprentices. In nineteen countries today, it is a crime to follow Jesus. Even in America, admitting to being a committed follower of Jesus can get you fired from many jobs. Many companies have unwritten rules to purge Bible believers.

Indeed, trusting Jesus requires dying to your old life. That is exactly what people around the world have had to do for the name of Jesus throughout history. Some have lost everything to follow Jesus. Sometimes, your loved ones refuse to come with you on the adventure or reject you completely.

Others will say, "It's fine to become a follower of Jesus, just don't change your identity." They will advise you to add Jesus to your life but not change. Right now, Jesus is asking you to have the courage to let go of your old life and follow Him without looking back. This is the price of apprenticeship.

Total commitment to Jesus? What if your dedicated love for Jesus inspires other people? What if you are the only one who influences for them to believe? You will never know unless you put Jesus above all and choose to love Him supremely; anything less communicates that Jesus is not truly worthy of their belief.

Many adventurers have wept tears of sadness for the loss of their family, friends, culture, and people, only to find that their steadfast dedication was the catalyst for their whole family to turn to Jesus and become saved!

PROMISES FOR BOLD ADVENTURERS THAT GO AND TELL

> How beautiful on the mountains are the feet of those who bring good news, who proclaim peace, who bring good tidings, who proclaim salvation, who say to Zion, "Your God reigns!"
> —Isaiah 52:7 (NIV)

> "Whoever finds their life will lose it, and whoever loses their life for my sake will find it."
> —Matthew 10:39 (NIV)

ADVENTURE MEDITATIONS FOR TELLING THE STORY

Jesus endured the cross willingly. He did not hold back one drop of blood or sweat because He looked forward and saw us. He saw what would happen to those who trust Him. He brought joy to the Father, obeying the Father's perfect plan.

It wasn't easy. Jesus asked the Father three times if there was any other way. The answer was no. If there was any other way, then Jesus died in vain. Since the Father said no, we can know <u>for certain</u> that there is no other way to come to the Father except Jesus.

Let's be real. There's an urgency. True adventurers want to make every bit of His sacrifice count by reaching everyone possible. We give every bit of devotion to Him since He gave it to us. What little effort is it to share the message with our friends, family, and even strangers we barely know? Jesus is worthy of our best.

Therefore, we throw off everything that weighs us down. We press forward and live out the life that Jesus gives with dedicated faith that speaks of better things to come. This is the adventure, this is the journey, and this is where Jesus walks the closest with us. Jesus has such a heart for lost people; reaching the lost brings him great joy.

MORE RESOURCES TO TRAVEL ONWARD

Since Jesus has commissioned us to do greater things, and we have an imperative instruction to go into the world with our testimonies and His teachings, we have to ask: how? That is a task much greater than is possible for mere humans. We cannot possibly fulfill it on our own. Fortunately, we are never on our own. In the next chapter, we discover resources, wisdom, and strength for travelers on the Jesus Adventure.

CHAPTER 9

EQUIPPED WITH SPIRITUAL WEAPONS

"Whatever you ask for in prayer, trust that you are receiving it."
—Mark 11:24, CJB, Jesus training His apprentices

SKILLFUL PRAYING ON THE JESUS ADVENTURE

There is a fact that escapes many religiously inclined people that Jesus wants His apprentices to be confident in: He came to accomplish the impossible for us, in us, and through us. This threefold truth is essential to know in these last days. We face impossible situations, and Jesus planned for us to succeed through those situations with supernatural resources.

This is not a trivial contest. This is the most epic drama of all history. Jesus intends for us to bring many other rebel souls into His Kingdom with us by doing great things in His name. To overcome evil and accomplish the impossible, we have to master the skills of this incredible spiritual system, which we casually call "prayer."

God cares about us. Nothing is insignificant concerning His children, whom He sent Jesus to save and restore. Prayer is how we obtain His power.

INEXHAUSTIBLE RESOURCES OF GOD

When praying, we always want to remember that God cannot be denied His purposes and will. We seek Him, and we seek His authorized power to do His will. He is working in this world in our times; if we are faithful to Him, we get to be a part of it! He will do as He has promised, in His timing, and for His purposes. This is emphasized in Daniel 4:35 (NIV):

> **He does as he pleases**
> **with the powers of heaven**
> **and the peoples of the earth.**
> **No one can hold back his hand**
> **or say to him: "What have you done?"**

And the point is driven home again in Psalm 145:13:

> **Your kingdom will never end,**
> **and you will rule forever.**
> **Our Lord, you keep your word**
> **and do everything you say.**

Our confidence is always in God. Nothing can resist when it's His will we seek. This is where prayer becomes the "prayer of faith." We're trusting that God will do exactly what He has already said. In the process, we find ourselves becoming an integral partner of His redemption epic.

We access supernatural resources by praying. This powerful system includes authority over all spiritual opposition to Christ. Most people are fearful of praying, as if praying is weird, like it's a spare part of the apprentice's life. This idea is a devilish lie. I was once like that. But I learned that the lie is designed to intimidate us away from prayer.

We access supernatural power and resources from the Father in Heaven by praying. It is how our Father works in us and through us. Praying is not an unusual aspect of the apprentice's life. Prayer is central to it. It's our main defense and our main weapon, fighting in a spiritual war against real, powerful, and oppressive enemies. Praying changes things, and Jesus teaches us to pray effectively. If you struggle with anything, the answer is to pray.

KNOWING THE FATHER'S PURPOSE

Jesus makes an incredible statement that still applies to modern apprentices: *"Fear not, little flock, for it is your Father's good pleasure to give you the kingdom"* (Luke 12:32, ESV). When He says this, He is not merely speaking of giving us a place in His Father's home (although that is part). He also wants us to know that He gives us the royal authority of Heaven—here on earth in this life.

There are rights, privileges, responsibilities, and royal authority granted to the children of earthly emperors or kings. Wherever they go, they have titles and rights of their realm. Our Father in Heaven is an authority far above all other authorities. And Jesus has become King and Lord above the realm of this earth and over the rulers of earth's spiritual realm. So, Jesus is granting us heavenly authority over spiritual evil in high places.

The more we learn to function under that authority, the more opportunity we have to operate as His apprentices. Some of that authority is absolute and immediate, but I also believe we receive more authority and rights as we learn to operate in Kingdom authority. He invests more resources into those who practice a powerful prayer life.

Jesus says, *"To him who has, more will be given"* (Matthew 13:12, author paraphrase). So when we are faithful to access what we already have, more access and more resources come.

Jesus says it is the Father's *good pleasure*. This means it is something that He gives willingly because He desires for us to grow in the proper use of this authority. He is not withholding it from us but working to vest us with all He has to offer. Everything Jesus teaches about praying and receiving answers to prayer is from within that promise.

However, the common prayers people pray often don't follow that model of authority—it is no wonder that some people do not get answers to their prayers. Getting that perspective right makes us more effective as agents of our Father's business—and brings us answered prayer more consistently.

REMOVING THE WRONG PERSPECTIVE

Most of what we hear people praying about, even demanding from God at times, is about what they will eat, what they will wear, where they will live, and what comforts they will have. Entire ministries and movements are teaching people how to think about these things first in their lives. But that is contrary to what Jesus teaches us. That is not the way of Jesus.

Let's read the full section around that verse 12:

> I tell you, do not be anxious about your life, what you will eat, nor about your body, what you will put on. For life is more than food, and the body more than clothing. Consider the ravens: they neither sow nor reap, they have neither storehouse nor barn, and yet God feeds them. Of how much more value are you than the birds! And which of you by being anxious can add a single hour to his span of life? If then you are not able to do as small a thing as that, why are you anxious about the rest? Consider the lilies, how they grow: they neither toil nor spin, yet I tell you, even Solomon in all his glory was not arrayed like one of these. But if God so clothes the grass, which is alive in the field today, and tomorrow is thrown into the oven, how much more will he clothe you, O you of little faith! And do not seek what you are to eat and what you are to drink, nor be worried. For all the nations of the world seek after these things, and your Father knows that you need them. Instead, seek his kingdom, and these things will be added to you. Fear not, little flock, for it is your Father's good pleasure to give you the kingdom.
> —Luke 12:22-32 (ESV)

God wants us to pray for the right things first. He already plans to meet our needs as we go! He provides when we're invested in His work.

Adventure Key: God has the resources we need to do the things He asks and richly rewards us for it.

GOD'S FOREKNOWLEDGE IMPROVES OUR GAME

When we're focused on praying and working for His Kingdom, it is amazing how regularly God answers our prayers. He already knows what we need and already plans to bless us generously.

Often, when people are praying for things, they are focused on themselves and their plans rather than on God's calling. God doesn't reward self-centered focus rooted in satanic pride and selfishness. God wants us to understand that when we are focusing on His purposes, we can pray and have more than is needed because we're working to meet the needs of others. If we live like His kids, He will treat us like His kids.

God assures us that He provides resources before we ask when we're doing His will. Even in times of great hardship and difficulty, God makes a way. Nothing encourages you more than sudden answers to prayer.

I know a minister and his wife who, as young evangelists, had run out of money and groceries while touring the country preaching on college campuses. They lived in a little camper, towed by a car, and could not go on without funds. They fell asleep that night praying.

In the morning, a single knock on the door revealed bags of groceries with the things they needed—the exact items they had run out of—including his favorite shaving cream and cash for gasoline. They had told no man of their need. They had prayed only to the Father.

REALIZING THE TIMES IN WHICH WE LIVE

These are no ordinary days. Since Jesus walked the shores of Galilee until now, there have not been as many fulfillments of Bible prophecy as we have seen in the past century. These are the times leading right up to the end, which Jesus and the prophets spoke of as "the last days." From now until He returns, there's marvelous adventure daily if you're trusting Jesus. In prophetic times, amazing works of God become ordinary for His people.

God intends to do great things in these days before Christ returns to Earth. The prophet Habakkuk speaks to this issue with a hopeful prayer, which pertains to us now:

> **LORD, I have heard of your fame;**
> **I stand in awe of your deeds, LORD.**
> **Repeat them in our day,**
> **in our time make them known;**
> **in wrath remember mercy.**
> **—Habakkuk 3:2 (NIV)**

God wants us to boldly pray for such things. This has been my prayer for several years, and I hope it will be yours also.

God planned these days long ago. He wants us to be empowered by His Holy Spirit for it all. As He said long ago:

> **Have you not heard**
> **that I determined it long ago?**
> **I planned from days of old**
> **what now I bring to pass.**
> **—2 Kings 19:25 (ESV)**

FORMS AND METHODS—SPIRITUAL KATA

In any martial arts system, there is a mixture of philosophy, forms, methods, and endurance training. Asian martial arts call this your "Kata." I believe Jesus similarly trained His apprentices for Spiritual Martial Arts, with all these tools to prepare and empower us for spiritual battles. He did not train them to fight with fists or material weapons!

Instead, He trained them with spiritual weapons to be spiritual champions—warriors of light—to tear down the false gods and enforce the victory of Jesus against the darkness. Today, people have mostly forgotten these things, and Jesus is calling us back.

Jesus's apprentices changed their world and defeated the principalities of darkness without bloodshed. This has been the way since He walked among us. His apprentices accomplish great things without human force, without wars.

In the first century, there were over sixty million slaves in Rome's empire alone; children were bought and sold like cattle for anything the rich wanted without restraint. Brutality was normal, murder was entertainment, rest was rare, compassion was scarce, generosity was weakness, charity was unknown, and equality was never considered. None but the richest could boast of peace.

In the hands of Jesus's apprentices, the Great News brought a whole new way of life—a community with no distinctions of people: no Jew or Gentile, no rich or poor, no slave or master. All were recognized as children of God; all had a place.

The poorest sat with the rich. Men served with women. Compassion was normal. Charity was for anyone who needed it. The church was the one place where people invested in each other. There was no clerical hierarchy; only servants qualified to teach by their dedication to prayer and study. Children were protected; innocence was preserved. It changed the world.

Within three centuries, the apprentices of Jesus defeated the cruelest empire without war.

Common men had fellowship with the rich; the first people ever to "speak truth to power" in the ancient world (without armies to back them) were followers of Jesus. That power derives from prayer. His movement changed the world until the world changed the movement.

God continues raising a Last Days Jesus Movement. We see greater things as we discover Jesus's Spiritual Combat Systems: prayer and worship.

A SYSTEM TO TRAIN AND EMPOWER

Martial arts training teaches you how to move, dodge, block, and subdue opponents using a Kata, the forms and tactics that train your body and mind so that you do not get injured. Every move is practiced. However, you rarely see a skilled martial artist using full forms in a fight.

In a similar way, I believe that Jesus's primary teaching on prayer (which is often called "the Lord's Prayer") is not meant to be a repetitious ritual. Instead, it is a form to memorize and practice, enabling us to pray effectively in our spiritual battles. Jesus specifically said <u>not</u> to pray with *"vain repetitions"* (Matthew 6:7, NKJV).

We also notice that Jesus's apprentices never repeat this entire prayer anywhere else in the Bible. If they believed that Jesus wanted it used that way, then we would see it used repetitiously later on.

Let's see what Jesus did say:

> **When you pray, go into your room and shut the door and pray to your Father who is in secret. And your Father who sees in secret will reward you. And when you pray, do not heap up empty phrases as the Gentiles do, for they think that they will be heard for their many words. Do not be like them, for your Father knows what you need before you ask him. Pray then like this:**
> **"Our Father in heaven,**
> **hallowed be your name.**
> **Your kingdom come,**
> **your will be done,**
> **on earth as it is in heaven.**

> Give us this day our daily bread,
> and forgive us our debts,
> as we also have forgiven our debtors.
> And lead us not into temptation,
> but deliver us from evil.
> For if you forgive others their trespasses, your heavenly Father
> will also forgive you, but if you do not forgive others their
> trespasses, neither will your Father forgive your trespasses."
> —Matthew 6:6-19 (ESV)

Jesus is telling us not to mindlessly repeat this. It's a form we are to learn, which enables us to move fluidly and effectively for God's business in every situation. If you study what His apprentices did after Jesus rose from the dead, I believe you will see that.

GOD HEARS AND REWARDS

So, do we pray the "form" regularly? Yes, privately. But we let that form guide our praying for specific needs. For example, an evangelist recently shared a story from his ministry where he encountered a very sick woman in a hospital looking for relief from suffering for a long time. She didn't care if she lived or died, but she desperately wanted the suffering to end.

The evangelist prayed calmly and simply, "Our Father, this lovely woman needs your help to answer this request. Let your Kingdom come, and Your will be done for her, in the name of Jesus." Her healing in that hospital room was immediate.

She went home that day.

How are we meant to apply this? We look at what Jesus taught and simply do what Jesus says. Shutting the door is important to building our confident, private relationship with the Father. Why? Because if it's private, you know the answers were not contrived by someone else.

When Jesus prayed, He went out to a private place. So, we do most of our prayer work in the secret place with the Father, not for the hearing of others.

Jesus says the Father will both hear and reward, so we pray with expectation. We don't wonder or wish. We know He hears and rewards us by faith in Jesus.

We have the privilege of being concise, even blunt, with honest communication with our Father. We can ask for what we need. We can tell Him how we feel! We can come and state what our purpose is. God is amazing to answer our prayers precisely and at the precise time in accordance with His Kingdom purposes through our relationship with Jesus.

Adventure Principle: God wants to hear us pray. When we conform to God's system, we can know that He will listen and the answers we need will come.

THE ANYTHING AND EVERYTHING OF EFFECTIVE PRAYING

Our Father in heaven, hallowed be your name. We start with a humble and worshipful attitude: God created and sustains the whole universe! He is worthy of great respect. He wants us to be familiar but not disrespectful. Jesus came to the Father with reverence and respect when He prayed. Should we do less?

Your kingdom come, your will be done. We pray for everything to be in His Kingdom and will. Every part of our life is Kingdom business. We are privileged to be on this adventure, so we want His Kingdom authority and power in all of lives.

Give us our daily bread. We pray for our real needs: Daily bread can be our food or our bills, as well as our daily revelation and relationship with God. Jesus said, *"I am the bread of life."* If we have Jesus, all that we need will get sorted out.

Forgive us our debts, as we also have forgiven our debtors. The fountain of the divine nature for us is forgiveness. We are the people of redemption! Forgiveness is the hub of God's work in this world. Forgiveness is experienced more clearly when we give it more earnestly. Jesus has total and perfect forgiveness for us. So, we take hold of that by forgiving others.

Lead us not into temptation, but deliver us from evil. We pray for deliverance from the enemy we face daily. Evil is ever hungry to destroy us. We actively oppose the real evil in this world. Whenever you see evil, pray for deliverance.

ADVENTURE PRAYING

Our goal is for God's name to be revered and praised throughout the world so that everyone may know Him and receive the redemption of Jesus. Our Father's name and Savior's name will not be worshiped if they aren't revered in our own lives. When we live to praise Him, we become part of changing the whole world. This is why followers of Jesus have always sung praise to lift up His name.

Did you notice that Jesus expects us to pray, expects God to hear our prayers, and expects the prayers to be effective? He said, *"When you pray,"* not <u>if</u> you pray. He said, *"Your Father, who sees in secret,"* not <u>may</u> see. He said, *"Will reward you,"* not <u>may</u> reward you. Jesus is teaching that we can approach Him, ask, be heard, and we will receive answers—these promises were provided through the cross and resurrection, if we are His own.

This model prayer is really comprehensive. It covers worship; kingdom, material, and spiritual needs, our emotions; and our attitude. Most of all, it covers our spiritual defense against the schemes of the devil. This is serious stuff. We have a powerful, committed enemy; an army of spiritual entities scheming against us (see Ephesians 6:12).

THE DEFENSIVE SHELTER

How do we defeat our enemy? By the Spiritual Combat System: prayer and worship in the name of our Lord Jesus. Praising His great name in this broken world, all by the faith He has given us. When we do that, our Father delivers us from trials, afflictions, temptations, and workings of evil.

Our Father's name cannot be denied. He has given authority through Jesus so that by the name of Jesus, every devil must flee. Every knee will ultimately bow—and Jesus has approved His apprentices to use His name for victory.

The problem with just repeating form prayers is that it is very general, and often we need specifics. Sometimes our prayer is just for worship and relationship with our Father. Other times it's much more. Sometimes we need to focus on our daily bread and be specific about those needs. If you are in desperate need of something, pray about that need specifically. The name of Jesus breaks down spiritual strongholds of evil in high places.

THE INTERCESSORY COMMUNION

Did you notice that this is not praying to "my father" for "my daily bread," "forgive me," or "deliver me from evil?" The essence of this spiritual Kata is **intercessory communion with all the apprentices** and praying for the whole gathering who follow Jesus. Sure, we pray for our own needs. Yet, the way of Jesus is to pray for the whole fellowship. We are part of something greater than ourselves.

We're privileged to be in this communion and pray for God's people as we pray for our own. God has united us by Christ's blood as one family. We dare not ignore our global family.

This is the relationship with the Most High God, where we have been granted a place in His work and His family. He loves all His children equally; none of us is greater. He has taught us to pray for all, and your fellow apprentices around the world are already doing that for you.

Our Father, Give Us, Forgive Us, Lead Us, Deliver Us. We are one in Him, by the Holy Spirit and the blood.

Our God is a refuge, a fortress for His people. His name and His presence protect us from more than we can see or understand. When we praise Him with reverent worship, it's like hitting the enemy camp with artillery. It makes the devil shudder because the devil was once the leader of worship at the throne of God. But now, worship is a weapon against the devil!

So, this is key for anyone under attack from the spiritual realm. We learn that praising and celebrating our Savior gives victory. There are many places we have been given examples of effective worship:

> "O LORD, our LORD, how majestic is your name in all the earth! You have set your glory above the heavens."
> —Psalm 8:1 (ESV)

> "Great is the LORD and greatly to be praised."
> —Psalm 48:1 (NASB, KJV)

> "God is our refuge and strength, a very present help in trouble. Therefore we will not fear."
> —Psalm 46:1-2 (KJV)

When we praise Him, we are declaring victory and participating in the victory that Jesus won against the kingdom of darkness.

LONG DISTANCE WEAPONS OF SPIRITUAL WARFARE

In the spiritual realm, we can overcome distance and frailty. The least among His apprentices outranks the fallen ones. The littlest woman and the weakest cripple receive power in worship and prayer.

So, we can pray for our persecuted family around the world. There is no limit to who we can help. We support and influence the battle for others at long distances, and they can do that for us. So always listen for God's promptings as to who has a need, then pray. God often reminds us of the needs of others who are enduring struggles against satanic forces. This is what His apprentices do and have always done. The more we become concerned about what God cares about, and the more we join the fight, the more God reveals His heart to us. If you want to really know what's going on in the world, start praying for all God's plans. God will reveal things nobody is reporting.

Adventure Key: God's people are in this fight together.

HELPS AND HINDRANCES FOR THE SPIRITUAL COMBAT SYSTEM

We hear and see teachings that are not based on the Bible. Many popular books and ideas contradict Jesus. We want to be careful not to get led astray by man-centered ideas. The Psalms are the very prayers and hymns that Jesus Himself prayed as a boy and young man. So, these are great foundational tools for building our prayer skills.

What was true for the original apprentices is still true today, especially with prayer. There are three plain things to guide us: what Jesus taught, what Jesus modeled, and what His apprentices did. We develop effective skills from these three points. In fact, don't trust anything I've said here or anyone else's teaching if you find it contradicts the Bible. That is the standard for all truth. Believe God's Word, not the words of men.

Above all, Jesus taught us to pray. He wants us connected to Him. Everyone starts the same way: we are weak and unsure. Jesus understands that. He's calling us to develop and grow in a real relationship where He trains us daily.

The Father delights in honest and open relationship with His children through prayer. You don't have to impress Him; He cannot love you more than He already does.

Everything that is happening in our lives is of concern to Him. In a way, our whole lives become a prayer to God, an offering of our faith. Praying is how we access the adventure.

THE PHILOSOPHY OF COMBAT PRAYER

Jesus gives many parables and examples, so we can learn how prayer works. Prayers are more than a memorized phrase to repeat but rather a process of communication with God until it becomes a communion of our soul with Him. So, we learn tactics from Him: the power of persistence, expectancy, trust, reverence, and positioning. All are part of defeating evil in this world.

Reverence is essential. We cannot defeat the forces of darkness without it. The enemy is arrogant, proud, boastful, and disrespectful to God and all that is holy. Our position must **be like Jesus—exactly the opposite of all that.**

Reverence is the tension between bold confidence in loving familiarity with our Father in Heaven and a humble full-hearted worship of the majesty of God. Ritual formality is wrong, but casual flippancy is also wrong. It seems that God is calling us to serious and respectful reverence, yet confident and familiar communion as His children.

Persistence is vital. Some matters take time, maybe even years. We have to be committed to praying through until we receive the promised results. The devils shudder when Jesus's apprentices get serious about persistent prayer. Can you stick with the process if it requires persistence?

Expectancy is knowing that God will ultimately do what He says. We are taught to pray for things with an attitude of anticipating the answers. This is a real relationship with the living God. It's also a matter of spiritual war against a committed enemy who is "dug in." Our faith is rooted in trusting in a God big enough to answer the impossible.

Positioning ourselves for answers is about being ready and able to receive. God says He will not regard our prayers when we approach Him with a prideful or wicked heart. So, we humbly trust God will answer our faithful prayers when we are humble enough to apply the conditions of reverence, persistence, trust, and expectancy.

Well, with God, there's always good news! Psalm 66:18-21 (NIV) says:

> **If I had cherished sin in my heart,**
> **the Lord would not have listened;**
> **but God has <u>surely</u> listened**
> **and has heard my prayer.**
> **Praise be to God,**
> **who has <u>not rejected</u> my prayer**
> **or withheld his love from me!"**

How can the psalmist say that? Was he perfectly sinless? Of course not. Only Jesus was perfectly sinless. The psalmist did not <u>cherish</u> sin, especially not pride.

We discover that living in a practice of sin—embracing a lifestyle of disobedience to God—is the devil's trap and restrains active communion with God. God forgives, but we harvest what we plant. Prayers are hindered when sin is cherished, especially pride.

The devil knows that God will not bless a lifestyle of rebellion against His authority. God will never encourage us to destroy our souls because it leads to bondage and destruction.

The right attitude is considering the cross of Christ and all that sin costs. Jesus loved us and gave Himself for us while we were still rebels who hated Him. From the cross, Jesus pronounced forgiveness and promised us to walk with Him in the afterlife.

MAINTAINING SPIRITUAL POWER IN PRAYER

Within any combat training system, we learn ways to maintain strength, flexibility, and endurance. This keeps us prepared for all challenges. In the Jesus Adventure, we remain vigilant against unseen but real forces that hate us. The enemy relentlessly works to diminish our effectiveness. We learn to guard against these tactics constantly.

There's a reason why Jesus gave us that order for prayer. He honors the Father first, followed by praying for God's Kingdom, our needs, forgiveness, and temptation—before we pray against the darkness. Jesus is saying we ought to be prayed up and empowered in the things we are FOR long before we engage the enemy of whom we are AGAINST. Stand in the light, and the darkness has no power. We have no power over the enemy when we stand in pride. But by faith, praise, humility, and forgiveness, we defeat the darkness.

THE NATURE OF SPIRITUAL WARFARE

Doubt. The enemy uses doubt to diminish us. He keeps us focused on ourselves rather than God. Jesus said: *"If you believe, you will receive whatever you ask for in prayer"* (Matthew 21:22, NIV). The word "believe" is better understood as "trust" or "depend." The kind of faith Jesus teaches is faith that relies on God, not ourselves.

Build confidence in God with truth from the Bible. Increase awe and reverence for God, and belief becomes action. If two farmers pray for rain in a drought season, how do you tell which one had faith? He's the one who plows his field and plants his seed after prayer—because he is trusting in God for rain.

Unconfessed Sin. Hiding and cherishing sinful things in our hearts keeps us ineffective. Remember that Jesus said if we have a conflict with a brother, we're to resolve that before we come before God with gifts or prayers (see Matthew 5:22-24). When we confess and humble ourselves to the person whom we have sinned against, God heals us, restores us, and answers our prayers.

I believe there is a ledger in Heaven of answers to prayer that were never received because of unconfessed sin and hardened hearts! Many people blame God when the real issue is that they cherished sin. When we humble ourselves, God pours out blessing.

<u>Unforgiveness</u>. Our ability to see answers to prayer is tied directly to our ability to forgive. It seems so easy to justify holding grudges. However, this impairs living by the divine nature of Jesus.

This is why He made it central to our prayer form, *"Forgive us as we forgive,"* and taught so much about forgiveness. Unforgiving hearts grieve the Holy Spirit. Sadly, many preachers teach more about faith than forgiveness. A forgiving heart opens the door to true power. God rigs things in favor of those who forgive.

<u>Deliberate Rebellion</u>. The devil tempts us to seek things that are offensive to God—sin that opens the door to evil. He does this because he knows this hinders our effectiveness. He will do anything to keep our eyes off Jesus.

Adventure Principle: God wants us to win, so we have to learn how to fight to win.

IN THE NAME OF JESUS

"All authority in heaven and on earth has been given to me" (Matthew 28:18, NIV). If you hang around many Christians long enough, you will hear people pray and add a phrase at the end: "in the name of Jesus." It's so common some people forget they've said it and repeat it. Is this some magical guarantee for our prayer? Is it a "stamp of approval" to force God to do what we want? God does not respond to that kind of thinking.

Praying in Jesus's name is about stewardship. It's about being an ambassador for God.

> "Oh give thanks to the LORD [Yehovah]; call upon his name;
> make known his deeds among the peoples!"
> —1 Chronicles 16:8 (ESV)

When we really grasp who He is and what He is saying to us, we begin to fathom the power of His name. He does not merely have authority; **He IS the authority!**

SEALED BY THE AUTHORITY OF HIS NAME

The power of the name of Jesus is the authority given to those who trust Him, follow His teachings, and do them. We are granted a position as adopted children in His Kingdom. In doing so, His royal authority is granted, and we are commissioned to fulfill His purposes in this world.

In ancient times, those commissioned by kings a sign of that authority. An emissary would carry letters from his king that authorized him to carry out a role. That commission carried the king's authority. The emissary could go anywhere that the king's name was respected to complete that task.

Jesus commissioned His apprentices and us to offer salvation to everyone who will receive it. Our letter of authority is the Holy Bible.

IN MY NAME, THEY WILL

Today, we don't see demons or fallen angels very often, although they sometimes reveal themselves in places where the Bible has little influence. The Bible calls them principalities, rulers of the darkness, and so on. One of the reasons they do not show themselves now is that they do not want Jesus's apprentices to realize how much authority we have over them in the name of Jesus.

So, we want to know what Jesus promised about praying and living in the power of His Name! He said:

> **Whatever you ask in my name, this I will do, that the Father may be glorified in the Son. If you ask me anything in my name, I will do it.**
> **—John 14:13-14 (ESV)**

> **I chose you and appointed you that you should go and bear fruit and that your fruit should abide, so that whatever you ask the Father in my name, he may give it to you.**
> **—John 15:16 (ESV)**

The reason for the authority is to set a broken world into order. What might that look like from the perspective of Jesus? In Mark 16:17-18 (ESV), He says:

> **And these signs will accompany those who believe: in my name they will cast out demons; they will speak in new tongues; they will pick up serpents with their hands; and if they drink any deadly poison, it will not hurt them; they will lay their hands on the sick, and they will recover.**

Our priority is to defy the works of the evil ones and defeat them. We commune with God and communicate the Great News to others. We are called to go to people who are different—foreigners. We are called to restore people who have been in bondage.

When is all that supposed to happen? When we're doing what He shows us in the previous verse, where He says, *"Go into all the world and proclaim the gospel to the whole creation"* (Mark 16:15, ESV). Where is that? Your home, your neighborhood, your job, your market. This power of Jesus's name is about setting people free from evil, sin, and its devastation.

This is the business of Jesus: setting people free by the grace and love of God. Just as Jesus has set us free, He is calling us to partner in reaching someone else. This is the business of Jesus.

DYNAMIC POWER IN THE NAME

His people have proclaimed it for centuries: there is power in the name of Jesus! Power for us to overcome and power to defeat the darkness in our lives, the lives of those we know and love, and the lives of strangers. As apprentices of Jesus, we are agents of the blessings of Heaven. We have authority to tear down spiritual strongholds!

Jesus Christ is the one name that the devil wants us to fear proclaiming. The power of the name is the power of all Heaven, accessed by the cross. The cross is what gives us access to God and to this authority.

We must never forget that. The enemy happens to hate all reference to the blood of Christ, and he scurries away when that is our focus. This is why it's so important to regularly and faithfully participate in Holy Communion.

The authority and calling of Jesus are to seek the power of His name. Ask the Holy Spirit to reveal our wrongs, heal our hearts, and help us to make things right.

> **God has surely listened
> and has heard my prayer.
> Praise be to God,
> who has not rejected my prayer
> or withheld his love from me!**
> —Psalm 66:19-20 (NIV)

With a heart that is right with God, no evil can stand against us. When we humble ourselves to one another, the unity of the Spirit makes us remarkably effective. Nothing can keep the will of God from being done when we have the unity of the Spirit. Each of us can be an instrument to defeat evil.

Adventure Principle: When we have God's authority, we can do the impossible.

SPIRITUAL COMBAT SYSTEM DEVELOPMENT

There are purposes for prayer, which may be summarized as exalting God, communing with Him, strengthening our faith, receiving support, establishing His authority, defeating evil, and interceding for these things on behalf of others. The most essential of these is **communion with God**. The rest are part of bringing Heaven to Earth, but the entire point is communion with our Creator.

The devil and his minions do not flee from a person who is cocky about their faith. Mountains do not move because someone can quote verses. The heart of God is not drawn toward the person who merely focuses on morality.

Instead, God is near to those who draw near to Him in prayers of faith. Miracles happen for those who humbly seek Him, and the evil ones flee from those who know by the practice of prayer and worship how to walk in the authority of Messiah.

True Adventurers don't pray flippantly. God knows our hearts, and He loves for us to be cheerful and familiar with Him, but we are here to establish God's authority and break the chains of evil. So, we pray earnestly with respect and loving adoration for the great God and Savior who redeemed us by the blood of Jesus. Discovering the Spiritual Combat System of Jesus reveals that *"with God, all things are possible"* (Matthew 19:26, NIV).

MEDITATION IN PRAYER AND WORSHIP

God has given us the ability to know Him, communicate with Him, and experience fellowship with Him that overcomes the evil in the world around us through prayer and worship. So what evil, what unbelief, what lies, what bondage are we personally called to defeat in His name?

PART 4

SEATED WITH JESUS

CHAPTER 10

SUPPLYING EARTH'S NEEDS FROM HEAVEN'S RESOURCES

Jesus said:

"You give them something to eat."
—Mark 6:37

FLOWING IN FULL ADVENTURE MODE

The Jesus Adventure is about receiving and growing in the dynamic and constantly moving "divine nature" of Messiah/Christ. This is the vitality and stream of the true spiritual nature and character of the Messiah, Jesus.

It is the spiritual essence that Jesus brought to us from Heaven and lived out in the presence of His apprentices every day and the divine wind that filled His apprentices at Pentecost. It is the very breath of God that He breathed into Adam, which we each receive when we are born from above in the new birth.

It is the essence of what He trained them to discover and what they were sent out to help us discover. This involves transformative healing of our broken self that is always in the context of lovingly trusting God as our Lord and loving others as we love ourselves.

Since our own souls can never be transformed other than when we participate in the "divine nature" of Christ, this is an essential part of true living faith in Jesus. This is about being empowered for a life of selflessness; not thinking less of ourselves, but instead, it is a life of thinking of ourselves less.

In the process, we discover the fountainhead of all life and strength—the creative and generative nature of God Himself, which enables us to be life-givers rather than takers. As we begin to flow in the divine nature of Christ, we are becoming in communion with the true nature of Jesus, the Messiah.

Rather than being wrathful mortals who have mercy, we become mercy. Rather than being self-serving sinners who have grace, we become grace. No longer wretched, prejudiced outlaws who learn justice, we become the just who love restoring the victims of injustice.

Rather than talking about forgiveness while condemning, we become the essence of forgiveness itself, keeping no record of wrongs. We become agents of the divine life-giving spirit.

In the process, we discover that God always gives more to the givers. If there is something you lack, give it away.

Do you lack mercy? Be merciful. Do you lack help with something difficult? Help others who have difficulty. Do you need to find the faithfulness of God's promises? Be the source of meeting someone else's needs according to God's promises.

We find this part of the adventure to be the most thrilling because, in this process, we become agents of God's nature to other lost mortals as we lay down our former identity. There is nothing more exciting than that.

No thrill in this life can match being the conduit of God's divine nature. It is what we were created for. While we're doing it, we find

God's provision for the very things we need. His empowerment flows to us because He knows it will flow through us.

FULL-THROTTLE ADVENTURES

We are the new creations in Christ who live life with gusto. We are amazed and see what God can do with our lives as we entrust ourselves to Him. We put our resources in His hand, letting Him guide us on how to use them. He does amazing things through us and for us when we do it with Him and for His glory. Proverbs states:

> **One person gives freely, yet gains even more; another withholds unduly, but comes to poverty. A generous person will prosper; whoever refreshes others will be refreshed.**
> **—Proverbs 11:24-25 (NIV)**

God has rules in the spiritual realm in which He governs people. One rule is that generosity leads to more, and being miserly makes you poor. We tend to think the opposite is true. When we judge this truth, we tend to look only at the short-term results rather than the long game of life.

As apprentices of Jesus, God pushes this rule into overdrive because He commits to bringing supernatural resources to our aid whenever we join in His work. It's just the way He runs His government, which we call the Kingdom.

LIGHTING ETERNAL FLAMES WITH HIS WORDS OF SPIRIT

When Jesus said, *"You are the light of the world. A city set on a hill cannot be hidden"* (Matthew 5:14, NKJV), it confused His apprentices. He had told them that He was the light of the world, and that was probably difficult to understand at first. Because, at that point, they had known Him just as a local preacher who grew up in a carpenter's workshop.

Jesus's claim that they were *the light of the world* and suggest that He would put them on display would have puzzled them. Yet Jesus was depositing something into them that would never burn out and never be extinguished. He was investing in them with His divine nature, speaking His words of Life and Spirit.

They didn't understand it at first, but He was making an eternal investment into their souls. Every day and every turn of events gave them more to be amazed about.

THE VALUE OF GIVING WITHOUT RETURN

Early in my life following Jesus, when I had a young family and very unreliable work, I had an offer to move to a new city and start a new job. I'd been doing well for a while, and then suddenly, work dried up without new options. Rent was due, and I could not afford to keep our little family in that home anymore. But I also didn't have enough money to move.

When I asked some of the men in my fellowship for prayer about what to do, they all agreed to pray. Later, the leader of the fellowship, named "Joe," handed me a wad of cash—more than a week's worth of earnings for me at that time. It was enough to get us to the new job.

I said, "Joe, I can't take it; I don't know how long it will take to pay you back." And Joe quickly replied, "My wife and I don't want you to pay us back. We want you to pay it forward."

I'd never heard a phrase like that before. I'd also never heard of anyone giving someone a large sum of money and expecting them to repay it to someone else. My mind was spinning.

Joe said to me, "The money all belongs to Jesus. It's up to you to send it forward to someone else who needs it." I had no idea that people did such things. Everyone who had money in my world expected to be paid back with interest, if they were willing to loan money at all.

Joe knew the power of giving without expecting anything in return. Joe and his wife have been givers in all the years since; they have never lacked resources for anything. They keep seeing God give them more to bless others more.

JESUS IS THE GREAT CONTRARIAN

It's a funny thing: the longer we know Jesus, the more we realize that He doesn't operate by the rules of this world. He asks you to believe what you cannot see and to do what seems the opposite of what works. He makes promises that are impossible from our perspective, and He gives peace in the middle of fearful challenges. He just doesn't do things like us, and He expects us to understand that we're the ones who have it wrong.

When Jesus commanded His disciples, *"You give them something to eat,"* it seemed absurd. They had 5,000 people following them across a desolate region with no stores or resources—just barren prairie around the Sea of Galilee. They were many hours' walk away from any village that had food, and there wouldn't be enough there for so many people, anyway.

His disciples told Him that they checked, but no one had food except for one kid with a basket of five loaves of bread and two fish—basically enough to make a few fish sandwiches. But Jesus is not restricted by our limitations. Here's what happened in Mark 6:39-44 (ESV):

> Then he commanded them all to sit down in groups on the green grass. So they sat down in groups, by hundreds and by fifties. And taking the five loaves and the two fish, he looked up to heaven and said a blessing and broke the loaves and gave them to the disciples to set before the people. And he divided the two fish among them all. And they all ate and were satisfied. And they took up twelve baskets full of broken pieces and of the fish. And those who ate the loaves were five thousand men.

So, Jesus was expecting them to learn something from this, and it wasn't just a lesson on how to feed a lot of people. In fact, the needs of those particular people were just the backdrop to what Jesus wanted them (and us) to discover. Later the next day, Jesus mentioned an important principle which He wanted them to apply to this experience—a principle often gets missed:

> **"Watch and beware of the leaven of the Pharisees and Sadducees."**
> **—Matthew 16:6 (ESV)**

His apprentices didn't get it and thought He wanted something to eat, so He said:

> **Do you not yet perceive? Do you not remember the five loaves for the five thousand, and how many baskets you gathered? How is it that you fail to understand that I did not speak about bread? Beware <u>the leaven</u> of the Pharisees and Sadducees. Then they understood that he did not tell them to beware of the leaven of bread, but of the teaching of the Pharisees and Sadducees.**
> **—Matthew 16:9, 11-12 (ESV)**

Why bring the Pharisees and Sadducees into it the next day? Those men were so focused on their training in Jewish law that they missed the point God wanted His people to discover: a relationship with Him marked by dependency on Him. A relationship with God to do the impossible. You see, the Pharisees and Sadducees followed the laws and regulations but missed the heart and mind of the God who gave them.

They knew all about the writings of Moses, but they had lost the faith of Moses. They forgot who led the Israelites out of Egypt! They studied all about the Moses of God, but they had lost perception of the God of Moses.

Jesus wasn't just feeding the 5,000 people following Him. He was showing us the heart of God. He was inviting us to join in His work and showing us <u>how</u> to join His work. We will never have enough resources in our own strength, wisdom, or abilities to do His work. We depend on Him because without Him we can do nothing.

ALL THINGS POSSIBLE WITH JESUS

We discovered in an earlier chapter that the miracle of crossing over is about trusting God for our needs through the storms we face while following Jesus. We also learned that those storms come just before God wants to use us to do something important.

In this case, however, *"You give them something"* is about trusting God to work through us for other people's needs. It's about doing that important work to **help other people experience God.**

As we walk with Jesus, He calls us to do something bigger than ourselves. He always does. The tasks that God gives us always require His hand. The true challenges are spiritual and require spiritual resources, and that means we must rely on God's empowerment. Jesus wants us to learn how to know a challenge is from Him and how to experience His supernatural provision.

All of life is ministry; every one of us is a preacher. The only question is, what are we preaching? The children of darkness preach sin and darkness.

Jesus calls us to preach life with more than words, to reach a deaf and dying world. In return for our participation, He gives rewards in this life and promises greater ones in the next. Speak the words of life and preach by demonstrating a life of sacrificial love. Create the Kingdom of Heaven in front of an evil generation.

THE PROCESS OF THE CALL

Notice there were two events of the feeding of the masses (as Jesus said in Matthew 16:9-10). Jesus asks them a question to make them aware of the need and His expectation. In Matthew, He says:

> **I feel sorry for these people. They have been with me for three days, and they don't have anything to eat. I don't want to send them away hungry.**
> **–Matthew 15:32**

So, Jesus's disciples asked Him, *"Where can we find enough food to feed such a crowd?"* (v. 33)

Jesus makes us aware of a dilemma we cannot solve. Most people quit as soon as they realize they don't personally have the resources. Some will condemn and criticize others, whether the government or the church, for not solving the problem; they can only find fault, which is just a way of deflecting the gnawing conscience inside them that is saying, *"You give them something"* (Matthew 14:16). To reconcile this, they silence that voice inside by blaming others. The natural man tries to ignore the problem and says, "It's too big."

Jesus is looking for those who will bring Him the challenge so that He can solve it for them. He doesn't expect us to have it all worked out. He expects us to start with something, as Andrew did in John 6:9: *"There is a boy here who has five small loaves of barley bread and two fish."* That's when Jesus can make things happen.

So, Jesus directs us to do what we can, as it says in Mark 6:39, *"Jesus told his disciples to have the people sit down on the green grass."* In other words, get organized and set up a means of achieving the goal.

Then He demonstrated how we achieve the impossible: *"Jesus took the five loaves and the two fish. He looked up toward heaven"* (v. 41). The work begins by putting some resources in Jesus's hands.

We bring God into it and activate our faith in Him with whatever resources we have.

> **And (He) blessed the food. Then He broke the bread and handed it to his disciples to give to the people. He also divided the two fish, so that everyone could have some.**
> —Mark 6:41; Luke 9:16; Matthew 14:19 (author paraphrase)

There was abundance left over both times after the work was done because God is rich and lavish toward His people.

Wishing doesn't accomplish the impossible. Faith in the living God through Jesus does something to meet the need. That's why Jesus said to them, *"YOU give them something to eat."* Mark's account is the second time this happened.

Jesus expected them to understand that this dilemma was given for them to **activate their faith and do something themselves.** This gives us insight: Jesus doesn't give up on us just because we fail the first time. He's committed to our growth.

FEEDING THE MASSES WITH SPIRITUAL FOOD

We live in a time like no other. We have more awareness of what's happening in the whole world and less interest in each other than ever before. We have more access to the Bible in more current languages, more access to current archaeology that continues to prove its accuracy, more access to science that validates the Bible's claims, and more churches ignoring the Bible than ever before. People have become entertained by worthless things and are living more selfishly than ever before.

Still, the Bible's timeless message and power are clear and more valid than ever as we see biblical prophecy coming to pass, pointing to the soon conclusion of this age.

God is calling us who have tasted and seen that He is good to boldly live and share the message. Jesus is looking for people who will take on impossible tasks in His name and trust Him to bring the resources.

The time is short until He returns; He wants as many to be saved as possible. That requires every one of us who knows Him to share the bread of life with a world that is starving spiritually.

Jesus told us, *"I am the living bread which came down from heaven; if anyone eats of this bread, he will live forever"* (John 6:51, RSV). The miracle of tangible food feeding thousands is not nearly as satisfying as the miracle of spiritual food that saves and purifies souls. It's not enough to meet the material needs of people; if we don't give them the Great News of Jesus, then we do a disservice. It is also true that people listen better when they aren't hungry.

SPEAKING IN THE DAYLIGHT

Sometimes we struggle to know what to share, how, and when to share it. As we continue paying attention to His Word and His Spirit, Jesus will teach us about our needs and the needs of others as we go. This is how He leads us. We learn to meditate on what He is showing us, which means to memorize it, repeat it to ourselves, and mull it over.

Often, when we give Him time in our day devoted just to Him, He speaks to us in the night as we rest and gives us a plan for what to do. Matthew 10:27 reports:

> **Whatever I say to you in the dark, you must tell in the light. And you must announce from the housetops whatever I have whispered to you.**

If we start sharing what He speaks to us with our neighbors, He will give us more to say. The problem isn't what to say as much as it is the willingness to say it.

Jesus warned that generation, according to John 9:4 when He said:

> **As long as it is day, we must do what the one who sent me wants me to do. When night comes, no one can work.**

In those days, there was a pending climactic conclusion to the nation of Judea and Jerusalem. Jesus knew that their rejection of Him and His teachings triggered judgment from the Father. It wouldn't be long after He left, and many of them would still be alive to see it.

Looking back, it's clear that all the prophetic signs had been triggered, and there was no going back. The apprentices had a limited window of time to reach their people with the message before their nation went into captivity.

The faithful fellowship did as He instructed and was completely saved from that horrible tragedy. Those who rejected Him suffered the most terrible times that we can imagine. Millions died; more were taken captive by the Romans and sold into slavery.

A time worse than that is coming, except it will impact the whole world. The night is approaching that will be greater than any of us can imagine. Like the first century, modern apprentices of Jesus will be spared the worst times on the planet Earth. The people who are left here will wish they had listened.

We want to get the spiritual food out to everyone. We each have that calling if we follow Him. We want to find meaningful ways to help the needs of people here and now.

A terrible night is coming when no one can work, called by Jesus and the prophets as "the Great Tribulation," the time when *"the Wrath of God comes on the whole world"* (Colossians 3:6, author paraphrase). So, we keep sharing what Jesus has spoken to us since the faith to believe in Messiah Jesus always comes through hearing God's Word shared repeatedly by those with true living faith.

STRIVING FOR A FEAST DAY THAT ENDURES

The meaning of these unexpected feasts in a field is not only to show us that we should expect God to aid us in meeting the spiritual hunger of humanity and consider the physical needs of people who will want to hear Jesus, but this was also so they would understand that God was doing something new. This foreshadows a big feast day that is coming with great multitudes in attendance, face-to-face with Jesus!

No one knows the timing but the Father alone. The great feast that is coming will happen without much warning, and it will be the most incredible event of human history.

Jesus said, in John 6:27 (NIV):

> **Do not work for food that spoils, but for food that endures to eternal life, which the Son of Man will give you.**

We find this "food that endures" by doing the will of the Father, abiding in Jesus, and doing what He teaches. We find it by being apprentices who live intentionally and sacrificially for the cause of Jesus. Our mission field may be the neighbor, our children, our coworkers, or even people in far-off places. It doesn't matter who because no person or mission is more valuable than another. What matters is faithfulness to trust Jesus and take action as He leads. This is the full-throttle way of Jesus.

MEDITATION

Those truly hungry for God find that Jesus offers an eternal banquet unlike anything we know. James 3:17-18 informs us:

> **But the wisdom that comes from above leads us to be pure, friendly, gentle, sensible, kind, helpful, genuine, and sincere. When peacemakers plant seeds of peace, they will harvest justice.**

CHAPTER 11

CROSS WALKERS OF A NEW IDENTITY

Jesus said in Mark 8:34:

If any of you want to be my followers, you must forget about yourself. You must take up your cross and follow me.

THE SUPREMACY OF SELF-DENIAL

It bears repeating: God's plan for His children is victory. That victory requires training to defeat darkness with an entirely different set of skills than we learned in this world as children of the rebellion. We are created to be children of the government/Kingdom of God. For that purpose, we take on a new citizenship, essentially a new identity.

Seeing someone discover this dominion over darkness for themselves is a total joy! There is no earthly pleasure that matches a person who fully trusts in Jesus and discovers her new heavenly identity. But we don't often see that because this dominion is a long-distance run. It's rarely discovered in a moment. For many, it's a cross-country marathon with stumbles, scrapes, and bruises before the finish line.

Maturing on the Jesus Adventure means growing in our comprehension and ability. It means realizing the true meaning of life and self. We discern the difference between popular ideas that do not work versus the way that gives life from the Master Himself. That maturing comes with trials, difficulties, and challenging experiences that require us to find the inner strength to resist everything begging us to turn back.

It's like a guitar player who would be great; she gives herself completely to the practice, dedicating all to that goal. A serious painter studies color, paint, texture, light, and the subject they're painting with obsessive patience. No artist became famous without extreme practice and study. In this same way, an apprentice needs total dedication.

The apprentice who takes Jesus seriously and accepts the call to partner with Him follows Him all the way to the cross. We seriously consider the work Jesus completed there. Only when we recognize that Jesus already gave His all for us can we imagine giving our all for Him.

At the foot of the cross, we find all the meaning and purpose we need because Jesus purchased our right to claim total amnesty and receive the magnificent beauty of redemption as His children.

SINCE WE'RE GOING TO BE WALKING ANYWAY

Everything we do and every choice we make is a decision to reject something in favor of something else. Sitting in front of the TV is a choice not to read a book or not to walk or pray. It's a decision to let someone else's ideas fill your mind rather than create something.

No one can be free from serving. At our core, we are worshippers. We each worship something, even if it's a sports team. Those who serve only themselves are simply doing the devil's work of rebellion. This is just the nature of reality; we cannot escape it.

Jesus shows what we already know: there is no reward without commitment. The price of any success is total abandonment of a goal. Everything from pop music to athletic shoe commercials tells us that. The price of half commitment is mediocrity and failure.

This should give us complete peace as we discover that following Jesus is higher, greater, more significant, and more fulfilling than all other pursuits.

We're going to walk and serve a brand or identity in this life anyway. Walking with Jesus and carrying our cross is a choice to build a life based on His identity, dying to all that this vain world may entice us with.

Denying ourselves opens up marvelous discoveries because we find out who we really are and what we were made for: a whole-hearted, enthusiastic relationship with our Maker. This gives greater satisfaction than natural minds can ever find.

It has been said that we are restless until we find our rest in Him. This is what we find when we abandon ourselves to know Jesus above all things: complete serenity. The freedom, peace, and purpose of life rolled into one, enthusiastically lived for the Prince of Peace.

KEEPING OUR HEADS UP

Sometimes Christians say, "It is my cross to bear," regarding some difficulty they face in life. They act as though being miserable is a path to spiritual growth or that God wants us to have lifelong aggravation.

This is totally misunderstanding God's method. This attitude is counter-productive to the working of the Spirit and grieves the Holy Spirit, who loves us.

Taking up our cross, denying ourselves, and following Jesus are about transformation and finding our true identity and calling. The Spirit restores us from the death curse to become a carrier of the life-giving Spirit. The person who laments carrying a burden has never considered the mind of Christ to see the total joy and commitment Jesus had going to the cross.

Yes, Jesus suffered—it was horrible. It was worse than we can imagine. But no one pulled Jesus onto His cross! No one forced Jesus to His trial. No one pushed Jesus into His ministry. No one pulled Jesus out of Heaven. He came willingly to seek and save the lost. He did it *"for the joy that was set before Him"* (Hebrews 12:2, ESV), and Jesus did not complain.

He looked to the greater good He would do. He demonstrated the joy of obedience, the total satisfaction of doing the will of the Father.

Jesus looked at the Father's joy to accept us as adopted children who were once the children of wrath.

Can you see His face? He endured it and kept His mind completely focused on what He would accomplish—bringing many to the Father! His suffering was not a failure! His crucifixion was the greatest achievement in history!

Every time we identify with Christ and resist evil, and every time we deny our rebel nature, we are doing the same: defeating the rebellion and adding to the ultimate joy of Jesus. We get filled with the same joy because we know that the Father has already given us His favor.

Adventure Principle: Identity in Christ in His death, burial, and resurrection is dying to our old identity and taking on His living identity.

SOLO BUT NEVER LONELY

When we discover the truth of self-denial is the point in which we realize we have never been alone, and never will be, in Christ. Finding yourself comes from losing yourself to follow Jesus.

> **For whoever would save his life will lose it, but whoever loses his life for my sake and the gospel's will save it.**
> **For what does it profit a man to gain the whole world and forfeit his soul?**
> —Mark 8:35-36 (ESV)

This can only make sense if we understand that there is much more to who we are than our bodies.

We are creatures of light, spirit, and soul, even though we do not see it. Even as mortals, God says we are complex beings, not merely bodies, with life that is given by God. He tells us that every thought and deed is recorded! Our hardware is temporary, but the software—the nonmaterial part of us—is eternal. How does that work? God knows.

People only see the hardware, our bodies. The real person is nonmaterial. The hardware is what we are given, but the software is fluid and develops based on our choices. Our experiences, hopes, and abilities are invisible, covered by temporary organic machinery. Those experiences, hopes, desires, and accomplishments will survive beyond the end of the body and are carried forward in the eternal realm.

As an example: a digital storage drive weighs about fourteen grams, whether it's empty or packed with ten gigabytes of data. That's because software has no mass. Software exists in a nonmaterial realm.

That data is captive and organized into energy patterns. If I lose the data on a device, I can retrieve it from a cloud storage facility through the internet that I never see. The hardware is just a temporary container. God is telling us that our bodies are temporary containers of our eternal data set.

In a similar way, God reveals that we have a temporary hardware called a body, but the software that makes up who we are—the password and the source code inside—is in His control. We will get new upgraded hardware later. God alone knows what goes on inside us and how we operate. God alone knows our hearts.

UNLIMITED CAPACITY OF A TIMELESS GOD

Since God is outside of time (but created time as a feature of our universe), He is not limited by time in His understanding. He knows everything about us. Jesus has spoken to us: *"I am with you always, even to the end of the age"* (Matthew 28:20, NLT). This can only be true if Jesus is also outside space and time. In Jeremiah 1:5 (NKJV), God says, *"Before I formed you in the womb I knew you,"* and Paul said in Galatians 1:15 (NIV), *"God . . . set me apart even from my mother's womb and called me by His grace."* So, God has always been with us, has always watched us, and continues to watch over us today. He is with us through every situation until the end.

Why is that important? When you understand this, then you can say: "I will take up my cross and follow Jesus." Since He has always been with us, we can confidently go with Him.

Adventure Principle: God is our Creator, who has always had a purpose for us far greater than we understood before we learned to walk with Jesus.

GIFTS GIVEN FREELY, NOT EARNED

We do not earn favor with God by denying ourselves. We deny ourselves because we already have favor with God. Denying ourselves is about learning to become like God, who has freely given us His favor.

None of us can do what Jesus did. But we can learn the principle of passing things forward to others without the expectation of compensation. In doing this, we become participants with Jesus and with the Father in the same plan.

Denying ourselves is just a way of emptying what weak identity we have so that God can fill us up with more favor to share with others who have not yet discovered God's favor.

THE CHALLENGE OF WHO YOU WERE

When Jesus was telling first-century Jews that they needed to take up their cross, deny themselves, and follow Him, He was calling them to lose their own identity as Jews. That's right: Jesus was commanding His fellow Jews to lose their identity. That sounds harsh, and it would be if I had said it. But Jesus also calls *us* to lose our identity! We are called to join the fellowship of the redeemed regardless of our history.

For a pagan Gentile, leaving behind all the idols and beliefs contrary to God is also required. We're called to set Christ Jesus apart in our hearts and consider Him supreme. We're called to make a change of identity from the empty ways we once lived. That change was just as hard for pagan Gentiles as it was for Jews. This is the way of Jesus.

While Jews saw their identity in the laws of God who spoke to Moses on Mt. Sinai, pagan Gentiles saw their identity in forces and idols of false gods. Today's atheists see their identity in self-help, self-sufficiency, humanism, and evolution. But those ideas lead souls away from the Creator. In turning allegiance to Him, we are welcomed as heirs of His Kingdom.

BREAD OF LIFE OR A LIFE FOR BREAD

Spending our lives working for things that perish, we work hard at getting food, clothing, shelter, and pleasure. We forget to think about the long game, the big picture. We generally fail to consider the eternal, which is vastly more important. We ignore the fact that at any time, in one moment, we could lose it all, even our own lives. For modern people, the end of physical life seems like an unexpected event.

Jesus is the only man who knew precisely when and how He would die. Can you imagine that? I'm actually glad I don't know when I'll die. It would make it impossible for me to really live well.

On the other hand, some people live like they will never die, like there is no day of accountability coming. They never consider what is ahead or how to be ready. Yet, it's true that we will all wake up in "the afterlife" soon. According to Jesus, we need to prepare! Today is the only day to prepare for the eventual tomorrow.

Jesus said in John 6:35, *"I am the bread of life."* And then He added:

> **Truly, truly, I say to you, unless you eat the flesh of the Son of Man and drink his blood, you have no life in you. Whoever feeds on my flesh and drinks my blood has eternal life, and I will raise him up on the last day. For my flesh is true food, and my blood is true drink.**
> **—John 6:53 (ESV)**

In those days, most people failed to consider what God had been showing them throughout their history through the Bible—that their Messiah would have to come and do the impossible for them. God cannot be good at all unless He is just. God cannot ignore the rebellion of sin and be truly just. God also cannot be good unless He is kind and merciful.

So, the rebellion of man creates a dilemma that causes the enemies of God to rejoice because no one in Heaven or on Earth ever imagined that God would pay the price for the death curse Himself. God chose to do this because man was never intended to die. God created man for eternity to have fellowship with Him.

God did it this way so that anyone who would humble themselves could receive Him without trying to work or earn that relationship. God wants us to choose it; it is a gift we receive without the temptation of pride.

God wants us to realize that the food and drink that feeds us with eternal life comes from recognizing the cost of our rebellion and, at the same time, realizing His total love for us. This is why Jesus gave us the sacrament of communion, which some call the "Lord's Supper."

This is a regular reminder that we should share this mysterious celebration of bread and wine every time we gather as His people, which reminds us of the cost of our redemption. Eating and drinking these elements remind us that we must internalize His death, burial, and resurrection as our identity.

The two choices of life are illustrated in this concept: we either work for bread and drink that perishes, or we internalize the gift of bread and wine that gives us eternal life. Because even as apprentices, sometimes we get so busy that we forget a judgment is coming.

HOW STRONG MUST WE BE TO CARRY OUR CROSS?

The truth is that **no one is strong enough.** Even Jesus needed help. Mark 15:20-21 (ESV) says,

> **And when they had mocked him, they stripped him of the purple cloak and put his own clothes on him. And they led him out to crucify him. And they compelled a passerby ... to carry his cross.**

Jesus was a strong man, a fit and able-bodied carpenter, working with His hands six days a week. He traveled on foot across mountains and deserts many times. But Jesus was so badly beaten that He could not carry His cross. Along the way, the soldiers forced another man to take it.

Do you think you have carry your own cross alone? **No.** Jesus is with you. We are not called to carry our cross; we're called to take it up and follow Him. Jesus strengthens us from that point on. Our strength doesn't impress God; that's backward. The point is to be committed to following Jesus, because one way or another, we're all going to lose this life one day anyway.

Three men went up the hill that day carrying crosses, and Jesus was crucified between two thieves. All three died that day. One died with confidence in God His Father; one died cursing God under the death curse. There was a third man, a thief. He repented, and Jesus promised that man that He would walk in paradise with Jesus that very day.

The point is not that God wants us to suffer. We already do that in this life, sooner or later. The mandate is to follow Jesus and die to our selfish rebellion against God. The thief on the cross died to himself and came to the defense of Jesus, recognizing that he was being punished justly but that Jesus was being punished unjustly. In other words, the thief acknowledged that Jesus was righteous. He also acknowledged that he was a sinner himself. He then took the only action he had left: to proclaim Jesus and ask for Jesus to remember him.

In that hour of misery, he was the first evangelist in the world; his heart had been changed. He took up his cross and identified with Jesus. Ironically, he may be the most fruitful of all evangelists in history since he reminds us that we are powerless before Jesus and that Jesus is more merciful than our sin is bad.

Adventure Principle: Realizing our true position means knowing that we were never equipped to live this life alone, but with Jesus we can overcome every struggle.

SHOW US YOUR ID

We may come from the weirdest family in the world, but there we have an identity. Jesus knew His identity and it didn't matter what anyone said about it. They could slander His ancestry, malign His hometown, attack His message, hit His face and pull out His beard. But Jesus knew He belonged to the Father; He knew that He had come from the Father and would return to the Father. Nothing would change that, and Jesus didn't need to defend it. This is what Jesus is calling us to—to maintain an unshakable confidence in our identity in Him.

In our world, we have to carry identification of some kind, everywhere. You can't drive a car, ride a train, fly on a plane, cross a border, open a bank account, get medical care, apply for a job, rent or buy a house, get married, stay in a hotel, buy medications or donate blood without proof of who you are in the form of a photo identification card or passport.

Does any of that prove who you are? Wherever we come from, Jesus is offering us the chance to gain a new heavenly identity and become who we were made to be. He is asking us to lay down the rebel life and take up His identity.

From the ancient prophets and the apostles, we know Jesus was much more than any mere man. He was the Son of Man, from beyond time, the Prince of Peace, and the Mighty God. He was twice declared the Son of God by a voice from Heaven described in the Gospel of Mark and declared the Word of God by His closest disciple John. Jesus said of Himself that He and the Father are one. So, we know that Jesus was fully in possession of His true heavenly identity without forgetting His earthly identity as a Galilean Jew.

Mark 8:34 (ESV) tells us what Jesus wants from us when He said, *"If anyone would come after me, let him deny himself and take up his cross and follow me."* This means taking on our primary identity as adopted children of God and seeing the old person we once were as dead and buried. We declare our mortal life has ended and receive an immortal life directly from Jesus, empowered by the Father, and strengthened by the Holy Spirit.

In other words, we are called to consider ourselves already resurrected into the new life. We begin walking in the resurrection of Jesus, here.

NO LONGER CAPTIVES TO CONDEMNATION

Many people imagine that in Mark 8:34, Jesus is demanding we become martyrs, beat ourselves up, and struggle and suffer through life to earn God's favor. That's a religious spirit tempting us to think God is impressed if we suffer and struggle more.

God is not condemning us nor waiting for us to suffer so that He can love us. The cross of Jesus is the final word that God has to say about judgment for sin. In Jesus, God pours out favor on us. The call to take up our cross is about being emptied of self so God can fill us with His gracious favor.

Keep in mind what Jesus said about it:

> **God did not send his Son into the world to condemn the world, but in order that the world might be saved through him. Whoever believes in him is not condemned, but whoever does not believe is condemned already.**
> **—John 3:17-18 (ESV)**

> "Do not think that I will accuse you to the Father."
> –John 5:45 (ESV)

> "The Son of Man came to seek and to save the lost."
> –Luke 19:10 (GNT)

Most people raised around religion have never considered this, but Jesus never once condemned any person who came to Him hoping for forgiveness or help. The only people Jesus rebuked were the proud and hypocritical religious leaders! Many of us are shocked to discover that. Jesus came offering redemption, forgiveness, and soul transformation, not condemnation.

Adventure Principle: God has already passed judgment, which Jesus paid in full. We can now walk in the power of His life with a restored identity, knowing we never need to impress God or win His favor—we already have it in Jesus.

WAGES OF THE DEATH CURSE

Students of the Old Testament and people who discipline themselves to do what is right struggle with the issue of redemption and forgiveness because they know there must be a judgment for evil, sin, and rebellion. It can't be ignored. Think of one person you know who has done real evil, and you're hoping they "rot in hell." We all know that there must be justice. We crave it for the "bad guys."

God is holy, just, and pure: He cannot allow sin to go unpunished. Mankind is a race that has committed treachery toward God and one another. We are all guilty at some level. We struggle to believe that we will suffer judgment, but we are "the bad guys" from God's perspective.

So, God pronounced death. Not just physical death, but spiritual and eternal death—God's wrath for rejecting the life and love of the eternal King. The weight of it was upon all. None could escape it. Yet, God is so rich in mercy that He had to provide an amnesty that did not violate His perfect justice.

This is why the wrath of God was poured out on Jesus <u>by proxy for us</u> and why He suffered such cruelty. He opened a way for our amnesty, if we humble ourselves.

We saw that God was thoroughly satisfied with Jesus's sacrifice; Isaiah 53:11 says so. Jesus is the bearer of all of mankind's judgment. First, He perfectly lived out the requirements of God's law, then became the substance of those requirements as an innocent substitution—a spotless firstborn lamb.

From the cross, Jesus made seven key statements. The first was forgiveness; the last was that "the debt is paid in full." This is the beginning and end of all that Jesus came for—to forgive us and to pay our debt. There is nothing more to be said about our sin debt for those who identify with Jesus and take up their cross.

So, rather than saying we have to carry on a miserable struggle of self-effort, Jesus has called us to end our struggle through His identity and power. We receive the new life of acceptance with His Father, now our Father. We live a life of favor and walk in the light of Jesus's perfect grace. Carrying this cross means we are now free in Him to walk in freedom, kindness, acceptance, and favor with God in the name of Jesus. Psalm 13:5-6 illustrates this:

> **I trust your love,**
> **and I feel like celebrating**
> **because you rescued me.**
> **You have been good to me, LORD,**
> **and I will sing about you.**

THIS IS THE WAY WE WALK NOW

This adventure of Jesus transforms even the worst among us, everywhere we go and every day we are alive. Whoever you are, wherever you come from, and whatever you have done, you can become a living cross-bearer. You can offer God's forgiveness and proclaim that the debt has been paid!

Do you see it? We are not called to walk hunched over carrying the burden of our mortal weakness! <u>That's what we were already doing</u>! Now, we stand up like children of the Most High—the King's kids—carrying a completed work. We've died to that old way. Now, we're walking by transforming grace. We have taken on His identity and His authority.

We're now agents of God's kindness and carriers of the gracious favor of God. We can do that because we know that <u>we are accepted by Jesus</u>, the Son of God. We are His; everything we have is His, everything we do is for Him, and everything we receive is from Him.

Everything else is icing on the cake, adding delight to the adventure. Once we know to whom we belong, no one can convince us otherwise.

HOW CAN WE BE DENIED?

You will find hostility from the religious crowd who <u>work hard to earn God's favor</u>. I tell you this to prepare you because it will happen—the most religious people you will encounter will try to condemn you and convince you that God will deny you for failing at their perspective of some standard.

Their religious spirit keeps them working hard to earn favor by keeping laws and commands. Their prideful minds find their identity in being strict, in trying harder, and in being more religious in their own power. As a result, they are certain that they know better than what Jesus said. They despise the idea that God gives full redemption to sinners through Christ.

So, they will grab verses out of context to convince you that you must keep their version of God's law.

First, let's look at what Jesus said in Matthew 7:21 (ESV):

> **Not everyone who says to me, "Lord, Lord," will enter the kingdom of heaven, but the one who does the will of my Father who is in heaven.**

This is a serious warning, and many of these people take it so literally that they refuse to refer to Jesus as Lord at all (even though His apprentices did).

Matthew 7:22-23 (ESV) will also point out to you that Jesus said a moment later:

> **On that day many will say to me, "Lord, Lord, did we not prophesy in your name, and cast out demons in your name, and do many mighty works in your name?" And then will I declare to them, "I never knew you; depart from me, you workers of lawlessness."**

Again, this is a very serious warning, and it should be considered diligently. Taken by itself, without looking at the whole context, it could appear that people who do miracles in Jesus's name but don't keep all the commandments will be cast away from Him into hell. But what is His real warning? What is the heart of this message? *"I never knew you."* Jesus tells us that is what He will say to those *"workers of lawlessness:"* *"I never <u>knew</u> you."*

So, the first question is, does Jesus know you? And do you know Jesus? Or are you a worker of lawlessness? Because Jesus Himself said <u>all people are lawless</u>. He said it to the most diligent lawkeepers—the Pharisees. Check out John 7:19 (ESV): *"Has not Moses given you the law? Yet none of you keeps the law. Why do you seek to kill me?"*

Not only did they miss His point, but they also immediately lied and said they weren't seeking to kill Him. So, not only did they deny they were lawbreakers, but they broke the law by lying about it. Do you see the irony?

This happens all the time with religious legalists today. While they are adamantly claiming that you need to keep the law, they will break it right in front of you, usually by slandering you or another person, or by outright lying.

God has already indicted all of mankind for being lawbreakers. He left no one out when He warned His people in the Books of Isaiah and Psalms:

> **All we like sheep have gone astray; we have turned—every one—to his own way; and the LORD has laid on him the iniquity of us all.**
> **—Isaiah 53:6 (ESV)**

> **They have all turned aside; together they have become corrupt; there is none who does good, not even one.**
> **—Psalm 14:3 (ESV)**

> **We have all become like one who is unclean, and all our righteous deeds are like a polluted garment.**
> **—Isaiah 64:6-7 (ESV)**

From these passages, we can be sure that Jesus will <u>not condemn anyone</u> for keeping the laws of the Torah, or the Ten Commandments, on judgment day. He could not give a more scathing review of mankind's nature than what He has already given. Anyone who believes they can correctly keep God's law is calling God a liar and kidding himself. If it were possible for anyone to perfectly and fully keep the law and be righteous, then Jesus did not need to go to the cross.

So, what is Jesus saying? He is challenging the idea that men can earn favor with God by works. Notice how He confronts their claim to godliness because they prophesied, casted out demons, and worked miracles. You see, they believed that works saved them. Jesus points out that we must do the will of the Father. And what did He tell us is the will of the Father?

> **My Father wants everyone who sees the Son to have faith in him and to have eternal life. Then I will raise them to life on the last day.**
> **–John 6:40**

The heavenly voice at Jesus's baptism and at the transfiguration made it clear that the will of the Father is that we should hear and believe Jesus. Does that mean we should break or violate the moral law (Ten Commandments)? Absolutely not. What it means is that we do not walk UNDER that law.

So, what law are we under? The Law of the Spirit. Look at those Old Covenant laws and consider the Spirit of the law. Love. Love does not harm its neighbor. Loving God means humbly respecting everything about Him and seeking to know Him in Spirit and Truth.

As Jesus said:

> **But the hour is coming, and now is, when the true worshipers will worship the Father in spirit and truth; for the Father is seeking such to worship Him.**
> **–John 4:23 (NKJV)**

VANQUISHING ALL CONDEMNATION

The Jesus Adventure is built from the beginning with Jesus's call to us to join Him on His journey and walk by faith with Him. We either go with Him by faith, or we are not His. At every point, He teaches a progressive walk of believing and doing His Word. This adventure, and the identity He offers, is a gift, not a payment.

At no point did Jesus tell us that He called us because of any virtue we had. Jesus called us despite our lack of virtues and merits. This was true of His original apprentices (just look at who they were) and is still true today.

Most people who strive to build their own virtue will struggle to believe they need His spiritual rebirth. Most people who believe they are good enough have already put this book down. The religious and self-righteous are <u>not interested in the gift of God's favor</u>. They don't believe they need it!

What God wants us to do is to completely rest in this gift. When Jesus died, proclaimed forgiveness, and called the work complete (or paid in full), the Son of God took all the condemnation against us and vanquished it. Forever.

For God to hold us accountable for our rebel nature or any of our rebellious acts would be a matter of double jeopardy. That is to say, He would be putting us on trial twice for the same crime, even though the sentence was already served. The punishment was already paid.

God cannot and will not violate His own justice! Those who have taken on the identity of Christ have already been judged, and the debt has already been paid. To follow Jesus means to follow Him not only to the cross but also to His grave and resurrection. Since we depend completely on Jesus, there is no chance we can lose it or fall short of it.

What about those people who say we will be rejected for lawlessness by not keeping the Torah? They fail to read the whole passage, as they often do. Because Jesus said in the next verses:

> **Everyone then who hears these words of mine and does them will be like a wise man who built his house on the rock.**
> **—Matthew 7:24 (ESV)**

Notice He <u>did not say</u> the teachings of Moses. Matthew reports that <u>He said His own teachings</u>.

> **Everyone who hears these words of mine and does not do them will be like a foolish man who built his house on the sand.**
> **—Matthew 7:26 (ESV)**

Our Father in Heaven has made it clear that Jesus is superior to all others. Therefore, we are instructed by God to do the following:
- Listen to Him (see Matthew 17:5, Mark 9)
- Believe/trust in Jesus, whom God has sent (see John 6:29-40)
- Obey Jesus the Son of God (see John 3:36)
- Become born of the Spirit of God (see John 3:3)
- Love Jesus and keep His Word (see John 14:23)
- Abide in Jesus and His love (see John 15:9-10)

To reject these instructions of Jesus is to be the epitome of lawlessness. It is to reject His blood.

DECLARATION OF CITIZENSHIP IN HEAVEN

Taking up our cross is not just a new way of life but a new life altogether; it means dying to the old self completely. It says, "I was bought with a price. The old person I was no longer lives, and now I live in Jesus as one of His own. So, I willingly choose to live as His, and I willingly choose to belong to Him and bear His reproach." We don't look back at all. What we were before does not matter.

In doing so, we are emboldened to walk the rest of this life as if we literally died and have been resurrected. We choose to be the new person, by faith, that we will be in reality in the time of the resurrection.

The formal declaration of these truths is called baptism for all apprentices since Jesus. As we look back at the final instruction that Jesus gave us, we see that He told us this is the step of faith we all must make:

> **Go to the people of all nations and make them my disciples. Baptize them in the name of the Father, the Son, and the Holy Spirit.**
> —Matthew 28:19

The formality of baptism is about personally choosing identity and community. This is a public declaration of an inner transformation. Baptism does not save us, but it is the first act of trusting obedience, declaring that we have died to the old life and are buried, and therefore when we are raised out of the water, it's a symbol of the resurrection.

You can think of this as "bathing in the new identity of being an apprentice of Jesus," because doing it means we choose allegiance to Christ and His community.

This is symbolic and yet also a mystical action. The baptism itself, outwardly, is nothing but a ceremony of getting wet in front of witnesses. The inner choice of taking this ceremonial action is a transformative and mystical event, being added to the ranks of God's faithful who identified with the death, burial, and resurrection of Jesus.

In doing this, we receive a fresh impartation of the Spirit, which leads to more inner growth. Believers who resist or reject baptism tend to have stunted walks, but apprentices who embrace this way of Jesus experience more of the Spirit, adventure, and fullness.

Adventure Principle: As we abide in the identity of Jesus and acknowledge Him, God will never deny us because He will never deny Jesus.

INTERNALIZING THE NEW IDENTITY TOGETHER

The second declaration is less formal but equally an act of faith: taking communion with the community of believers. This is also both symbolic and mystical. On the night Jesus was arrested, He took the Passover meal with His apprentices.

After the dinner, Jesus took a slice of unleavened (flat) bread which He broke, and a cup of wine to share with the apprentices, saying, *"This is my body. . . . and this is my blood"* (Mark 14:22-23). At that moment, they did not understand it.

Today we know He was talking about His pending crucifixion. This simple ceremony becomes a symbolic and mystical impartation of the presence of Christ, which should be a regular practice for us. Jesus said, *"Do this in remembrance of me"* (Luke 22:19, NKJV). But what is it that He's asking us to do?

We are called to share this in community as Jesus did with His apprentices. Part of what makes it mystical is that Jesus said, *"Whenever two or three of you come together in my name, I am there with you"* (Matthew 18:20). So, when we share communion in the community of believers to celebrate Jesus, He is joined with us in Spirit. We also remember that Jesus said:

I am that bread from heaven! Everyone who eats it will live forever.
My flesh is the life-giving bread I give to the people of this world.
—John 6:51

Communion reminds us that there is a life-giving impartation from Jesus in this celebration because of the completed work on His cross.

We want to remember that our admission into God's family came from the perfect sacrifice of Jesus on the cross. It was His own body and His blood that ended the death curse of rebellion. Our entire hope is established upon His death and resurrection. As He said:

Truly, truly, I say to you, unless you eat the flesh of the Son of
Man and drink his blood, you have no life in you. . . . Whoever feeds
on my flesh and drinks my blood abides in me, and I in him.
—John 6:53, 56 (ESV)

Jesus is obviously not talking about cannibalism. He's teaching us to recognize that we depend on internalizing His sacrifice, His body, and His blood as an acceptable offering before God. These symbols of communion with Him, in community with our fellowship of other apprentices, **remind us that God has said He is satisfied.** That's the symbolic part.

The mystical part is what the Spirit does with us **when we are faithful to honor the blood of Christ** as total sufficiency for the penalty due. The Father is pleased, and the Spirit moves in us powerfully when we declare Jesus's sacrifice as sufficient.

Acknowledging that Jesus's blood is enough, we agree with God that we cannot add to Jesus's work and don't need to. We agree that we depend completely on God and not on ourselves—and are willing to follow the Spirit as Jesus did. Here, Holy Spirit works His power in us.

I have seen the Holy Spirit work through this practice and it's miraculous. True healing and transformation of lives, true spiritual gifting, and true prophetic works come as a result of people trusting the words of Jesus and, more so, the blood of Jesus.

THE GOLDEN KEY OF ABIDING

There's one more part to this cross-walking new identity, a treasure that is generally missed. It may even be the most important part of taking up our cross: Jesus said this is how to abide in Him. Many read the call to abide in Jesus from John chapter 15, and they wonder—how? What is the secret? Well, Jesus told us, and it's recorded in John 6:56 (ESV): *"Whoever feeds on my flesh and drinks my blood* **abides in me, and I in him.**"

So, Jesus is telling us, in a mystical form, that we abide in Him when we internalize taking up the cross and embracing His identity. We recognize His redeeming sacrifice and total redemption for us in that sacrifice every moment. We should never think of ourselves more highly.

We are never in a place where we do not need that covering. We cannot add to it, and no one can take away from it. His blood and His body are our total covering.

This is how we abide; it produces every good thing that Jesus wants us to live out. Every act of faith, every good work of love, every bit of patience, every answer to prayer, and all of the relationship the Father wants us to experience flows from Jesus's act of redemption—the cross.

When we feel we're really doing great, we remember that it's only by His sacrifice. When we feel like unworthy losers? We remember God's total love for us. There is no greater love—abiding in that remembrance is a mystical and real union.

Then, when temptation comes, we realize we are dead to sin. When we feel condemned? We know we were already judged. When we feel prideful so that we may boast? We see Jesus on that cross and know that we must cling to the splinters of that timber because we need Christ's death to cover our pridefulness even on our best day.

This abiding becomes the resurrected life of following our risen Savior. As we see the old life dead and judged, once and for all time, we are now free to follow Jesus into His resurrection in every situation.

This life is only chapter one of the endless Jesus Adventure. We will soon receive the ultimate upgrade: new resurrected bodies which will never suffer, never shed tears, never know rejection, and never commit a rebellious act against our great loving Creator. So, this key of abiding through the body and blood of Jesus is the key to filling all emptiness and completing every hope. We take hold of it all by faith, that is, by trusting Jesus and our Father in Heaven for our whole lives.

Jesus wants us to be a joyful part of what God is doing in this world. We may see hard times, as some already have, but Jesus wants us to remember that He is with us through it all. He does not want us to become weary in doing the will of God.

We are the children of the eternal God. He never tires of ways to help us and bless us. God has riches and resources that never end.

So, we can reject the darkness and be freed from bondage. We can see miracles, receive the unbelievable, and learn to be apprentices of light.

Adventure Principle: We maintain the identity of Jesus the same way we obtained it, by trusting and walking in the Spirit.

MEDITATIONS ON INTERNALIZING JESUS—THE BREAD OF LIFE

The Jesus fellowship grew, as the early apprentices:

> **Were continually devoting themselves to the apostles' teaching and to fellowship, to the breaking of bread and to prayer.**
> —Acts 2:42 (NASB)

The example is given to us as a pattern to follow. None of us is truly a follower of Jesus alone. We are called to become part of His precious body, His precious fellowship in this world. That is a thing that can only happen by faith, together.

What about us today? Our fellowship is not about being a passive audience in a big room hearing an expert talk about Jesus. This happens in small groups, house to house, sharing the life of internalizing Jesus and His cross.

It sounds wrong; it seems like we should all follow a few chosen experts. It seems like we all just need a guru or two who know it all. My dear friends: Jesus is our Guru. Jesus is the only Master.

The rest of us are mere learners taking up His training and walking it out in total dependence on Him. Whether we gather in a big group or small, we trust that we don't have to be masters because we hear and follow the voice of the Shepherd.

THE ORIGINALS—WALKING RESURRECTED

The original apprentices were amazing people. Part of what is so amazing about them is how little we know. They changed the world **by focusing on Jesus**. Only a few of them "preached." Most of them witnessed of the risen Lord. They told the world what they saw and heard, and they lived enthusiastically like Jesus was with them.

The ones who wrote the gospel accounts seem to have focused on their own weaknesses to better reveal Jesus to us. The ones who did not write are mostly left as footnotes in history's record, humbly willing to let Jesus be the focus of all the attention. They humbly accepted that their purpose was to be living witnesses of His majestic story.

CONSIDERING THE NEW IDENTITY'S FIRST TRAVELERS

The eleven men and several women who comprised the core of the original apprentices and followed Jesus faced incredible dangers. They went forward in the world with Jesus's message of love, peace, hope, faith in an everlasting Father, and perfect redemption by Jesus's sacrifice. The record of what they did and how it changed the world is the continuation of the greatest epic of all times.

As we consider what God did in their lives, we can see what He may also do in our lives if we trust Him. What is the Holy Spirit speaking to you about this? How does your identity in Messiah/Christ shape what you will do next? How can your witness be a part?

CONFESSION FOR THE RESURRECTED LIFE

These three lines from a simple hymn by an Indian man who had chosen to take up his cross and trust Jesus completely capture the heart of every apprentice who has accepted Jesus's call:

I have decided to follow Jesus; no turning back, no turning back.
Though none go with me, I still will follow; no turning back,
no turning back.

The world behind me, the cross before me; no turning back, no turning back.

MEDITATION FOR THE RESURRECTED LIFE

Only one life will soon be passed; only what's done for Christ will last. There is no higher goal, no more important ambition than to live for Christ and seek His reward at the final interview, when He says: "*Well done, you good and faithful servant.*"

Psalm 13:5-6 and Psalm 16:7-8 illustrates this, respectively:

> But I have trusted in your steadfast love;
> my heart shall rejoice in your salvation.
> I will sing to the LORD, because he has dealt bountifully with me.
> —ESV

> I bless the LORD who gives me counsel; in the night also my heart instructs me. I have set the LORD always before me; because he is at my right hand, I shall not be shaken.
> —ESV

CHAPTER 12

THE TREASURE CHEST OF CHRIST

"The kingdom of heaven is like treasure hidden in a field. When a man found it, he hid it again, and then in his joy went and sold all he had and bought that field."
—Matthew 13:44 (NIV)

THE APPRENTICE'S BANK ACCOUNT

As with any journey or adventure, the Jesus Adventure requires resources and a treasury of something trade-worthy. This world requires money to acquire or accomplish anything. In the same way, we need a treasury of spiritual resources to carry us through this journey.

There is a treasury for us, with immeasurably valuable resources granted to us by God for the sake of Jesus. What treasury is this? The promises of God. Fortunately for us, the promises of God will carry us through every aspect of this adventure and keep us filled with answers for every need. We have real substance available through God's treasury of promises given to us through Jesus, the Messiah's unlimited bank account.

God fulfills His promises as always, in His perfect timing. **When we're walking by faith, we become part of that perfect timing.** We have seen through history how He has kept His promises precisely for His people.

Everything we have learned in this study, and everything we count on as we go forward, comes down to our ability to trust in the character of God through His promises. God's promises enable us to navigate and succeed through this adventure with Jesus.

Therefore, we go forward boldly, relying on God's promises that have been made to us. To do that, we want to know them correctly. If it was promised to someone else, we need to know whether that promise extends to us. As a general inclusive promise to all of God's people, the Bible says:

> **"For He satisfies the longing soul, And fills the hungry soul with goodness."**
> **—Psalm 107:9 (NKJV)**

So, we look to the promises of God to do just that: satisfy and fill the areas of hunger and thirst we encounter in life!

FINDING THE UNLIMITED RESOURCES

Worldly treasures, royal crowns, and crested emblems are kept locked up in vaults and fortresses and transported secretly in locked chests to be preserved from theft or fire. In this way, a king may preserve that treasure for his heirs or send it somewhere for special occasions.

God has done something similar to protect the spiritual treasures for us so that cults and false teachers cannot steal them, and the devil cannot create a false system of redemption.

The devil made and continues to. make counterfeit spirituality systems. So, God hid His plans and locked away His purposes in the Bible's deep treasury of promises. Every page and every story are shadows of a greater reality we discover in Jesus Christ.

Within God's treasury of promises and prophecies are authentication systems: the types and patterns in the historical narratives of the Old Testament. Here, God reveals His plans to His people. An example is how Jesus explains that His death and resurrection are paralleled by the "sign" of the prophet Jonah (see Matthew 12:38-41).

The first prophecy of a coming Messiah is given in Genesis 3 at the fall of mankind, yet man did not understand it. We can only begin to unpack that brief promise by considering Jesus's miraculous birth and then considering Christ's completed work of suffering on the cross, leading to His glorious resurrection. In retrospect, we see that Jesus fulfills the Bible's promises and prophecies with every word and every action.

The Bible is full of more promises rather than mere predictions. His promises are found in the typologies. For instance:

Jesus is rejected and seems to be the least among His people/brothers, yet He ultimately rules over them, like Joseph, the patriarch, found in Genesis 37-50.

Jesus is a prophet like Moses who speaks directly with God but greater than Moses because He came directly from the Father.

He is a king like David and a descendant of David, yet He is David's Lord and is greater than David.

He has wisdom like Solomon, yet none of Solomon's wisdom could match Jesus's wisdom and knowledge—and unlike Solomon, Jesus lived out Heaven's wisdom in perfection.

In this manner, we find that page after page speaks of Jesus in prophecy and pattern. For instance, we see that Cain represents the natural man who rebels against God, and Abel is a type of Christ, the spiritual man who brought a faithful sacrifice.

Cain killed Abel (which is saying that the natural man killed the spiritual man), yet God forgave Cain and, in that forgiveness, gave Cain a mark of redemption so that no one could harm him. In this way, Jesus is both a fulfillment of Abel's faithfulness and also of God's mercy to the murderer, just as Jesus forgave His torturers while on His cross.

We discover that the great and precious promises of God were preserved—hidden away in God's Word—transported through time in a message that requires His Spirit to teach and guide us. We can participate in the fulfillment if we are seeking these treasures in His promises.

DISCERNING THE TRUTH IN A CONFUSED ERA

There has never been a time when so much information is available. Yet it is so difficult to discern and understand what is true and what we can do with that truth—because such an abundance of false information is circulating. This is where we must become constant users, discerners, and hearers of God's Word! He reveals His wisdom to those who seek it and are willing to do it. God has given us great and precious promises to help us discern truth from lies and distortion.

God knew that the final era of mankind on earth would be the most confusing time in history. <u>This is why He gave us these promises</u>! God wants us to sift everything through the filter of His promises. This way, we can discern and keep trusting Him, no matter what lies or half-truths we hear. He wants us to become full possessors of the promises. That is the endgame of the Jesus Adventure.

HOLDING TIGHTLY WHAT IS VALUABLE

The time is late, and the scenario is unfolding. The devil once tried to keep Bibles away from common people so that we would not know God's promises. Now the devil wants us to believe counterfeit ideas or be so overwhelmed that we can't think about God's promises. So, the devil is raising tens of thousands of false teachers so that we miss the one true Teacher. Now more than ever, God wants us to go to His Word.

This is why it is important to learn and memorize what God has given us in this treasury of promises. Through the promises of God, we are sustained, empowered, and protected from false teachings that appeal to the natural mind. The promises of God keep us steadfast, filled with faith and unwavering belief.

Adventure Principle: We look for the eternal treasures and place no value on things that God says are worthless.

THE SIX PROMISE TYPES/CATEGORIES

Implied: These are promises that are not directly made but are precepts or principles that we should apply to maintain our relationship with God.

For instance, Psalms says, *"I sought the LORD, and he answered me; he delivered me from all my fears"* (Psalm 34:4, NIV). This is an implied promise that is true for anyone who will seek Him because it is God's character. It later challenges us to *"taste and see that the LORD is good!"* (v. 8, NIV). This is an indirect promise for all who will accept it.

Highlight and memorize implied promises whenever you find them. Pray over them and see how God responds to you.

Extended: Another kind of promise is the extended promise. We know these are extended to us because while the Old Testament says those promises were made to Israel and the people of the Old Covenant, Jesus has reiterated them and given them to us.

For instance, we saw earlier that Jesus has given us a New Covenant confirmed by His blood (see Luke 22:18-20), so we know the New Covenant announced by Jeremiah (see Jeremiah 31:31) pertains to us today by extension, even if we are not Jewish. If you are Jewish, praise God because you have a double confirmation if you trust in Jesus!

Inclusive: Some Bible promises are very inclusive. These are promises that God makes to <u>anyone who will receive them</u>. For instance, Peter says that God is *"not willing that any should perish but that all should come to repentance"* (2 Peter 3:9, NKJV). And by this, we learn that the heart of God is so big that He will include anyone willing to turn to Him; He will not reject anyone who comes to Him.

This provides us with a point of discernment: <u>what is not promised also becomes a promise</u>. Even though God is not willing that any should perish (be condemned to hell), the unrepentant will surely go anyway—because they reject God's redemption.

Exclusive promises to His apprentices: This is the best part! Those first three categories are intended for our learning so that we can develop perseverance and hope through the Bible's demonstration of God's character, but they are not explicit promises made directly to us in this era.

However, this fourth category gives us total confidence in Him. We trust these promises because Jesus rose from the dead. If God would keep such an audacious promise, we can trust all His promises.

He wants us to have strength for endurance and confidence that no challenge can erase. This exclusive category is specifically for the apprentices of Jesus of all times, but especially for these last days.

Exclusive promises to Israel: It's important to review the <u>exclusive promises that only pertain to Israel</u>, the natural-born descendants of the twelve tribes of Jacob (the natural descendants of Jacob's twelve sons). To them, God said:

> **This is what you are to say to the descendants of Jacob and what you are to tell the people of Israel: "You yourselves have seen what I did to Egypt, and how I carried you on eagles' wings and brought you to myself. Now if you obey me fully and keep my covenant, then out of all nations you will be my treasured possession. Although the whole earth is mine, you will be for me a kingdom of priests and a holy nation." These are the words you are to speak to the Israelites"**
> **—Exodus 19:3-6 (NIV)**

Notice how God says that this is exclusive in <u>four ways</u> to <u>a specific people</u> that He made into a nation. It is not for all people! We dare not call God a liar by saying He will break His Word. We say: "Lord, have your way."

Promises to unbelievers: It should be noted that this is the last category. God's only favorable promise to unbelievers is that He will receive them if they turn to Jesus. Now is the time, and today is the day to receive those promises if you have not yet done so. Otherwise, the rest of the promises to unbelievers are of judgment and condemnation!

Since we have learned that God is not willing that any should perish, there is an open door to all who will repent and come to Jesus with the slightest bit of faith; God is serious with those who will receive Jesus. We have discussed that in detail throughout this book, so if you have not read that yet, please start at the beginning.

Otherwise, Jesus says in Revelation:

> **But as for the cowardly, the faithless, the detestable, as for murderers, the sexually immoral, sorcerers, idolaters, and all liars, their portion will be in the lake that burns with fire and sulfur, which is the second death.**
> **—Revelation 21:8 (ESV)**

Since Jesus has done so much to save us from that judgment, I implore you to make peace with God through Jesus.

EXCLUSIVE PROMISES FOR THE APPRENTICES OF JESUS

This is the time of God's greatest promises. We have the distinctive thrill of living during the greatest age of all history (so far); it also happens to be the most perplexing time in all history.

Followers of Jesus have received the results of fulfilled promises of the Old Covenant era but also have new, greater, and precious promises to hold onto until Jesus returns. In fact, Jesus's return is one of the great promises we hold. Completing our roles here requires knowing what promises we have been exclusively given and holding on to them tightly. There are many such promises, so this is meant to **be a starting point and a guide for your own discovery,** not an exhaustive resource.

END-TO-END PROMISES FOR LIFE WITHOUT END

Essentially, because Christ was raised from the dead, we can know that death has no power over Him and since it has no power over Him, He extends that to us. Since He was resurrected to an indestructible life, so shall we be. As Jesus said:

> **For my Father's will is that everyone who looks to the Son and believes in him shall have eternal life, and I will raise them up at the last day.**
> —John 6:40 (NIV)

So, these promises explain the new relationship God gives. From that relationship, all blessings and opportunities flow out to us, and those are only available to us who have that relationship.

> **God loved the people of this world so much that he gave his only Son, so that everyone who has faith in him will have eternal life and never really die. God did not send his Son into the world to condemn its people. He sent him to save them!**
> —John 3:16-17

Unlike under the Torah (God's Law), God is offering a personal relationship with Himself, apart from a national identity. This is the "whosoever" part. Jesus is creating a global community. Jesus confirms:

> **Everyone who has faith in the Son has eternal life. But no one who rejects him will ever share in that life, and God will be angry with them forever.**
> —John 3:36

Anyone who does not receive this gift of God's Son is <u>already under judgment</u> from God. See other references giving some insights into this passage: *Mark 10:45, Matthew 20:28, John 6:40, John 5:42, and Isaiah 9:6.*

JESUS PROMISES THE ULTIMATE REWARD

Jesus alone promises us eternal redemption and the ultimate position: a place in the Father's house. There was no promise of Heaven in the Old Testament. Their promises were for this earth.

Jesus makes us an incredible composite promise in John:

> **Don't be worried! Have faith in God and have faith in me. There are many rooms in my Father's house. I wouldn't tell you this, unless it was true. I am going there to prepare a place for each of you.**
> **—John 14:1-2**

Where did Jesus go to prepare a place for us? Forty days after His resurrection, He ascended to the Father's throne in the highest Heaven.

So, these two promises teach us a lot about what has happened already and what is coming for us who trust in Jesus in these last days. Everything between now and Jesus's return is covered and prepared for us by these two incredible promises.

THE FILLING—EVERYTHING SPECIAL THAT WE NEED IN BETWEEN

When I was a little kid, I liked getting pastries with frosting in the middle. The tasty filling between the beginning and end of being an apprentice of Jesus is the filling of the Holy Spirit. He has been sent to guide us, help us, comfort us, teach us, and empower us. This is the joy of being a disciple: the sweet presence of God Himself makes it possible to be joined with Jesus in constant communion and to take this journey confidently.

We have continual conscious contact with God by the Holy Spirit and communion with other apprentices. His presence is a fulfilled promise for many of us, but for those outside, it's a promise yet to be fulfilled: the Spirit of Christ in you.

In this section, let's consider a short list of some of the key verses teaching us of the Holy Spirit, who is promised to us for our journey through this dry and weary world:

> **"He will baptize you with the Holy Spirit and fire."**
> **—Luke 3:16**

> **The true worshippers will worship the Father in spirit and truth, for the Father is seeking such people to worship him.**
> **—John 4:23 (ESV)**

> **But when the Helper comes, whom I will send to you from the Father, the Spirit of truth, who proceeds from the Father, he will bear witness about me.**
> **—John 15:26 (ESV)**

So, the gift of the Holy Spirit came on the day of the feast of Pentecost, forty-nine days from the day Jesus rose from the dead.

This collective gifting of the Holy Spirit had never happened before. And since then, He is now available to all who believe and trust in Jesus. This is called being *"born of the Spirit"* or *"born again"* (John 3:6, ESV).

Since the Holy Spirit is available to us and is actively keeping us for Himself, we want to live for God and follow Jesus faithfully—because the power to do that is given to us so that we can fulfill our destiny.

Ultimately, the Holy Spirit will bring us a perfected love for Jesus, a love that fills and empowers us every day. When we have that, nothing prevents fulfilling His instructions because Jesus is for us and loves us with an everlasting love.

As you study and pray on your journey with Jesus, ask the Father to increase your awareness and reliance on the Holy Spirit He sent you. Seek His comfort; seek His guidance. Seek His empowerment for your journey.

FEARLESS FAITH AND STRENGTHENED FEET

You may have noticed that every step of this adventure builds on the last and strengthens you for the next so that as you go, it becomes easier to take on greater challenges. We become strengthened and conditioned with endurance and power from Heaven's throne. It builds progressively, the same way Jesus did with His original apprentices.

Some who want to serve God get very hung up on the idea that they will have to be perfect keepers of the Torah or even just the Ten Commandments. But that's not how God sees the matter. Jesus said, *"If you love me, you will keep my commandments"* (John 14:15, CEB). Some people think He said, 'If you keep my commands, I will love you!' which is completely wrong.

The goal is to come to a place of loving Jesus, which happens when we realize He has removed every barrier to be fearless apprentices—fearless toward Him, and fearless for Him. This is why Jesus repeatedly said, *"Fear not,"* and why He challenged His apprentices, *"Why were you afraid?"* It's fascinating because the most religious people become very fearful—they put too much confidence in self and so little in Christ.

We have been given a promise that we should not fear nor hide from Him, and we should not think of ourselves as unworthy. Jesus wants us to be confident—even bold, maybe too bold—in knowing Him. This is why Jesus said:

> **I no longer call you servants, because a servant does not know his master's business. Instead, I have called you friends.**
> **—John 15:15 (NIV)**

Jesus gives unshakable confidence. This is the gospel, the Great News: The feet that brought us great news were nailed to a Roman cross to deliver us from darkness. The mountain He offers that good news from is the mountain of His crucifixion, where He nailed every offense we have ever done to a cross and became judged as the penalty of sin for us. The voice that calls out that Great News is the voice of the Good Shepherd, seeking His sheep, who cried out from that cross, *"It is finished!"*

There can be no condemnation for us if we trust and walk in sacred reverence for the blood and resurrection of the Son of God. Now God promises a relationship that gives everlasting life, a home with Our Father at the end, and the Holy Spirit to baptize, fill, guide, comfort, and help us along the way. What shall we fear? Well, this is why Jesus reminds us repeatedly that without Him, we are naturally given to fear. He understands we won't pursue our adventure with Him if it's dependent on us.

> **Peace I leave with you; my peace I give to you. Not as the world gives do I give to you. Let not your hearts be troubled, neither let them be afraid"**
> **—John 14:27 (ESV)**

By these promises, we can be fearless. Jesus wants us to understand that nothing that comes in this life should bring us terror. Our destiny is in His hands, and He is for us, not against us. He knew at the beginning this would be a concern for us even more as we near the day of His return, so He said: *"And surely I am with you always, to the very end of the age"* (Matthew 28:20, NIV). To the end of the age. This age.

Assurance

> **And this is the testimony, that God gave us eternal life, and this life is in his Son. Whoever has the Son has life; whoever does not have the Son of God does not have life. I write these things to you who believe in the name of the Son of God, that you may know that you have eternal life.**
> **—1 John 5:11-13**

THE PROMISE OF THE GREATEST REWARD

Ultimately, God Himself is our reward for those who trust in Jesus. In Genesis 15:1, God tells Abraham that God Himself is his *"exceeding great reward."* Thirty-six times we're told in the New Testament that those who trust in Jesus and follow His teachings will have great rewards, but we want to remember that having a restored relationship with God Himself is the ultimate reward. God is a *"rewarder of them that diligently seek him"* (Hebrews 11:6, KJV).

Jesus tells us repeatedly, in many ways, that there are special rewards coming for even the simplest acts in His name. He warns us not to miss the rewards or let ourselves be cheated out of the rewards by seeking the praise of people.

Jesus says that we are to work for the praise of God, who sees all and rewards secretly (for now) but will reward openly later. In my experience, the less people know about our works of charity, the more glory God receives.

He loves for people to know that He is watching them and blessing them. If we get in the way, it hinders His ability to speak directly to another person's heart. He also wants to speak to us privately and say, "I saw what you did in secret for my glory," so that we know He's watching. If we don't keep it secret, we don't hear God speaking secretly to us.

IF WE ONLY KNEW WHAT'S COMING

There are so much greater rewards for true sacrificial living than we comprehend. The Book of Revelation tells us there are special crowns prepared for those who die for the faith. I believe that **if we could see** what is really awaiting us on the other side, we would willingly sacrifice everything and eagerly accept being tortured for our faith in Jesus here. Did I really say that? Yes.

> **God will bless you when people insult you, mistreat you, and tell all kinds of evil lies about you because of me. Be happy and excited! You will have a great reward in heaven. People did these same things to the prophets who lived long ago.**
> —Matthew 5:11-13

Peter and the guys were so convinced of this that they celebrated that they were "considered worthy to suffer" for the name of Jesus (see Acts 5:41); they had prayed to have the boldness to speak of Jesus publicly after being arrested and warned.

What those men endured for Jesus is incredible, and they leave us a legacy to follow. But what can we do? If God is willing to reward us for giving a cup of cool water in the name of His ministry (see Matthew 10:42), what might Jesus do if we seriously work for the reaching of lost souls for salvation?

THE GRAND FINALE: THE PROMISED GLORIOUS RETURN

The promised final grand miracle we will receive is pending and could happen at any moment. I believe we are the generation that will see this one final event. Are you watching carefully?

> **"I am going . . . And . . . I will come back"**
> —see John 14:1-3

There is one great hope, one great final promise that we are given that surpasses all the others. It is the one promise, given multiple times, that has energized the followers of Jesus for these 2,000 years.

He has promised to return for us, not as the humble Teacher or even the miracle-working Healer. He promised to return as a glorious reigning King, a King who dwells in glorious rainbows of light, a King who will sit on a throne on earth but is no longer an earthly mortal.

NOT A HUMBLE GALILEAN TEACHER ANYMORE

Consider these verses that tell us about Him today:

> "Behold, He is coming with the clouds, and every eye will see him."
> Revelation 1:7 (NKJV)

> His eyes looked like flames of fire. His feet were glowing like bronze being heated in a furnace, and ... His face was shining as bright as the sun at noon.
> —Revelation 1:14-16

> A throne stood in heaven, with one seated on the throne ... and around the throne was a rainbow that had the appearance of an emerald ... From the throne came flashes of lightning.
> —Revelation 4:2-3, 5 (ESV)

He promises to return and bring order and peace to this world, ruling in perfect justice for a thousand years before creating new heavens and a new earth.

FAITHFUL AND RELIABLE FRAMEWORK

Since He kept His promises precisely in the past, we can know that He will keep His promises in the future. Since He warned us to watch for signs of His near coming, we can know that signs tell us of the nearness of His return.

These are the days that all the prophets and holy people of God have looked forward to throughout all of history. We now live in a truly interconnected global community with perplexing challenges affecting the whole world. This is exactly what Jesus told us it would be like right before His return.

What does He want us to do? Watch, pray, and be diligent in walking the Jesus Adventure until He returns. Be an active and engaged participant in bringing the authority and power of God to your world. Live His Word, as He taught, because it is more necessary now. Be engaged. Be proactive. Be the light, as He is the light. Be the doer of His Word, faithfully expecting Him to return at any moment. Be ready to be found doing His work.

> **Be like men who are waiting for their master to come home. . . . Blessed are those servants whom the master finds awake when he comes . . . You also must be ready, for the Son of Man is coming at an hour you do not expect.**
> **—Luke 12:36-40 (ESV)**

> **Who then is the faithful and wise manager, whom his master will set over his household, to give them their portion of food at the proper time? Blessed is that servant whom his master will find so doing when he comes. Truly, I say to you, he will set him over all his possessions.**
> **—Luke 12:42-44 (ESV)**

Many places in the Bible have prophetic words for us. Some are long; some are very concise. This one captures the heart of the Jesus Adventure for our day:

> **"My soul thirsts for God, for the living God. When shall I come and appear before God?"**
> **—Psalm 42:2 (NKJV)**

The Holy Spirit speaks to the heart that is thirsty for and craving the living God. When will we finally come and appear before Him? Sooner than most people think.

Even when the bottom has dropped out, we hope in God. Because with God, our hope is not a wish <u>but an assurance</u>. It is a certainty; Jesus will come.

DIFFERENT PERSPECTIVES BUT ONE SURE CONCLUSION

The past fulfillments of biblical promises happened exactly as promised. The future ones will also.

The prophets, Jesus, and angels told us He's coming from the sky, on clouds:

> I saw what looked like a son of man coming with the clouds
> of heaven, and he was presented to the Eternal God.
> He was crowned king and given power and glory, so that all
> people of every nation and race would serve him. He will rule
> forever, and His kingdom is eternal, never to be destroyed.
> —Daniel 7:13-14

> "And then they will see the Son of Man coming in
> clouds with great power and glory."
> —Mark 13:26 (ESV)

> "You will see the Son of Man seated at the right hand of
> Power and coming on the clouds of heaven."
> —Mark 14:62 (NKJV)

> And when he had said these things, as they were looking on, he
> was lifted up, and a cloud took him out of their sight.
> And while they were gazing into heaven as he went,
> behold, two men stood by them in white robes,

> and said, "Men of Galilee, why do you stand looking into heaven? This Jesus, who was taken up from you into heaven, will come in the same way as you saw him go into heaven.
> —Acts 1:9-11 (ESV)

So we are taught to expect the real Jesus from Heaven above us, riding on clouds. We don't accept an imposter coming another way. If someone claims to be Jesus, the Messiah, or the Son of God, and you didn't see Him riding down from the sky on a cloud, then He's not Jesus! He warned that false prophets and deceivers would come, but we watch for our master in the sky!

THE ORDER OF EVENTS

Based on over thirty years of comprehensive Bible study, I have concluded that Jesus will remove His faithful apprentices before the final era of events on this earth, which is called by various phrases, including *"the day of Vengeance of our God," "the Great Tribulation," "the day of the Lord,"* and *"the time of Jacob's Trouble."* I have drawn this conclusion on the basis of Jesus's teachings, the prophets' declarations, and the teachings of Jesus's emissaries.

But my purpose here is not to be dogmatic about the timing of events. There are different opinions, so we should study to understand what the Bible teaches. My point is that we should do what Jesus said to do, which is to faithfully <u>watch</u> and escape what is coming. I'm going with what Jesus said:

> Watch therefore, and pray always that you may be counted worthy to escape all these things that will come to pass, and to stand before the Son of Man.
> —Luke 21:36 (NKJV)

Jesus said and did everything in His life and ministry precisely as the prophets foretold. This is how we know He is the Messiah!

At the beginning of His ministry, Jesus quoted Isaiah 61:1-2, **but ended with a comma**—in effect, He said that He had come for the first part but not the second part of the promise <u>at that time</u>. At the end of this passage, He said that Scripture was fulfilled simply by Him being there. The promise goes like this:

> **The Spirit of the Lord GOD is upon me, because the LORD has anointed me to bring good news to the poor; he has sent me to bind up the brokenhearted, to proclaim liberty to the captives, and the opening of the prison to those who are bound; to proclaim the year of the LORD's favor, and the day of vengeance of our God; to comfort all who mourn.**
> —Isaiah 61:1-2 (ESV)

Since Jesus didn't read the second part, He was saying, "I have come for the first, but the second part of that prophecy is for later." Jesus showed God's favor during His ministry. But He has not brought the vengeance of God, yet.

Which is exactly what the prophet Daniel said would happen in Daniel 9. Therefore, there remains an unfulfilled seven years of time from Daniel's prediction, which is called *"the day of vengeance of our God."* We are still living in that gap of time before day of vengeance begins.

THE HIGHEST HEIGHT OF ALL PROMISES

I do not believe that God will leave us here for the day of His vengeance. That would be out of character. He has given us a window of time to complete the work of making disciples. The time is short, and we have a lot to do. In Revelation, Jesus promises:

> **Because you have kept My command to persevere, I also will keep you from the hour of trial which shall come upon the whole world, to test those who dwell on the earth.**
> —Revelation 3:10 (NKJV)

And shortly after that, in Revelation 3:21, He also promises:

> **To him who overcomes I will grant to sit with Me on My throne, as I also overcame and sat down with My Father on His throne.**
> —Revelation 3:21 (NKJV)

So, it seems to me that Jesus is offering something incomprehensible: to both escape His outpouring of wrath on this world and also to sit with Him on the Throne of Heaven.

CONCLUSION

The Jesus Adventure continues until He returns or calls us home. The adventure is for those who humbly trust Him and activate their faith in Him. His ultimate plan for us is to become possessors of the promises. As we do, He frees us from every evil that binds us.

Since we have been set free, we walk by trust; we celebrate Him, sit at His feet, and listen and do His Word. He gives us these amazing promises for life, hope, love, joy, peace, and a heavenly home that we want to share. So, we tell others about His amazing favor. Let it become your lifestyle, and rest confidently—because Jesus will not deny us; Jesus will never reject us if we trust Him.

Jesus's authority from Heaven brings a God-ordered way that destroys the chaos of the spirit of rebellion.

Knowing that God has given us exceedingly great and precious promises, we hold them tightly, because we know He is returning soon, and we want to be found faithful when He does.

THE NEXT REAL STORY OF THE ADVENTURE

The next step is all **about you and Jesus**. That is no longer a step in the dark because, as we have discovered, *"you know the way"*—and that way is Jesus. Search out His many promises to you in the Bible. Find them all with Jesus guiding you. That is the point of this book: to stimulate you to discover the truth for yourself with Jesus. There are many more than I have listed.

Pray seriously and let the Spirit of Messiah/Christ guide you. As you hear what Jesus teaches, be ready to do amazing things. What are your next steps? Pray, read, and take notes as you go. Now is the time to dig in and hear Him more carefully than ever—get into the Bible daily. Pray as you go. Write down the questions that come to you; Jesus will answer you along your journey. Take action. Our faith is not theory; it is faith-filled engagement.

> **Jesus came and said to them, "All authority in heaven and on earth has been given to me. Go therefore and make disciples of all nations, baptizing them in the name of the Father and of the Son and of the Holy Spirit, teaching them to observe all that I have commanded you. And behold, I am with you always, to the end of the age."**
> **—Matthew 28:18-20 (NKJV)**

www.ingramcontent.com/pod-product-compliance
Lightning Source LLC
Chambersburg PA
CBHW050104170426
43198CB00014B/2454